HümCA

Uncollected Early Prose of Katherine Anne Porter

UNCOLLECTED

EARLY PROSE OF

Katherine Anne Porter

EDITED BY

RUTH M. ALVAREZ AND

THOMAS F. WALSH

UNIVERSITY OF TEXAS PRESS   *Austin*

FOR THOMAS F. WALSH, 1925–1991

Copyright © 1993 by the University of Texas Press
All rights reserved
Printed in the United States of America
First edition, 1993

Requests for permission to reproduce material from
this work should be sent to Permissions, University of
Texas Press, Box 7819, Austin, TX 78713-7819.

∞ The paper used in this publication meets the minimum
requirements of American National Standard for
Information Sciences—Permanence of Paper for Printed
Library Materials, ANSI Z39.48-1984.

Library of Congress Cataloging-in-Publication Data

Porter, Katherine Anne, 1890–1980.
　[Selections. 1993]
Uncollected early prose of Katherine Anne Porter
/ edited by Ruth M. Alvarez and Thomas F. Walsh.—1st ed.
　　p.　　cm.
Includes bibliographical references (p.).
ISBN 0-292-76544-4 (alk. paper)
　I. Alvarez, Ruth M.　II. Walsh, Thomas F.
(Thomas Francis), 1925– .　III. Title.
PS3531.0752A6　1993
813'.52—dc20　　　93-3361

FRONTISPIECE:
Katherine Anne Porter in the early 1920s. This
may be the photograph Porter had taken for her
passport in the summer of 1920; in a July 4, 1920,
letter to her sister Gay she described that
portrait as the "best likeness I ever had made."
Rare Books & Literary Manuscripts Department,
University of Maryland at College Park Libraries.

Contents

Preface

This collection grew from my relationship with Professor Thomas F. Walsh. We met in Spring 1986 when we were both doing research on Katherine Anne Porter at the University of Maryland at College Park. As our individual projects progressed, our relationship grew more intimate, intensified by our common interests in Katherine Anne Porter and Mexico. We shared Porter's belief that her experiences in Mexico were crucial to her development as an artist. In a talk entitled "The Mexico I Knew," Porter asserted, "I am perfectly certain that my time in Mexico was one of the very important times of my life. I think it influenced everything I did afterward" (undated manuscript, circa 1968–1976). In the course of our research, we turned up previously unknown early work of Porter in newspapers: *El Heraldo de México*, the *New York Call*, and the *Christian Science Monitor*. Quite by accident, we located a copy of the first issue of the *Magazine of Mexico*, which Porter edited during her first Mexican trip. Professor Walsh was able to confirm the contents of the second (and last) of these issues among the intelligence files at the National Archives. As the list of these finds lengthened, we conceived the notion of putting together a collection of Porter's early work, most of it on Mexico, which deserved more attention. We decided to republish other early work which Porter for one reason or another had not seen fit to use in her *Collected Stories* or *Collected Essays*. With the generous permission of Isabel Bayley, literary executor of the estate of Katherine Anne Porter, we were able to include unpublished fiction and nonfiction from the Katherine

Anne Porter Collection at the University of Maryland at College Park Libraries. Although Professor Walsh's life was tragically cut short before the work of editing was completed, the collection contains his contributions, to editing as well as to the introduction and headnotes.

This collection provides evidence of Porter's artistic growth. She went to Mexico in November 1920 having written four derivative stories, which open this volume, and a body of newspaper pieces. Shortly after her arrival in Mexico she produced "The Fiesta of Guadalupe," which was entirely hers and in her own distinctive voice. Mexico contributed in some mysterious way to her development into an artist, and this volume is a small attempt at chronicling that development. The aim of this collection is to contribute to a better understanding of Porter, enlarging the record of her early career as well as delineating a partial picture of her process of composition. Professor Walsh and I attempted to steer a rather conservative course in editing the pieces collected here. We did not want to mislead the reader to believe that the previously unpublished pieces had been polished by Porter for publication. We attempted to make our editorial efforts transparent by using angle brackets to indicate insertions from among Porter's various drafts and square brackets for our insertions. For the details of procedures as well as specific decisions, the reader should turn to the Notes on Texts at the end of the collection.

Professor Walsh and I are indebted to many individuals who helped bring this project to fruition. Isabel Bayley granted us permission to publish Porter's unpublished work and made useful suggestions about the editing of some of that work. The staff of the Special Collections Division of the University of Maryland at College Park Libraries, especially Blanche T. Ebeling-Koning, the curator of Rare Books and Literary Manuscripts, made research in the Porter collection a pleasure. The photographs that illustrated the *Outline of Mexican Popular Arts and Crafts* appear in this volume because of her efforts. Her department generously granted us permission to publish the pieces from Porter's unpublished manuscripts as well as photographs from the Katherine Anne Porter Collection. Sue Presnell of the Lilly Library at Indiana University in Bloomington bore patiently my requests for information about the photographs from the Sergei Eisenstein papers. The photographs from that collection are printed here with the permission of the Lilly Library as well as that of Jean Sinclair, the heir of the Estate of Upton Sinclair. We are indebted to the Nettie Lee Benson Latin American Collection, University of Texas, Austin, Texas, for making available the essay and photographs from the *Magazine of Mexico*. "Hacienda" is published with the permission of the *Virginia Quarterly*

Review, where it was originally published. The Miguel Cabrera portrait of Sor Juana Inés de la Cruz appears by permission of the Instituto Nacional de Antropología e Historia and the Museo Nacional de Historia, Chapultepec Castle, both of which are located in Mexico.

Joan Reuss of Georgetown University provided invaluable assistance in transcribing, from confusing photocopies, many of the items that appear in the volume. I have also had the assistance of a number of friends, some of whom number among the Porter scholars. Mary Titus shared her transcription of the story "The Princess," which helped us make our final editorial decision on that story. Joyce Ann Joyce, Jane Krause DeMouy, Janis Stout, and Nina Fay read the manuscript at various stages and made helpful suggestions. Neither Professor Walsh nor I would have been able to complete this project without the assistance of María A. Walsh. She served as assistant in Mexico at the Hemeroteca Nacional de México, where the issues of *El Heraldo de México* are housed, as proofreader, and as consultant on Mexico and the Spanish language. I am especially grateful to Roy D. Alvarez for his support and encouragement throughout.

R.M.A.   November 1992

Uncollected Early Prose of
Katherine Anne Porter

Introduction

Three volumes, *The Collected Stories of Katherine Anne Porter*, *The Collected Essays and Occasional Writings of Katherine Anne Porter*, and *Ship of Fools*, all published in the author's lifetime, constitute the heart of Katherine Anne Porter's opus. *My Chinese Marriage*, her ghostwritten account of American Mae Watkins's marriage to Chinese national Tiam Hock Franking, and *"This Strange, Old World" and Other Book Reviews*, a collection of her reviews, augmented that core in 1991. This volume provides yet another piece of her literary identity, presenting some of Porter's earliest writing. These items provide a heretofore unavailable perspective on her developing skill as a writer as well as an entree to her later work.

Porter began her career as a journalist in Fort Worth in 1917 and pursued that profession in Denver from 1918 to 1919, but her development into a creative writer did not begin until she moved to New York City in late 1919. Evidence of that development appeared soon after her arrival in Mexico in 1920. Nineteen of the twenty-nine pieces in this volume were written between 1920 and 1922 (the year when "María Concepción," the earliest among her *Collected Stories*, appeared); six others were written before 1929 and the remaining four in 1930–1931. The volume includes both fiction and essays, published and unpublished. The published fiction consists of four stories "retold" by the author ("The Shattered Star," "The Faithful Princess," "The Magic Ear Ring," and "The Adventures of Hadji") and the first version of "Hacienda." The unpublished fiction found among Porter's papers at the University of Maryland at College Park provided six pieces complete enough to merit inclusion in this volume ("Trinidad," "The Dove of Chapacalco," "The Lovely Legend," "The Evening," "The Princess," and "Return"). The remainder of the volume consists of eighteen published and unpublished essays. Among them are her monograph, *Outline of Mexican Popular Arts and Crafts*; her first two political essays ("Striking the Lyric Note in Mexico" and "The New Man and The New Order"); her first two book reviews (on books by Blasco Ibáñez, W. L. George, Jeanette Lee, and Leonard Merrick); and several literary sketches ("The Fiesta of Guadalupe," "In a Mexican Patio," "Xochimilco"). Eight of these works were recently discovered among the pages of *El Heraldo de México*, the *New York Call*, and the *Christian Science Monitor*. All of them have intrinsic merit and provide an interesting view of Porter's personality and her creative process.

All but five of the pieces in this volume (the four "retold" short stories and "The Princess") focus on Mexico, the country where Porter first began to realize her creative potential. Persuaded by artist Adolfo Best-Maugard that Mexico was about to undergo exciting social and political changes after ten bloody years of revolution, Porter entered her "second country" on November 6, 1920, and straightway contacted Thorberg Haberman, who, like Porter, had lived in Greenwich Village. Haberman was at that time English language editor of *El Heraldo de México*, but she soon surrendered this position to Porter. In *El Heraldo*, Porter published her first two book reviews and "The Fiesta of Guadalupe," her first published literary effort, later included in her *Collected Essays*. Porter also met Thorberg's husband Robert Haberman, a lawyer and the only U.S. citizen who was a member of CROM (Regional Confederation of Mexican Workers). This labor union was headed by Luis Morones, the third most powerful man in the country and, at the time, the political ally of Alvaro Obregón. Thus, the Habermans gave Porter access to the political world of Mexico. She attended the presidential inauguration of the newly elected Obregón, accompanying Luis Morones to one of the inaugural balls. Soon after, she went to work for Morones in an informal capacity.

Although Porter gave many reasons for visiting Mexico, her principal one was to write. After *El Heraldo* terminated its English language section, Porter became editor of the *Magazine of Mexico*, financed by American businessmen to encourage investment in Mexico. The magazine folded for want of funding after issues in March and April 1921, but not before publishing two of Porter's political essays (on Obregón and on Morones) and another literary sketch, "In a Mexican Patio." Invited by friend Ernestine Evans to contribute to the *Christian Science Monitor*, Porter published

Porter with an unidentified group of fellow passengers on board a ship returning from Mexico in June 1922. She had just completed writing the text for the *Outline of Mexican Popular Arts and Crafts*. Rare Books & Literary Manuscripts Department, University of Maryland at College Park Libraries.

there a third literary sketch, "Xochimilco," in May 1921, three months before her departure for Texas. The *Monitor* published two more Porter essays in 1922, one during and the other after her second trip to Mexico ("A Letter from Mexico and the Gleam of Montezuma's Golden Roofs" and "Two Ancient Mexican Pyramids"). She had returned in April 1922 at the invitation of the Mexican government to participate in preparations for an exhibition of Mexican folk art to be shown in the United States. Her contribution was the *Outline of Mexican Popular Arts and Crafts*, a fascinating commentary on both the art and the indigenous people. She returned to Mexico a third time in summer 1923 as art editor of the Mexican issue of *Survey Graphic*, to which she contributed two essays ("Corridos" and "To a Portrait of the Poet"). All of these pieces except the political essay on Luis Morones are included in this volume. (The Morones essay was published in the second issue of the *Magazine of Mexico*; the editors were unable to locate a copy of the issue or of the essay.)

During this period her creative work was beginning to emerge, clearly reflecting her Mexican experiences. In December 1922 *Century* published "María Concepción," Porter's first totally original work of fiction. Prior to that she attempted but did not complete two other Mexican stories, "Trinidad" and "The Dove of Chapacalco," included in this volume. In 1923 she published "The Martyr" and in 1924 "Virgin Violeta," the latter based on her experiences during her second and third visits to Mexico. "The Lovely Legend" (published here) and "The Martyr" both have as their central character Rubén, who shows a remarkable resemblance to prominent Mexican painter Diego Rivera. During this time she attempted to write a novel she later called *Thieves' Market*, but the only unified works salvaged from this effort for inclusion in this volume are "The Evening" and "Return." The heroines of these works anticipate the character of Laura in "Flowering Judas," which Porter finished in 1929 and published in 1930. Her most accomplished work to that date, it mostly reflected her disillusioning experiences with politics and love in Mexico in 1920–1921.

Porter visited Mexico a fourth time in April 1930 after several unsuccessful attempts to return. She arrived armed with a contract for her Mexican novel, but it never advanced beyond the note-taking stage. Awarded a Guggenheim fellowship that would take her to Europe, she sailed from Mexico in August 1931, but shortly before leaving she visited the Hacienda Tetlapayac, a visit which inspired her masterpiece of despair, "Hacienda." The first version of this work concludes the selections in this volume.

Porter's complex reactions to Mexico have long been the subject of critical speculation. The assumption has been that she entered the country idealistically committed to the political changes that the revolution promised but eventually lost hope in the few dedicated idealists in government, who were hamstrung by implacable forces from without and within. She implied as much in "The Mexican Trinity" (August 1921; republished in Porter's *The Days Before* and *Collected Essays*), indicting the *hacendados*, the Roman Catholic Church, and the foreign oil interests for their exploitation of the country. In 1943 she wrote her friend Mary Doherty that her "childlike faith in the Revolution was well over in about six months" (unpublished letter dated 1 November, 1943). Her remarks are misleading, because they suggest an all too simplistic version of her experience in Mexico. They suggest that the failure of the revolution was the sole source of her disillusion, omitting Porter's own psychological state before she set foot in the country.

The works included in this volume provide another perspective. For instance, "Xochimilco," published in May 1921, depicts the Indian village as a kind of Eden. One might assume that it was written before she lost

mexico 1923

Porter dated this photograph of herself dressed as a China Poblana dancing the Jarabe Ta-
patío, "Mexico 1923." Rare Books & Literary Manuscripts Department, University of Maryland at
College Park Libraries.

her "childlike faith in the Revolution." Yet "The Fiesta of Guadalupe" and her review of W. L. George's *Caliban*, published in mid-December 1920— only five weeks after her arrival and presumably too soon for that loss of faith—express a despairing view of Mexico and the world. The answer to this apparent inconsistency is that Porter, as she wrote to Josephine Herbst in 1931, suffered all her life from a "deep, incurable (apparently) painful melancholy" (*Letters of Katherine Anne Porter*, ed. Isabel Bayley [New York: Atlantic Monthly Press, 1990], 44). Her cure for this state of mind was to escape to a new place or into a love relationship, in which she would realize her hope in the way she thought the world should be. Mexico was such a place, and while there she oscillated between hope and despair. She hoped it would be an Eden, but, as she wrote Mary Doherty in that same letter of 1943, she remembered it as "mostly hell." Ironically, that was its fatal attraction, for it gave her artistic reason to objectify and justify her despair.

The works included here reveal Porter's other artistic and psychological concerns. Her feminist stance, which may have arisen from her failed first marriage at age sixteen, is apparent in her four earliest published stories, "The Shattered Star," "The Faithful Princess," "The Magic Ear Ring," and "The Adventures of Hadji." That stance can be traced through much of the fiction and nonfiction published here, most notably in "The Dove of Chapacalco," "The Lovely Legend," and "The Princess." Her ambivalent attitude toward politics and politicians comes clearly into focus in the contrast between her previously collected political essays and those published here. "Striking the Lyric Note in Mexico" and "The New Man and The New Order," which appear here, are enthusiastically partisan; the formerly collected works, "The Mexican Trinity" and "Where Presidents Have No Friends," are skeptical and suspicious. This disillusion with Mexican politics also surfaced in "Leaving the Petate" and "Hacienda." Her use of mythology and legends, so overt in those four early stories published in *Everyland* and *Asia*, became understated and virtuosic by the time she penned the first version of "Hacienda." First expressed in "The Mexican Trinity," Porter's anticlericalism pervades all her work with Mexican subjects, especially "The Fiesta of Guadalupe," "Notes on Teotihuacan," and "The Dove of Chapacalco." The exploration of art and aesthetics, which Porter began with the *Outline of Mexican Popular Arts and Crafts* and continued throughout her life, is evident in "Corridos," "The Lovely Legend," and "The Princess." Finally, her alienation, a defining feature of her best fiction, suffuses most of this collection but especially "In a Mexican Patio" and "The Evening."

The individual works are arranged chronologically by date of publication or, if previously unpublished, by date of composition. Comments on each appear as headnotes to each and identify their sources wherever possible.

T.F.W.
Cuernavaca, Summer 1991
R.M.A.
March 1992

The Shattered Star   *Everyland* 2 (January 1920): 422–423

The Faithful Princess   *Everyland* 2 (February 1920): 42–43

The Magic Ear Ring   *Everyland* 2 (March 1920): 86–87

Porter, following in the footsteps of Eva Chappell—a fellow journalist of Denver's *Rocky Mountain News*—moved to New York City and settled in Greenwich Village in the autumn of 1919. Although New York served as the setting of only two stories, "Theft" and "A Day's Work," it became the intellectual center of Porter's life. Her friends included Bessie Beattie, editor of *McCall's*; Ernestine Evans, correspondent for the *Call* and soon to be an editor of the *Christian Science Monitor*; poet Genevieve Taggard; Helen Black, who wrote for the *Nation*; Kenneth Durant, first correspondent in the United States for the Soviet Union and editor of *Soviet Russia*; and Berta and Elmer Hader, illustrators for the children's magazine *Everyland*. Through the Haders, Porter contracted to write children's stories derived from various sources. Porter later disowned these, stating that there was nothing of hers in them, but the crisp prose is hers and her choice of tales reveals a good deal about her thematic interests—interests that would reappear in her own stories.

Each of these retold stories centers on a woman who, in the make-believe world where mortals commune with gods, gets her own way. In a world of magic, each woman becomes the subject of legend as the women in her own stories become. She called one of her own stories "The Lovely Legend" and entitled the stories based on her family history "Legend and Memory." Her "Old Mortality" is about the family legend of Miranda's Aunt Amy and, by extension, about Miranda, Porter's mythologized alter ego. In the retold "The Magic Ear Ring," Saila becomes a sorceress in her search for her lost husband; in Porter's own later stories some of her women characters work their sorcery on men for the opposite effect, as her essay "In Defense of Circe" makes clear. And in "The Shattered Star," Nayagta, kidnaped by demons in the service of the Moon-man, becomes a cultural heroine and eventually a goddess, anticipating the desire of Porter's women to be, if not adored, then admired from afar. When Nayagta brings the wonders she has learned from the gods back to her people, they reject them, perhaps indicating Porter's early suspicion that her family would never truly appreciate her talent. Nayagta's place in the firmament expresses Porter's desire for artistic immortality.

The Shattered Star

Some children of *Everyland*, we know, must have seen the Northern Lights, or Aurora Borealis, as the scientists call it—long, slender fingers of light wavering their faint blue or violet or white illumination from the northern horizon to the top of the sky. And of course everyone has asked the cause of this beautiful and mysterious radiance. When WE were small they told us it was the reflection of the sun shining on the ice of the Polar seas. Now they say it is the discharge of electricity through the atmosphere, influenced by the magnetic poles of the earth. Perhaps there are other theories. But we are sure that no explanation can be so delightful as this one of "The Shattered Star," which Miss Porter tells here to the children of *Everyland*.   —The Editors.

In the days of long ago when fairies and demons were powerful, and everything in the world was a marvel, the Eskimo people lived on the side of the earth which is winter for nearly all the year, and they live there to this day. They loved their snow and icebergs, and long, still, frozen edges of the sea. They built their *igloos* (huts) of snow and burned their whale oil lamps with moss wicks, and made their garments of fur from the seals and the polar bears; and they treated their demons kindly, for fear of harm.

But in doing honor to the goddess of the ocean floor who loosed the fish to the Eskimo in the springtime, and in offering food to the visitors from the lower world who whistled in their ears on dark nights, they sometimes forgot the Moon-man, a very powerful deity. In revenge he touched Nayagta, an Eskimo girl-child, when she was but a minute old, and claimed her for the people of the Moon.

Wrapped tightly in her swaddling clothes, Nayagta lay and watched the light from the oil bowl rippling in shadows on the walls of the ice hut until they shone with blue and green and silver light like stars shining in the sea. Sometimes they flowed like water tipped from side to side in a bowl. Nayagta loved this almost as much as she did the warmth of her mother's neck and shoulders as she lay cuddled into the furry *parka* (hood) that covered her mother's head. And she loved to hear her mother sing in a low voice, the same song always, that had only three notes in it.

But the demon who obeys the will of the Moon-man came and looked at the forehead of Nayagta. There was a mark, shaped like a seal, over her left eyebrow, which the finger of the Moon-man had drawn there. So the demon took the child, and stole from the igloo. The wolf dogs rose, bristling and shuddering, and howled as he passed.

Beyond the spaces of the Moon the demon carried Nayagta, and the spirits who inhabit that world received her, and made her their own. They taught her all they knew of magic, until at last she had more power than they, and they no longer had their will over her. And she wished to return to earth.

At this time, the demons were making their world anew, having tired of the old one. They had destroyed many things, but three treasures they could not give up. These were a star of surpassing brilliancy that glowed with all colors, a garden of warm pools and green trees and black shadows and scarlet birds, and a palace of white marble with ebony floors. They quarrelled among themselves as to where these things might be placed. They quarrelled among themselves with bitterness, and wrought spells upon each other, and still they could not find places for the treasures.

So Nayagta leaped up from among them. She seized the garden and the star and the palace, and tucked them under her robe of white fur and cried, "I will give them all to my people!" So she returned to earth, through clouds and gray winds.

But she was changed beyond the knowledge of all those who saw her. Not even the oldest women of the great igloo remembered her. For time among the demons is not measured like our time, and Nayagta had been a thousand years growing up.

"See, I bring gifts!" said Nayagta, while they regarded her with wonder. And she drew forth the marble palace. They looked at it and shouted with joy, for they thought it was of snow. But when they went within and found it was made of strange substance, full of dark caves and many corridors, they were lost, and went about wailing.

Then Nayagta spread out the fair green garden, with its black shadows and scarlet birds, but the people languished and sickened beneath the green, lowering branches of the trees, and drooped with the fragrance of the thick-petalled flowers. Last, Nayagta drew forth the white-hot star, and it shone so radiantly that they were blinded, and wept with terror, hiding their faces and calling to her, "We do not know these things! They are evil!"

Nayagta wept also, when she saw how her people did not know her, and that her gifts were bringing them sadness. She gathered them up and went away again, earth-weary and troubled. This was strange, too, for she had not learned of these pains among the Moon-demons.

Merah, an Eskimo boy who loved Nayagta, came after her and plucked at the sleeve of her fur robe, saying, "Do not go away again to the Far Off places. Abide here in our igloo; my mother shall call you daughter, and I will call you wife. You shall harpoon whale and hunt the reindeer with me, and the *brix* (ledge) of our igloo shall be heaped with the fur of bear and the fur of seal."

But Nayagta answered, "You and your people have not wanted my star nor my garden nor my palace, nor any of the magic I brought you from the spaces of the moon. So I go again."

And Merah said, "Take with you your memory of us." And she answered, "No, I take only my magic and my star and my palace and my garden." But her heart grieved and she remembered.

She went, and she walked in grief and wrath, her feet left the earth, and with each step she rose higher. With her toe she kicked the stars in passing, and a shower of them went flying over the sea, scattering on the icebergs that lay along the edges of the world. As she went, she grieved, saying, "Since my people will not have my gifts, neither will I have them."

Then she cast the palace into the sea, where it turned to ice and stands forever with towers and minarets flashing in the sunlight. She cast the green garden another way, and it slipped over the sides of the earth into a place where no Eskimo has ever been. It is told in old tales that a strange race of folk dream and sing beneath its black shadows forever. She hurled the star into the heavens, where it shattered against the wall of the sky in fragments of fire, and there it blazes and dances and flames forever.

The Eskimos saw it and said, "Nayagta is remembering. Merah can also make magic!" Thereafter whenever a great gray cloud with black edges came whirling down in the time of deepest winter, howling with a great voice, the Eskimos said again, "Nayagta is remembering!" And they smiled as they smile now, for the Eskimo loves the blue ice, and the heavy sea, and the slow-moving bergs where the white bears climb and prowl. They sleep warmly in their huts of ice, and cook their food of fish and oil over the lamps with the moss wicks. They do not long for the vanished gifts of Nayagta.

But Nayagta, wrapped in a great whirling cloud of black and gray, comes up screaming her homesickness in the storm rack; or lies at peace on the edge of the sea watching her shattered star as it is mirrored deeply in the snow and frozen seas. It ripples like the light of the whale oil lamp on the walls of the igloo where Nayagta's mother used to sing three little notes as she swayed with Nayagta in her hood. And Nayagta remembers forever.

The Faithful Princess

Once upon a time there lived a beautiful princess of the land called Indra (India). Her name was Damayanti, and she was the daughter of Bhima, a great *rajah* (king). She lived in a fair garden in her father's court, attended by a hundred handmaidens who loved and served her. She was slender as a young moon in a clear sky, and graceful as a narrow boat on a calm lake.

She sat behind her lattice in the drowsy days of summer and dreamed of the world that lay beyond the walls of her garden of roses and cypress and lotus blossoms. In the bright mornings she laughed with her maidens as they peered into the depths of her bathing pool that mirrored their smiling faces through tiny ripples. No human creature except her father and mother and maidens had ever beheld the face of Damayanti, for she was a Hindu princess of old times, and was sacred from the sight of the world.

In a neighboring state lived another great rajah, a young and glorious warrior who commanded a shining army, and tamed fierce horses, and was skilled in archery. He was high and brave, and he loved truth, for his heart was the heart of a great king. His name was Nala. He had heard tales of the beauty of Damayanti, and his thoughts flew toward her like swift birds.

In his palace court there lived a flock of golden swans who glided upon the waters of the lake, their feathers gleaming in the sunshine. Nala captured one of these for sport one day, and was stricken with awe when it spoke to him in a human voice, saying, "Do not harm me, mighty prince.

Leave unruffled my golden plumes, and I will go to Damayanti, the jewel of Indra, and tell her of your beauty and splendor. She will hear me, and love you."

So Nala loosed the swan and said, "Go quickly."

The swan went to the hidden garden of the rajah's daughter, and saw Damayanti walking a little distance from her maidens. She wore a thin scarlet robe that fell to her silver anklets, and her scarlet veil was sewn with pearls. Her feet were whiter and softer than the lotus flowers she trod upon.

The swan drew near and whispered to her, stretching up his neck. "There is a rajah who dreams of you, fairest of maidens. The heart of the great warrior, Nala, is stirred because of you. The commander of armies is defeated by your beauty. The lover of truth gives his pledge of faith to you."

Damayanti was amazed to hear this but answered, "Go to the glorious lord and say that a Princess keeps her heart a flowering garden for him!"

Then she told her handmaidens, who went to her father, the rajah, and said, "The time for the *Swayamwara* has come." This is the name of a ceremony in old Indra when a Hindu princess chooses a husband from among many rajahs.

So her father sent out a messenger who cried to the four corners of the land, saying, "Heroes of Indra, come! Mighty warriors and princes, come! Damayanti would choose a husband!"

From all over Indra there was heard the sound of elephants and horses tramping, and the rumble of many chariots and the march of feet as the stately rajahs came to the court of Bhima, hoping to be chosen of his daughter. They swept into the court, and were made welcome with feasts.

It happened that two ancient wise men went up Mount Meni, to *Swarga*, the heaven of the Hindu, and bowed before the Cloud Compeller who sat upon the mountain with three other powerful deities, called Agin and Varun and Yama. The Cloud Compeller frowned and asked about the warriors and rajahs saying, "Why have they not come to my feast this day?" And the wise men told him of Damayanti, the lily maiden, the bright jewel in the crown of Bhima, who was on this day to choose a husband. They described her beauty, saying she was like the cypress tree, or the early morning, or a pearl in a golden casket. The deities wondered, and they said, "We will go also to win this maiden." Then the air was filled with the noise of their chariots as they swept through the sky and alighted on earth on a low hill that shook under the hoofs of their horses.

At this moment Nala strode toward the court robed in blue and gold, and the deities saw him. "Go now as a messenger," they told him, "even into the presence of the maid Damayanti and say to her that she must choose for her husband a god rather than a rajah of the world—let it be either Indra, lord of the mountains; Agin, lord of fire; Varun, king of the waters, or Yama, king of darkness."

But Nala answered, "The gates of her court are closely guarded, I cannot enter." And then, the first deity, said, "Go, and the gates will open to you of themselves." So Nala went, fearing the wrath of the gods, and lo! by magic he found himself at Damayanti's lattice. He looked through, and she was more beautiful than he had dreamed.

Then his heart broke within him for sorrow, and he said, "I am Nala," and she smiled and said, "So be it." And he gave her the message from the deities.

Damayanti looked at him, and answered, "Unto you I have given my faith, and I am yours." Then Nala pleaded with her, saying, "Oh, my beloved, with me you choose death, for the gods will not spare us if we disobey them." And Damayanti smiled again and answered, "Behold, sun of my heart, I have chosen. How can I choose a second time? But hear me—when the gods come into the court, come you among them, and I will choose you as though you were a deity, and no sin can be charged to me."

Then Nala returned to the gods and told them what Damayanti had planned.

In the great outer court of the palace, the rajahs of Indra gathered. On gold thrones they sat, their necks hung with garlands of flowers, their ears heavy with jewels. Damayanti stood veiled in the center of them all, and the name of each rajah was called in turn as she looked at him.

Then she searched for Nala among the deities, and behold, each one of them had taken the form of her beloved, so that she could not say which was Nala and which was a deity, for there were five men all of one form and dress.

She bowed her head and wept, and said, "Oh, when I heard the sweet words of the swan, my heart left me. To Nala have I given my faith, and I will choose no other. Hear me if you love truth—I pray thee, oh, reveal my lord!"

The deities heard her, and marveled at her faith and holiness. So in pity they made her eyes to see clearly the signs that mark the deities from men. And she knew the four gods because their faces were without moisture, their eyes did not wink, their garlands did not fade, their feet did not touch the earth, and they cast no shadow. And she saw that Nala's garland drooped, his eyes winked to keep back tears, his feet were covered with dust, and his shadow fell far behind him. Damayanti threw a fresh garland of roses around his neck, touched the hem of his garment, and chose him from among the deities. Then all the people in the court cried, "Well done, well done, brave daughter!" and the palace was filled with joyful laughter and singing. The glory of the faces of Nala and Damayanti was like the glory of the sun and the moon.

The gods were pleased with them, and gave them power over the mountains and fire and water and darkness, because they loved faithfully.

The Magic Ear Ring

This folk-story of Kashmir is very old. When you read it you will see how different it is from our own tales. By knowing a little of ancient India, you will have a better understanding of that country today.

Saila, a beautiful Princess of Kashmir, was betrothed by her father the King to Tasar, a noble Prince. An old woman made the match, according to the ancient custom. She went first to the father of the Prince, and sang a song about the lovely lady in the next country who had a palace of her own, but no husband. Afterward, she went to the father of the Princess and sang a song about the handsome Prince nearby who was friendly to the gods, and had many possessions, but no wife.

The two kings straightway called their children to them, blessed them, and a great wedding feast was held in the white palace of the Princess Saila.

At noon of the day the Prince and Princess left the palace, each wearing robes of silver and blue with many jewels. They rode on the backs of elephants, and their maids and attendants followed, also riding on elephants.

A group of mischievous fairies was hidden behind a bush, watching the procession, and the Fairy Queen fell deeply in love with the Prince.

"Let us steal the husband of Princess Saila," she said to her fairy guard. At her word they all flew into the air like swift birds, circled down over the Prince with a buzzing noise, and made away with him into the dark forest.

The Princess saw them and slipped down from the back of her elephant and ran after the wicked fairies, calling to them to loose the Prince. The fairies fled, leaving Prince Tasar on the ground, but the Fairy Queen cast her spell on him first, and when the Princess Saila reached his side he was lying in a sleep as deep as Death.

The Princess was very sad and wept tears as large as her thumb, but the Prince did not waken.

"Sorrow, a thousand sorrows!" cried the Princess, "What shall I do now?"

At this moment Sudabror and Budabror, two wise brother crows, came and perched on a limb above the unhappy Princess. They live in many parts of the world, and go everywhere giving good advice to unhappy mortals. They now spoke to the Princess, saying, "Why shed tears as large as your thumb, lovely lady, since the Prince is not dead, but asleep? Go back to your home and return here at midnight; hide behind a bush and watch carefully, and you will be able to outwit the evil fairies."

The Princess thanked Sudabror and Budabror for their kindness and returned to her palace with her followers. When night fell she went back to the place where the Prince lay sleeping and hid behind a bush so that she might see him.

Soon the Fairy Queen came and knelt by the Prince. She was a tall woman with yellow eyes and pale green hair that hung to her knees. She took a magic wand from under the feet of the Prince and placed it under his head, and he awoke at once. The Queen talked with the Prince a little while, then placed the wand under his feet and he fell back into slumber.

As soon as the Fairy Queen was gone, Princess Saila rushed out, took the magic wand from under the feet of the Prince, placed it under his head, and awakened him. "Come with me quickly," said the Princess.

"I cannot," said the Prince, sadly, "For if I did the fairies would harm you. We must find a way to defeat them, for you know the saying of the wise men, that magic must be fought with magic."

"Then I will learn magic," said the Princess. "Farewell for a little while." She took a beautiful rose from her girdle and gave it to the Prince. She then placed the wand under his feet and he fell into slumber.

She was no sooner hidden in the bush than the Fairy Queen returned in haste and cried to her train of maidens, "A mortal has been here! Make haste and carry the Prince to the castle of the great Dev (demon) where I may cast a deeper enchantment on him!"

The fairies lifted the Prince and bore him away. As they went, petals from the rose the Prince held in his hand dropped along the path. The next morning Princess Saila followed the trail the fairies had made to the Dev's castle, picking up the rose leaves along the way.

At last she came to the mighty castle, set in the deep green woods. The Dev sat on a high throne. His face was sad, for he was remembering his daughter who had been stolen from her cradle by deep green woods. The Dev sat on a high throne. When he looked up and saw the Princess Saila standing before him, he thought it was his daughter who had returned to him, and he greeted her, saying, "Welcome, a hundred welcomes, beloved daughter! What a wonderful Fairy Queen you will be when the present one retires!"

So the wise Princess pretended to be his daughter, and said, "My father, before I may be Queen of the Dark Folk, you must teach me your magic, so that I may be able to defeat the fairies in their evil tricks against me."

So the Dev taught her the first magic, which is seeing in the dark. And she looked everywhere for the Prince and the Fairy Queen, but she could not find them, for the Queen hid herself and the Prince in a thick dungeon.

Then the Dev taught her the second magic, which is seeing through walls and stones and shields. And she looked everywhere for the Prince and the Fairy Queen, but she could not find them, for the Queen turned herself and the Prince into leopards.

Then the Dev taught her the third magic, which is turning folk into animals, and animals into folk. And she looked everywhere for the Prince and the Fairy Queen, but she could not find them, for the Fairy Queen made herself and the Prince invisible.

Then the Dev taught her the fourth magic, which is the power of making oneself invisible. And she became invisible and looked everywhere for the Prince and the Fairy Queen, but she saw only the Queen, who wore large gold ear rings, and smiled at the Princess as she said, "You will not find your Prince, for I have hid him safely."

Then the Princess went to the Dev and said, "I pray you, teach me more magic yet, for my enemies are destroying me." At last the Dev taught her all the enchantments of the fairy world, and the Princess became wiser than the Fairy Queen and as wise as the Dev himself.

She looked again for the Prince and the Fairy Queen and saw that the Prince was made small as a gnat, and was concealed in the ear ring of the Queen.

And the Princess said, "Give me your ear rings quickly." She stepped forward boldly and loosed the ear rings from the Queen's ears, while the

Queen wept and tried every one of her evil spells on the Princess. But they all fell away harmless.

"Come forth, beloved Prince of the Morning," said Princess Saila to the Prince in the ear ring. And Tasar rose, on the instant restored to life-size. Falling at the feet of the brave Princess, he thanked her.

In a few days the Prince and Princess wished to return to their home. So the old Dev gave them a magic rug that flew through the air, in order that they might travel safely and quickly to the Prince's country.

Early next morning the Prince and Princess seated themselves on the rug, which rose swiftly in the air, and sailed over white clouds high up in the sky until it came to the palace of the Prince. There it settled gently upon the earth. All the people gathered around to greet the lost pair, laughing for joy that they were returned to them.

The Adventures of Hadji:
A Tale of a Turkish Coffee-House

Asia 20 (August 1920): 683–684

✳ When Porter arrived in Mexico in November 1920, she advertised herself as a writer for *Asia* because of this tale and *My Chinese Marriage*, which she finished in Mexico. In the tale, the adventures are Hadji's, but his unnamed wife is clearly the heroine, giving the lie to the old proverb, "Once in forty years is it given to a woman to speak with wisdom." This tale is also "retold," but it is not for children. It is the first example of the mordant irony Porter musters to describe a wife's triumph over her unfaithful husband, roughly the same plot Porter employed two years later in "María Concepción." In both stories, the husbands are awed by the seemingly supernatural powers of their wives.

The Adventures of Hadji:
A Tale of a Turkish Coffee-House

Ali, the *medak* (story-teller), spoke to the effendis as follows:

There is an old saying among the Osmanlis, O Company of the Faithful, that from a woman nothing is to be had but foolishness and vexation.

So abiding is this truth that there is even a proverb among us saying, "Once in forty years is it given to a woman to speak with wisdom." But whether it is at the end of her first forty years, or at the end of the second, or at what moment this inspiration may come, no one among us can know. It is wise, therefore, to take no heed of the words of women, for they are as dry peas rattling in a pod, and like nutshells cast upon a roof top.

Once in many centuries, likewise, does there arise among us a woman of understanding, but how can a man know which woman this may be? It is good on this account to go your ways in peace, with ears deaf to the deceptions of woman, for even when she speaks with knowledge, it is all folly. She sets her words as stones in our paths for our undoing.

It is thus recorded of Hadji, who in old days had a spice-shop in the Great Bazar in Constantinople where he sat daily and sold to all that came to him.

His *hanoum* was a woman of energy and much speech. Hadji loved her tenderly, as it is the habit of all good Osmanlis to cherish those feeble creatures who live by our grace. Hadji was in this wise an exemplary husband, never lacking in kindness. Although the hanoum was long past her time of beauty and fruitfulness, Hadji cherished her. But ofttimes in the night when his wife lay at his side talking of many things, his ears grew faint with listening, and his eyelids were weighted with sleep.

One day in midsummer, when Hadji was seated beside his wares in the Great Bazar, a tall woman came to him and bought spices. Her hands were fair as wax and her nails were stained with red. Her eyes swam in light and her eyelids were painted black with kohl. Hadji perceived instantly that she was the most beautiful and desirable woman in the world, and moreover he saw that she smiled behind her *yasmak*, for her eyelids moved up and down. This warmed him as he measured spices for her, and he thought within himself, "Surely my youth and handsome appearance are yet with me, for this lady smiles upon me!"

He followed the lady to the street when she went away, but he did not have courage to speak to her. When he returned to his stall, a great mournfulness came into his heart. He dropped his head, and sighed for the tall lady. He thought of his faithful hanoum who talked, and his vitals were bitten with longing for other things. In this state he continued throughout the day.

When he reached his home in the evening, his wife met him at the door and began to question him as to his sorrow, for indeed anyone could see he was not himself. She asked him many questions, and he listened with patience, waiting for her to take breath. When she had taken this breath and was about to resume, he said, "Salaam, O Beloved! you have not stopped talking for many minutes, questioning me about this and that.

And all last night you talked. And this morning, likewise, your voice rang in my ears like a brass kettle that is beaten with hammers of copper. Now it is my turn. Here is the cause of my sorrow. Today a woman of surpassing beauty and stateliness and richness of dress came to my shop and bought many measures of spices, all of the finest quality. Her face was like a full moon in a sky without stars, besides which your face is as a mirror dimmed by many breaths. I gazed upon her with all my eyes, but I gave no sign of my admiration, remembering, O Beloved, that you are a faithful and jealous wife. Yet she smiled, as I could not help perceiving by the way her eyelids crinkled, painted black as clouds on a stormy night. Best of all, O Beloved, she spoke not a word. She pointed with her red-stained fingertips to the spices she wished to buy, and received them from my hands and paid me, and went away in silence. A woman above price, without doubt— lamentations upon it! But she left, by accident, this little black bag containing twelve grains of wheat, and I know not why she should be carrying such a trifle about with her."

The wife of Hadji took the bag, and examined it and said, "Alas, thou man of little wit. The woman left this miserable bit of rubbish for you, and the meaning of it is very plain. She lives in the Wheat Market, in the twelfth house, which has a door painted black. Go there, and tell me if I am not right."

Hadji did not believe this, for it was indeed too simple to have much truth in it. Besides, O Company of the Faithful, when did truth come from the mouth of a woman? Nevertheless, Hadji went at once to seek for the house in the Wheat Market.

When he returned, his wife met him and said, "O Hadji, what did she say?"

And he answered, "It was even as you told me, O Beloved. But why did she meet me at the door, without a word, and instead of inviting me into her house, throw a basin of water into the street and straightway make the door fast again?"

"O Hadji of little wisdom," cried the wife, pityingly, "she means by that you are not to come to the door, but by a running stream at the back of her house."

And Hadji said, "Mashallah! I will test your words for the truth that is in them," and he went away in great haste.

In a short time he returned, and said, "O Wise Woman, it was even as you told me. But that veiled and beautiful creature came and stood at her window after I had leaped the running stream, and she looked upon me a moment, saying not a word. Then she leaned forward and took a round mirror from her breast and turned its face from me and went away again. Tell me the meaning of all this!"

The wife answered, "O thou of exceedingly poor wit, she means that you are to visit her in her garden tonight when the moon has turned its face from the earth, that is, at the hour of midnight."

At the time appointed, Hadji set forth, smelling of sweet unguents, with oil of jasmine in his hair, and wearing his coat embroidered in red. The wife of Hadji waited until he was gone, watching him from behind her screen, then set forth also to inform the guards of the city.

It happened by reason of this, O friends, that no sooner had Hadji met the silent lady under her trellis of grapes, nor had he even approached her more than to kiss her hand, than there came over the wall six of the city guards, who seized Hadji and the beautiful lady and bore them away to prison. The guards refused to say what their fate would be, or why they were thus cruelly snatched from their delights in the seclusion of the garden. At the prison, they were flung into cells far apart from each other, yet Hadji could hear the voice of the lady complaining in tones more loud and shrill than the tones of his hanoum, and she continued this until sleep descended upon her. Hadji slept not, but pondered well the ways of women all the night through.

The next morning early, Hadji's wife baked seven little cakes and took them to the prison. She showed them to the cell-keeper, and said, "Let me now take these to the most wretched of your prisoners, for the repose of the souls of my beloved dead."

This request they could not refuse her, and she entered the prison without hindrance from anyone. She went to the cell of the lady and looked through, then entered with a strong step, saying, "The peace of Allah abide with you. It is here I find that face like a full moon in a sky without stars." And the lady said, "Mock on. You are the wife of that thief Hadji!"

The wife answered, "True, Hadji is but a man. Else he could have seen that you are far from your youth and, moreover, have a slight cast in the left eye. And the bones in your neck are like the branches of a fig tree in wintertime. Nevertheless, here is food, for it is not good for the aged to fast. I have a plan whereby you may escape the disgrace of a public trial for having enticed the husband of a virtuous woman, and for having forgotten your vows to your own husband, unfortunate man that he is! Give me your robe and yasmak, and take mine instead. Draw your veil over that face of yours that is like a moon in the last quarter, and leave this prison. But from this day forward, let my husband be as a dead man to you!"

"He is well dead, for my part," answered the lady. She took the robe and yasmak of Hadji's wife, and left her own. Then she went away, without looking back.

When the time came for the trial of Hadji and the lady, the prisoners were brought before the *kadi* (judge). Hadji's knees doubled under him when he saw his wife standing on the other side of the kadi. But wisdom bade him keep silence. His wife stepped forward, and made a speech to the kadi. She talked at great length and the burden of her discourse was this: It had come to a great case in Turkey when a faithful married pair might not embrace in the shade of their own vines without being molested by the guards and haled to a vile prison! For herself, she knew her place in the world and she asked nothing better than to live in peace under the rule of her husband, to whom she had been a faithful, submissive, uncomplaining wife, bearing everything in silence. As she had no thought save the good of her husband in this life, so also her husband had forgotten all women save her since the day she left her father's house, and had lived with her in kindness, without a bitter word. And if such a married pair were not an example to the whole of the empire, she wished to know if goodness existed anywhere. And if they were not safe in the exercise of their domestic virtues, but subject at all times to the danger of having their holy seclusion destroyed by any passing guards, what assurance had they that their very lives were not in danger? And she had nothing further to say, beyond the fact that she hoped this foolishness would soon be made an end of, and she be allowed to return home with her lawful husband.

She then called her servant and *imam* (priest) to testify that she and Hadji were in truth wedded by law, and the end of the affair was that the kadi implored her to take her husband and her imam and her servant and depart in peace with the blessings of Allah—only let his ears be free from the sound of her voice.

At this, Hadji, still speechless, followed his wife from the prison. When they had gone some distance, he said to her, "O Beloved, thou art indeed a marvelous woman." She did not answer, but walked on. And Hadji said, "Thy wisdom is like that of the Prophet himself." And he said, "Thou art a pillar of the virtues, O Beloved, and thy name is a sweet taste on my tongue." And he said, "O Beloved, for worldly knowledge thou art better than a vizier to the Sultan!" And he said, "Thy discretion, O Beloved, is a match for thy wit!" But still the hanoum walked on and would not answer.

Then Hadji said, "Thy face, O Beloved, is like a full moon in a sky without stars, whereas the faces of all other women are mirrors dimmed with many breaths!"

The wife of Hadji wept for joy, and fell upon his neck and said, "O Hadji, Hadji, thy wit is small and thy understanding is mean and thou speakest untruths, but my heart rejoices at thy words!"

And Hadji said nothing.

Blasco Ibanez on "Mexico in Revolution"

El Heraldo de México (November 22, 1920): 7

✴ This is, as far as we know, Porter's first book review. Intending to write a book on Mexico herself, but realizing that it would take considerable time to know the country, she became increasingly contemptuous of those who, as she pointed out in "The Mexican Trinity," dash in to Mexico, take copious notes, dash out again, and in three weeks produce a book to prove themselves Mexican experts. In this scathing review, she attacks Blasco Ibáñez for his superficiality and cynicism. (In her notes she repeats the story that he had proposed to President Carranza and later to President Obregón to write a favorable account of Mexico for 50,000 pesos.) Although she defends revolutionary leaders against his attacks, she soon assumed his jaundiced view of Mexican militarism. In fact, his observation—"No one knows with certainty on whom he can count. You never know whether a friend on embracing you will not stab you in the back"—inspired the theme of "Where Presidents Have No Friends," published in *Century* 104 (July 1922): 273–284, reprinted in *Collected Essays and Occasional Writings of Katherine Anne Porter* (New York: Delacorte, 1970), 404–415.

Blasco Ibanez on "Mexico in Revolution"

Newspaper notes gathered into a book make patchwork reading. Even Lafcadio Hearn's republished "Fantasies" could not survive the test. Six months after they are written, Blasco Ibanez' hurried observations on Mexico in Revolution are staler than even half year old news has any right to be. Tacit forgiveness is extended to daily potboilers in the swift forgetfulness accorded them. When the reporter seeks to revive and perpetuate his mistakes as literature, or even as propaganda, he invites the irritation of the reader.

Ordinarily, one does not review newspaper notes, even though the writer of them is "the most magnificent reporter in the world" as some sly critic dubbed the prolific Spaniard, who has discovered there is money in writing if you write fast enough and badly enough. Yet for one blazing moment when he was younger, he was an artist. He wrote "The Cabin." He was a revolutionary in those days, too, and spent eighteen months in prison for the sake of his political faith.

No doubt as one grows older things are different. Even a fellow countryman of Don Quixote tilts with no windmills at sixty or thereabout. It is better to stand solidly with editors and publishers who buy much and pay well. It is better to write racy, clever stuff: to tell quarter-truths amusingly and convincingly, than to content one's self with the obscure honor of having created "The Cabin."

I read portions of Ibanez' notes on Mexico when they were appearing serially in a New York newspaper. I read them again this week in a book decorated on both sides of the slip cover with an inconsiderately homely photograph of the late Carranza posing with Ibanez. They are evidently conversing on a subject painful to them both. Cordial intent is not visibly established. Ibanez is blinking in that strong light he claims Carranza always forced the visitor to face during interviews. Carranza's manner is nicely divided between boredom and suspicion.

The boredom was his personal affair, but he did well to be suspicious. It would have been better for many other Mexicans if they had been a little less frank in their welcome of the visiting third cousin who embraced them in order to feel of their pistol belts: who led them on to talk about themselves with humorous carelessness in order that he, the visiting third cousin, should be enabled to prove afterward in print what a very clever, knowing sort of chap he was. "See how I understand these people," you may imagine Ibanez saying. "Note the ease with which I tripped them up, and obtained their simple secrets. Really, dear friends, I was as amusing as a weasel in a Rat hole!"

I marvel again at his inverted Latin wit, his gift for stripping the personal dignity from a fellow creature, with deliberate intent so to strip him before as wide a public as he can muster. I resent his not dealing clean wounds that bleed freely. I protest against his sadistic pastime of removing an inch of skin at a time with a razor edge.

He attacks all of us insidiously at points where we are without protection. Who believes in militarism? Who does not feel for the sufferings of the poor peon? His indignation against the one, his proper sympathy for the other are sentiments beyond reproach. Who can help smiling over his sardonic account of the Mexican "soldierette," or laughing outright over the infernally amusing story of Don Jesús Carranza and the Red Cow in Hell?

That is the trouble with this affair. His malice touches the kindred spark of malice in all of us. Blasco Ibanez brought with him to Mexico—Blasco Ibanez. He carried about with him his taste for scandal—his will to believe evil of all he saw. He talked with everybody who had a shady story to tell. Over cafe tables and on street corners he gathered together the most trivial and scandalous untruths ever put between book covers as a serious account of a nation, carefully mixed with an occasional grain of fact when its exclusion would have been too glaringly obvious. Any one like-minded could spend a short time in any capitol of the world and come away with a similar collection of anecdotes.

He brought with him intellectual snobbishness—witness the "Belasco" story—and racial hatred he owns to in words between words. For six whole weeks he sat at cafe tables or stood on street corners discovering the truth about Mexico in Revolution. Then he went away and wrote a delightful, an informing, a profoundly truthful mental autobiography of Blasco Ibanez!

If the reader knew nothing of Mexico except the political propaganda published for years in American journals, it might be very easy to believe nearly all of this book.

It races along so fluently, never at a loss for a word, with a keen and poisonous little anecdote capping each incident sharply. He speaks fairly well of the dead—of Díaz, of Carranza, of Zapata; indiscriminately he scatters a few kindly, condescending words upon these harmless graves. But it is nearly always in order to point more precisely the villainy of some one now in power. Living men at work he hates, it seems.

For young de la Huerta he has a sentence of praise to stress his contention that there are no other idealists in all the government of Mexico. Reading his book, one remembers acquaintance with enough flaming and disinterested revolutionary idealists to employ the fingers of two hands in naming them, and is willing on the strength of that knowledge to admit the existence of numberless others one has never met, and will never hear of. But one feels that somewhere along the road, late or early, Ibanez has laid down his burden of faith in his kind, and groaningly cannot make shift to take it up again. He has taken masters, and serves them excellently well.

He writes always with a weather eye on these masters. Now and again he tucks in sweet pilules of flattery for the delectation of the great northern public for whom he wrote. Deftly he tickles the ear of the white man who indirectly made it worth his while to write this book.

And, ironically and caustically, with relish and innuendo, with much dropping of the eyelid and sweet turning of phrase would he delight a Spanish audience with an account of that so-amusing America he has just discovered if a Spanish publisher decided to make it worth his while.

It is not likely to happen. They have never made it worth Ibanez' while in Spain. Let him fill American platters with his spiced and vinegared scandal-mongering between nations. That is the logical place for it. But it should be devoured and forgotten by the third day.

The Fiesta of Guadalupe

El Heraldo de México (December 13, 1920): 10

On December 12, 1920, Porter attended the feast of the Virgin of Guadalupe and wrote up her experiences for publication in the following day's edition of *El Heraldo*—a remarkable overnight accomplishment for a work of such literary merit. The date of publication is also noteworthy because Porter incorrectly dated it 1923 when she included it in her *Collected Essays*. She made about forty stylistic changes in the second version, mostly for the better, but it contains a confusing error: one passage reads, "They have parted a carved bit of wood and plaster, I see the awful hands of faith . . ." instead of "Over that painted and carved bit of wood and plaster, I see the awful hands of faith. . . ." The second version completely obscures Porter's lament about the Indians' misplaced faith in the Virgin, who is nothing more than a painted statue. Her anticlericalism and out-and-out spurning of religion, which would not alleviate the suffering of the natives, conforms to revolutionary thought, but her consistent anticlericalism in other works in this volume and in later letters to her family and friends argues that she had reached some unfavorable conclusions about religion before coming to Mexico even though she was baptized a Catholic during her first marriage.

"The Fiesta of Guadalupe" is the first of Porter's literary sketches, which she hoped to assemble into a book. It resembles those of Nathaniel Hawthorne, such as "Sights from the Steeple." The first person narrator, presumably Porter, situates herself for a short, continuous period of time in a particular place and recounts what passes before her, creating in the process a unified emotional impression. The impression Porter creates is, of course, of the unrelieved suffering of the Mexican Indians—so great that she expresses, at the end of the sketch, the thought that it might cause them to awake from their dormancy and erupt like a volcano, as if she had forgotten that a revolution had already taken place.

The Fiesta of Guadalupe

I followed a great crowd of tired burdened pilgrims, bowed under their burdens of potteries and food and babies and baskets, their clothes dusty and their faces a little stained with long-borne fatigue. Indians from all over Mexico had gathered at the feet of Mary Guadalupe for this greatest *fiesta* of the year, which celebrates the initiation of Mexico into the mystic company of the Church, with a saint and a miracle all her own, not transplanted from Spain. Juan Diego's long-ago vision of Mary on the bare hillside made her Queen of Mexico where before she had been Empress.

Members of all tribes were there in their distinctive costumes. Women wearing skirts of one piece of cloth wrapped around their sturdy bodies. Women wearing gaily embroidered blouses with very short puffed sleeves. Women wearing full gathered skirts of green and red, with blue *rebosos* wrapped tightly around their heads. And men in great hats with peaked crowns, wide flat hats with almost no crowns. Blankets, and *serapes*, and thonged sandals. And a strange-appearing group whose men all wore a large square of fiber cloth as a cloak, brought under one arm and knotted on the opposite shoulder exactly in the style depicted in the old drawings of Moctezuma.

A clutter of babies and dolls and jars and blind people lined the sidewalks, intermingled with booths, red curtained and hung with paper streamers, where sweets and food and drinks were sold. Here we found their simple clean craftsmanlike potteries and jars and wooden pails bound with hand wrought clasps of iron, and gentle-looking lacework immaculately white and unbelievably cheap as to price.

I picked my way through the crowd looking for the dancers, that curious survival of the ancient Dionysian rites, which in turn were brought over from an unknown time. The dance and blood sacrifice are inextricably tangled in the worship of men, and the sight of men dancing in a religious ecstasy links one's imagination, for the moment, with all the lives that have been.

A woven, moving arch of brilliant-colored paper flowers gleaming over the heads of the crowd drew me near the gates of the cathedral as the great bells high up began to ring—sharply, with shocking clamor, they began to sway and ring, their ancient tongues shouting notes of joy a little out of tune. The arches began to leap and flutter. I managed to draw near enough to see, over the fuzzy poll of a sleeping baby on his mother's back. A group of Indians, fantastically dressed, each carrying an arch of flowers, were stepping it briskly to the smart jangle of the bells. They wore tinsel crowns over red bandannas which hung down their necks in Arab fashion. Their costumes were of varicolored bits of cloth, roughly fashioned into short skirts and blouses. Their muscular brown legs were disfigured with cerise and blue cotton stockings. They danced a short, monotonous step, facing each other, advancing, retreating, swaying the arches over their crowns, turning and bowing, in a stolid sarabande. The utter solemnity of their faces made it a moving sight. Under their bandannas, their foreheads were knitted in the effort to keep time and watch the figures of the dance. Not a smile. Not a sound save the mad hysteria of the old bells awakened from their sleep, shrieking praises to the queen of Heaven and the Lord of Life.

Then the bells stopped, and a man with a mandolin stood near by, and began a quiet rhythmic tune. The master of ceremonies, wearing around his neck a stuffed rabbit clothed in a pink satin jacket, waved the flagging dancers in to line, helped the less agile to catch step, and the dancing went on.

A jammed and breathless crowd of pilgrims inside the churchyard peered through the iron fence, while the youths and boys scrambled up, over the heads of their elders, and watched from a precarious vantage. They reminded one irresistibly of a menagerie cage lined with young monkeys. They spraddled and sprawled, caught toeholds and fell, gathered themselves up and shinned up the railings again. They were almost as busy as the dancers themselves.

Past stalls of fruit and babies crawling underfoot away from their engrossed mothers and the vendors of images, scapulars and rosaries, I walked to the chapel of the well, where is guarded the holy spring of water that gushed from beneath Mary's feet at her last appearance to Juan Diego, December twelve, in the year of grace fifteen hundred and thirty-one.

It is a small darkened place, the well covered over with a handsomely wrought iron grating, through which the magic waters are brought up in a copper pail with a heavy handle. The people gather here and drink reverently, passing the pail from mouth to mouth, praying the while to be delivered of their infirmities and sins.

A girl weeps as she drinks, her chin quivering. A man, sweating and dusty drinks and drinks and drinks again, with a great sigh of satisfaction, wipes his mouth and crosses himself devoutly.

My pilgrimage leads me back to the great cathedral, intent on seeing the miraculous Tilma of Juan Diego, whereon the queen of Heaven deigned to stamp her lovely image. Great is the power of that faded virgin curving like a new moon in her rigid blue cloak, dim and remote and immobile in her frame above the soaring altar columns.

From above, the drone of priests' voices in endless prayers, answered by the shrill treble of boy singers. Under the overwhelming arches and the cold magnificence of the white altar, their faces lighted palely by the glimmer of candles, kneel the Indians. Some of them have walked for days for the privilege of kneeling on these flagged floors and raising their eyes to the Holy Tilma.

There is a rapt stillness, a terrible reasonless faith in their dark faces. Their eyes strain toward the picture of their beloved Lady, printed on the garment of Juan Diego only ten years after Cortes had brought the new God, with fire and sword, into Mexico. Only ten years—but it is probable Juan Diego knew nothing of the fire and sword which have been so often the weapons of the faithful servants of our Lady. Maybe he had learned religion happily, from some old gentle priest, and his thoughts of the Virgin, ineffably mysterious and radiant and kind must have haunted him by day and by night for a long time; until one day, oh, miracle of miracles, his kindled eyes beheld her, standing, softly robed in blue, her pale hands clasped, a message of devotion on her lips, on a little familiar hill in his own country, the very spot where his childhood had been passed.

Ah well—why not? And I pass on to the steep winding ascent to the chapel of the little hill, once a Teocalli, called the Hill of Tepeyac, and the scene of other faiths and other pilgrimages. I think, as I follow the path, of those early victims of Faith who went up (how slowly and heavily, let the old Gods themselves tell you) to give up their beating hearts in order that the sun might rise again on their people. Now there is a great crucifix set up with the transfixed and bleeding heart of one Man nailed upon it—one magnificent Egoist who dreamed that his great heart could redeem from death all the other hearts of earth destined to be born. He has taken the old hill by storm with his mother, Mary Guadalupe, and their shrine brings the Indians climbing up, in silent groups, pursued by the prayers of the blind and the halt and the lame who have gathered to reap a little share of the blessings being rained upon the children of the faith. Theirs is a doleful litany: "In the name of our Lady, Pity, a little charity! For the clear love of God, help me! In the name of Our Pitiful mother, charity for the poor—for the blind, for the little servants of God, for the humble in heart!" The cries waver to you on the winds as the slope rises, and comes in faintly to the small chapel where is the reclining potent image of Guadalupe, second in power only to the Holy Tilma itself.

It is a more recent image, copied from the original picture, but now she is lying down, hands clasped, supported by a company of saints. There is a voluptuous softness in her face and pose—a later virgin, grown accustomed to homage. From the meek maiden receiving the announcement of the Angel Gabriel on her knees, she has progressed to the role of Powerful Intercessor. Her eyes are vague and a little indifferent, and she does not glance at the devout adorer who passionately clasps her knees and bows his head upon them.

A sheet of glass protects her, or she would be literally wiped away by the touches of her devotees. They crowd up to the case, and rub their hands on it, and cross themselves, then rub the afflicted parts of their bodies, hoping for a cure. A man reached up and rubbed the glass, then gently stroked the head of his sick and pallid wife, who could not get near enough to touch for herself. He rubbed his own forehead and knees, then stroked the woman's chest. A mother brought her baby and leaned his little face against the glass for a long time, the tears rolling down her cheeks.

Twenty brown and work-stained hands are stretched up to touch the magic glass—they obscure the still face of the adored Lady, they blot out with their insistent supplications her sweet remote eyes. Over that painted and carved bit of wood and plaster, I see the awful hands of faith, the credulous and worn hands of believers; the humble and beseeching hands of the millions and millions who have only the anodyne of credulity. In my dreams I shall see those groping insatiate hands reaching, reaching, reaching, the eyes turned blindly away from the good earth which should fill them, to the vast and empty sky.

Out upon the downward road again, I stop and look over the dark and brooding land, with its rim of mountains swathed in layer upon layer of filmy blue and gray and purple mists, the low empty valleys blackened with clumps of trees. The flat-topped houses of adobe drift away casting long shadows on the flooding pale blue sunlight, I seem to walk in a heavy, dolorous dream.

It is not Mary Guadalupe nor her son with his bleeding heart that touches me. It is Juan Diego I remember, and his people I see, kneeling in scattered ranks on the cold floors of their churches, fixing their eyes on mystic, speechless things. It is their ragged hands I see, and their wounded hearts that I feel beating under their work-stained clothes like a great volcano under the earth and I think to myself, hopefully, that men do not dream forever.

Book Review: *Caliban* by W. L. George, *The Chinese Coat* by Jennette Lee, and *The House of Lynch* by Leonard Merrick

El Heraldo de México (December 15, 1920): 10

With her visit to the Villa de Guadalupe fresh in her mind, Porter wrote her second book review. In reviewing George's novel, she describes his "profound pessimism," but her switch to the first person—"And out of it all the solitary victory that any of us can wring from life is the triumph of having achieved birth and the right to our day of sweat and confusion and half attained desires"—proves that the profound pessimism is hers. Like the novel's heroine, Porter has "that deadly female accuracy of vision that cannot be deceived. That would believe if it could, and knows it cannot do so." Already Porter had relinquished the tenuous optimism about life her visit to Mexico was intended to nurture. When depressed, she sometimes described hope as a self-deception.

Porter clearly had little enthusiasm for the other two books included in this review. Her obvious distaste for contemporary popular fiction is conveyed in her skillful choice of adjectives and adverbs to characterize the works. The "light and sweet romance of marriage," *The Chinese Coat*, is damned by faint praise as "a pleasant story very quaint and nicely told." Porter's view of Merrick's widely read fiction, as epitomized by *The House of Lynch*, is more sharply critical. Like his earlier novels, this work is "very light, very facile and easy, very charming in manner" and "told cleverly, not too deeply, with an air of romance." Porter's underlying pessimism also colors her negative assessments of these works.

Book Review: *Caliban* by W. L. George, *The Chinese Coat* by Jennette Lee, and *The House of Lynch* by Leonard Merrick

W. L. George is reversing the process of most of the younger British writers, by writing better and better instead of terribly worse and worse. His latest book, *Caliban*, excels either *The Second Blooming* or *Blind Alley*.

In *Caliban*, George gives us a thorough study of a very modern man, headlong in the pursuit of material success, which he does not know what to do with when he gets it. George's writing method is a realism, so-called, that grows naturally out of the very story he has to tell. Without enthusiasm, in a first rate homely style, he strips his characters down to the raw nerves and lets you see for yourself what they are, why they are that way, and what inevitably comes of it. I said "nerves" on purpose, for the whole book is a study of neuroses, the living pulp writhing under the excruciating pressure of life as it has evolved. He tells a little why it has become like this, too.

He begins with Richard Bulmer when he is a boy of fifteen in school girding at his enforced study of the Latin classics which are of no possible value in his scheme. He was born a frankly utilitarian person—if a thing had not obviously usable, practical qualities, available for the present instant, it was not for him.

We are given, as a foundation, a scathing study of his desolate, neargenteel family life, with his futile mother and his boasting, wavering father; his emotionally starving sister Hettie and his miserly sister Eleanor. The drab struggle to keep up appearances on an inadequate income, with the furtive family pinchings and strivings, are set before us as a background for the boy's first venture into the magazine publishing business, his first passion, his impossible marriage.

Already you see rising slowly to his surface those innate qualities later to be summed up in analysis by an employee of Bulmer: "You know, Alford, the Boss is a marvelous man. He's got no brain. He's not clever. He's got no common sense. He never thinks . . . but he never thinks twice, and that's the making of him. He's just one great big desire; and as most men can't conceive desire, he gets his way. . . . His mind is the middle class maximum, and it never evolves. . . . He thinks he leads because he follows. . . . That's the secret of his success . . . the boss's readers are all alike. . . ."

Thirty years afterward, when Bulmer has become the owner and publisher of a net of middle class newspapers, society magazines, sports weeklies and Town Tattlers thrown all over the United Kingdom, his Ego has become ferocious and bloodthirsty. He becomes a peer, he harries the government, he makes and unmakes politicians with a Caliban-like malice and intractable personal animosity. This part of the book contains a remarkable study of the immature temperament, goaded by an inferiority complex and a manifold defense mechanism growing out of his early struggles and the unhealing wounds he suffered in them.

He tramples and froths, he squanders lives and energies, he swings with the winds of popular opinion, he follows the latest fads in politics, always believing himself the Man of Power, the Molder of Public Belief. At last he espouses Labor because Labor is the Thing. It has become a popular issue, with a countess or two and the sprinkling of Intellectuals supporting its cause. Labor distrusts him and his old middle class adherents turn from him. But he can see nothing, and believes in nothing, and loves nothing save himself, until he meets Janet Willoughby.

He loves Janet late in life. She is written into the story with a gentle, crisp affection by the author, who evidently admires Janet very much. She is really admirably drawn—surface-wavering, innerly resilient and firm, feminine and calm, not to be swept off her feet. Horribly clear as to mind, analyzing Bulmer mercilessly, seeing him as he is, brutal and childish and boastful and strong. She has that deadly female accuracy of vision that cannot be deceived. That would believe if it could, and knows it cannot do so. That loves illusion, and cannot endure it. Janet is fearfully modern, really—firm and humorous, rationalizing life and emotion consistently unto a certain point, when she, with all the other people in the book, does the natural inevitable thing at last.

Bulmer's attitude toward the war, and all that rises from it, are set down with implacable quiet bitterness that you feel welling up from sources darkened with disillusion. All the way through it grows steadily upon you that George, himself, sees plainly that the world is in a bad way, with nothing much to be done about it. He offers no remedy and indeed he hints that there is none, for his conclusions are rooted in the profound pessimism of a thoughtful man who looks on a world in chaos, and hears the shrieking of a million Messiahs bent on setting it to rights each in his own way.

He looks back on a world clamorous with war, and looks forward to a world clamorous with war pursued in many causes into the next Glacial Age. And out of it all the solitary victory that any of us can bring from life is the triumph of having achieved birth and the right to our day of sweat and confusion and half attained desires. Under his calm style you sense the hot revolt against an unendurable fact that must be faced out.

"After all, what's it got to do with me?" asks Bulmer, at the last. "I am what I am. I'm alone, like most people. . . . One slips into life easily enough and one slips out. . . . One's not missed, because one doesn't hitch into other people." And here one sees the stain of a truth that will not wash out. Bulmer is merely a fiction prototype of Northcliffe, and Hearst, and Pulitzer and the war lords and the politicians and all the rest of them, who play the great game of molding public destiny. And George quite reasonably sees not much hope for a world run by the Bulmers.

This is a solidly written, honest and thoughtful book, worth several readings.

The Chinese Coat
by Jennette Lee

This little story of the symbolic Chinese coat is a light and sweet romance of marriage, wherein Mrs. Lee tells a slightly incredible tale with much sentiment and graceful writing.

Eleanor More, a bride, sees a Chinese coat at a sale one day, marked a price she cannot afford. She adores the coat, naturally, and her husband attempts to purchase it for her. The adventures growing out of this, which follow him into middle life, involve their grown up children and take the pair on a long pilgrimage into the hills of China, make a pleasant story very quaint and nicely told.

The House of Lynch

The story of an artist who fought a winning battle against the power of money was published serially about ten years ago in an American magazine. It has been included in the recent uniform collection of Leonard Merrick's works, published by E. P. Dutton & Co., in what is called the Author's Edition. Each book has been prefaced by a notable British writer, including Barrie and H. G. Wells. "The House of Lynch" has a preface by G. K. Chesterton somewhat more grave in tone than the book itself. For though Merrick deals with a more sober subject than is his usual habit, he cannot help being very light, very facile and easy, very charming in manner. He is that within himself: so if his artist is poor, and marries a rich girl, and discovers that she cannot bear his poverty, and he will not share her riches for honor's sake, and if the arrangement almost goes to smash on that account, it must all be told cleverly, not too deeply, with an air of romance. Merrick does it like that.

If you like Merrick—and almost everyone who reads him loves him—you will be charmed with his book.

The Funeral of General Benjamín Hill

El Heraldo de México (December 17, 1920): 7

General Benjamín Hill, Minister of War and nephew of Obregón, mysteriously died of food poisoning while attending a banquet in his honor. Porter probably met him during the inaugural festivities. Her impressionistic report, consistent in mood with "The Fiesta of Guadalupe" and her review of George's novel, is the earliest exploration of death, her favorite theme.

The Funeral of General Benjamín Hill

Under a brilliant morning sky, clean-swept by chill winds straight from the mountains; with busy people thronging the streets, the vendors of sweets and fruits and toys nagging gently at one's elbow; with three "ships" circling so close above the trees of the Alameda one could see the faces of the pilots; with the air live with the calls of bugles and the rattle of drums, the Minister of War, General Hill, passed yesterday through the streets of the city on his final march, attended by his army.

Life, full and careless and busy and full of curiosity, clamored around the slow moving metallic coffin mounted on the gun carriage. Death, for the most, takes his sure victories silently and secretly. And all the cacophony of music and drum and clatter of horses' hoofs and shouts of military orders was merely a pall of sound thrown over the immobile calm of that brown box proceeding up the life-filled streets. It sounded, somehow, like a shout of defiance in the face of our sure and inevitable end. But it was only a short dying in the air. Death, being certain of Himself, can afford to be quiet.

Striking the Lyric Note in Mexico
(co-authored with Robert Haberman)

New York Call, "The Call Magazine" (January 16, 1921): 1, 3

In an enthusiastic letter of December 30, 1920, to her family, Porter wrote that she had met Felipe Carrillo Puerto and J. H. Retinger at the Habermans' on Christmas day. Carrillo Puerto was the charismatic socialist delegate (and later governor) from Yucatán, while the Polish-born Retinger was adviser to Luis Morones and, for a brief time, Porter's lover. In her letter Porter also announced that she was to write a socialist textbook with the Habermans and was the editor of the newly established *Magazine of Mexico*. In early January she attended the Pan-American Federation of Labor conference, meeting Samuel Gompers, president of the Federation. Her new lover, new job as editor, and the excitement engendered by the labor conference account for her hopeful mood: this is the only optimistic politically partisan essay she wrote. The essay is also the only collaborative work in Porter's canon—the socialist textbook never materialized. The prose of the essay is clearly Porter's, as well as the point of view—witness the reference to a labor strike in Denver—while Haberman supplied the past history of another strike in Mexico, encouraged her partisanship, and arranged publication in the socialist *Call*, to which he contributed articles. The colorful descriptions and sympathetic observations of the contemporary scene and Porter's good-humored skepticism of the political purposes of the Mexicans connect this early piece with "Where Presidents Have No Friends" (*Century*, July 1922), which she included in her *Collected Essays*.

Striking the Lyric Note in Mexico

by Katherine Anne Porter and Roberto Haberman

Armistice Day! On either side of Avenida Juarez, which becomes Avenida Francisco I. Madero, at a curve near the Teatro Nacional corner, the houses were messy in draperies of Allied buntings. The yellow sunshine washed everything clean, even the gaudy banners, shouting of things one aches to remember, even the rags of the peon who stands under a tree in the Alameda, near a crowd of foreign holiday makers, easing the leather thongs of his pack away from his forehead as he listens to the military band playing a hot, drum-agitated war march.

Children in white dresses, with their Indian nurses, skip the rope through the shaded pathways of the old park. Decorated automobiles whirl through the streets, filled with gaily dressed people out for festivity. Armistice Day is being celebrated with appropriate gestures by the colonies representing the Allied victors in Mexico.

On the Alameda side of the avenue there emerged from a side street a long, straggling procession of strange looking Mexican men and women—strange, that is, in the midst of the rushing cars which they dodged aside for at intervals: strange in the brilliant, searching morning sunlight, leaving not a line in their dark faces, a single rent or mend or stain in their working clothes unilluminated. In the bands of their wide straw hats they wore red placards, lettered in black. Their banners did not wave in the breezes because they were merely other placards, slightly larger, carried on the ends of short sticks. They rambled along, two and two and three and three abreast, sometimes surging up to the sidewalks, sometimes strolling off to the street again. Small boys ran along with them. They were all smiling and talking among themselves, with an air of good humor. One decided they were celebrating an obscure little holiday of their own.

A small brown boy gave an adventurous shout, snatched a placard from a marcher's hat and stuck it in his own. He ran up the sidewalk. One read the legend in Spanish: "While the Allies celebrate victory their workers are starving!"

So that is the meaning of this gathering of thin and shabby, cheerful men. One followed along unobtrusively, keeping step to the war march blared at one's back in military brasses. It receded gradually in distance, but the morning was charged with its rhythm. One remembers similar demonstrations in America, with police riding down the marchers, ripping banners from their hands, carrying struggling workers away to jail. One remembers the militia lounging about, guns in hand, during strikes, in the streets of Denver. A curiosity prompts one to see this parade to its conclusion.

At a corner, several blocks down, the procession paused at the gesture of the traffic policeman, spiffy in his immaculate uniform of black, trimmed with green. As they went forward again, the policeman waved them on with a fraternal swing of his club. They waved at him and called out greetings. They passed a group of soldiers and exchanged a volley of good mornings! Passersby on the sidewalk turned to watch them, smiling.

The head of the parade passed around a corner. Immediately there floated back to us of the rear guard a curious and unpeaceful medley of shouts, growls, yelps, the clatter of booted heels mingled with the thud of sandalled feet. We rushed around the square into chaos. The marchers had met a group of Allied picnickers on their way to the Tivoli del Eliseo, there to celebrate peace with fireworks and brass bands. Exchanges of incivilities ensued, in the form of words and blows. An Allied celebrant, fired with liquor and patriotism, seized the placard of one worker who was peaceful but not a pacifist. The worker insisted on having his placard. Everybody mixed in joyously, and the orderly, humorous procession became a monopoly of bad intentions all around.

This happened near an army barracks. Now, peace is trying to professional militarists. When they looked out into the lately vacant day and saw their working brothers being molested, a group rushed out spontaneously, headed by a colonel. They mingled among the fray with expert technique, scattered the picnickers, who at first thought the soldiers were on their side, and the colonel himself restored the tattered placard to the worker.

Being American, one hardly believed the evidence of the eye at this juncture.

It was the marchers who were being protected—impossible! There must be a mistake somewhere. A state of affairs warranting immediate investigation presented itself.

Threading back to headquarters, there was unraveled a tale of subtle international complications which somehow should have been very serious and wasn't—the warp of humor and sanity in the Mexican mind is laid too straight to tangle in smaller complexities.

This demonstration, we were informed, was one phase of a strike by employes of the Palacio de Hierro, a great department store with its own furniture and clothing factories, employing about 400 laborers and owned by a French concern. And through this strike we went back to a strike of a short while previous, where the owners of the works were British.

We will begin there. Three hundred workers of the Excelsior Lumber Company struck for an increase of pay, recognition of their union, reemployment of their agitators. They belonged to the Federation of Syndicates of the Federal district, the Mexico City representative of the Mexican Federation of Labor. Before declaring a general strike, the union asked its fellow unions how far it might depend on them for help in the event of a strike. They received the regulation answer given to every striking organization: They would be given all material help, which means money; and all moral help, which means striking with them. Every union, down to the smallest group, receives this assurance as a guaranty of solid organization among the workers.

But the striking wood workers decided to help themselves, too, and impose no burden on the federation treasury. They quietly went out and got other jobs, with the exception of a picket committee of 30. Thus secured, they sent a delegation to confer with the manager of the Excelsior.

With true British courtesy and tact, he received them. He assured them he would be damned before he would let any bunch of workers tell him how to run his factory. They would all be in hell, he hoped, before they got a single penny more wages from him.

With these kindly sentiments refreshing their ears, the workers marched out. The factory doors were closed, the pickets formed, the red flag was flung across the gates. Nobody could enter or leave the place. The strikers departed to their new jobs. The pickets leaned against the walls and talked and smoked.

When night came they built large bonfires for warmth and cheer. Their wives brought them food in large baskets. Their brother strikers returned from their day's labor and kept them company. The bonfires increased, taking on the complexion of triumph. They sat about in groups and sang popular songs, harmonizing to the accompaniment of guitars and mandolins. Later on they danced with their wives and "novias" around the replenished blazes. The strike turned into a fiesta.

The British employers got their Consul by telephone, informing him of this scandalous state of things. The Consul called on beleaguered President De la Huerta, the natural storm center for this sort of trouble. The complaint was amusingly personal. The workers had not only the temerity to strike, but, dash it all, they were making a party of it, with red flags, bonfires and guitars!

President De la Huerta referred them, quite properly, to the Department of Labor. Celestino Gasca, the shoemaker Governor of the Federal district, appointed a delegate to look after the strike, and see that order was maintained. This delegate was Capt. Pio Quinto Roldan, and his exquisite impartiality in the discharge of his new duties was destined to call forth curses from the British. They demanded that he call off the strike or permit strikebreakers and material to be sent past the red flag into the factory.

Being Mexican, Capt. Pio Quinto Roldan is truly polite. He would love to aid the British Consul, but there is an article in the Mexican Constitution permitting Mexican laborers to strike whenever it is necessary to better their economic condition—a legal snag on which he professed himself fairly caught. How could *he* amend the Mexican Constitution, even for the sake of the British Consul? Unhappily, strikebreakers were not mentioned. It would, therefore, not be advisable, etc., etc.

The strike lasted nearly two weeks, for, though Britons never, never, will be slaves, they have a natural taste for the enslavement of others, and, being unaware that the strikers were romping on light hearts, supported by full stomachs and steady wages from other jobs, they hung to the hope that they would all starve or give in. But some ray of light penetrated at last. They may have found out about the other jobs, or discovered that the unions were backing the demonstrations. At any rate, the strikers won their demands entirely and returned to work.

This victory breathed the breath of life into the employes of the Palacio de Hierro, the French concern. They asked for 75 per cent increase for piece workers and 50 per cent for day workers. They followed the ritual of the strike, were refused everything, got other jobs, walked out and spread the red flag over the gates. And we see them a few days later marching down the Avenida Francisco I. Madero, where they encountered disapproval from the Allied picnickers with surprising results, as we have told.

The really lovely joke of this incident—the stinger, as it were—occurred almost simultaneously. The French colony had its flags and bunting stored in the Palacio de Hierro, sealed with the scarlet banner. When the French committee called for them the pickets would not let them pass. The French rushed away and returned with a deputation of police. The police took the pickets aside for a chat. At the end of five minutes they returned. Good will, within certain defined limits, was to endure for an hour or two. The French could go in and get their flags, but the police and a group of strikers must go, also, to make sure no other materials were removed with the buntings. With maddening exactitude, every flag was unfolded before it was delivered to the holiday committee.

In the meantime, the French owners of Palacio de Hierro were also following a ritual. They and the French consul called on De la Huerta, who referred them to Celestino Gasca, who passed them on to a specially appointed labor delegate, none other than the indomitable Pio Quinto Roldan, still engaged in his favorite pastime of upholding the Mexican Constitution.

"Can't you do something about it—any thing at all?" requested the committee, with Gallic emotion.

"It is nothing to me personally," answered Captain Pio Quinto, in that polite, detached official manner of his, "but it says here," and his finger came down squarely on the line beginning: "Strikes shall be lawful when by the employment of peaceful means they shall aim to bring about the balance between the various factors of production, and to harmonize the rights of capital and labor. . . ."

"As long as they are orderly and commit no violence," he finished, "we cannot possibly interfere." And the strikers steadfastly refused to even hint at violence.

Under the outraged and uplifted noses of the owners, whose respective governments, by the way, still refuse to recognize the new Mexican regime, the bonfires and singing and dancing went on nightly at the factory gates, with the red flag blazing handsomely in the firelight.

In two weeks they won. Two weeks seem to be the time limit of endurance in the owners' minds. They could not part with all that precious money at one crash—the workers very reasonably conceded they had asked for too much on the first occasion. They compromised on a 40 per cent flat increase for everybody, with re-employment of their agitators, a donation of 2,000 pesos toward their co-operative society and medicine and medical attendance for all employes during illness, which does very well as a beginning.

During this time baffled representatives of those governments that cannot see Mexico as a republic—or probably see her too plainly as such—spent days rushing about trying to get something done about it. Nothing was done about it. The officials refused to order out the soldiery to shoot the workers. They even seemed shocked at the suggestion. The policemen did not interfere. They wigwagged their traffic signs on street corners and otherwise followed their arduous vocations with becoming concentration. Nobody minded.

And the singing party went on before the gates, to the thrumming of mandolins—lovely and tuneful native melodies, with their lovely and tuneful names—"La Pajarera," "Cielito Lindo" and "Estrellita."

The New Man and The New Order

Magazine of Mexico (March 1921): 5–15

After at least a month's delay, the first issue of the *Magazine of Mexico* appeared, with a photograph of President Obregón, "The New Man," gracing the cover. Porter's admiration of Obregón is evident throughout. In a country that oscillated "between despotism and revolution," he is the man to lead Mexico—if he cannot do it, there is no man who can. She does not predict but hopes for his success despite the fact that his enemies will stop "at no thing to accomplish his downfall." This ominous observation Porter enlarged on a few months later in "The Mexican Trinity," in which she was skeptical that he could indeed overcome the enemies of Mexico. In "Where Presidents Have No Friends," Porter returned to the idea with which she opened this essay: "It would be useless to deny that a man throws dice with death when he becomes president of Mexico."

The New Man and The New Order

It would be useless to deny that a man throws dice with death when he becomes president of Mexico. "He plays blind man's buff with La Muerte" says a Mexican writer. It is a high adventure, not to be undertaken lightly. Tremendous inner compulsion forces a man into the presidency of the

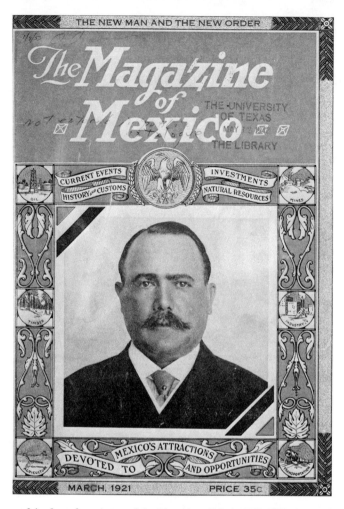

Front cover of the first of two issues of the *Magazine of Mexico*. Edited by Porter, the magazine was intended to encourage investment in Mexico. The featured article of this issue was her essay on President Alvaro Obregón, "The New Man and The New Order"; Obregón's picture appears on the cover. All illustrations for this article courtesy of Benson Latin American Collection, University of Texas General Libraries.

Mexican Republic. In the past, this official has been infallibly one of these things—an egoist without horizons, an adventurer who loves danger, an idealist with a self sacrifice complex, a steel nerved dictator sure of his butchering strength. Once or twice it has been a fantastic combination of these qualities. But in all of them, the flair for personal magnificence, has made one-half of the formula. All things considered Mexico has borne with her presidents leniently, a divine patience has marked her dealings with her chance-appointed Chiefs. Some of them were aristocrats and all of them were opportunists. There was a dreamer once, hands raised in ineffectual blessings, dictators more than once, and the beautiful gold laced seekers of glory were the most numerous of all. But they shared ineluctably one glittering assortment of qualities—a baffling self sufficiency that blinded them to the importance of pacific international relations; a racial arrogance that made them not fusible with their neighbors; a personal pride that forbade them to learn the practical problems of their country; a startling ignorance of the conditions of labor and commerce and economics and industry that are the very life fluid of a nation.

It was high time Mexico had a simple working president with his feet firmly set in his native soil. After the scintillating procession of remote and inaccessible rulers, there came up from the land a farmer, Alvaro Obregon, prosperous and well acquainted with his country in its working dress; a man of straight literal mind, with a detached legal passion for setting disorder to rights. He became a soldier when the need for an honest fighting man became all too plain. He kept himself clear of the intricacies of professional diplomacy and politics through several years as general when Carranza was Chief of the Army. Later he became minister of War with this same Carranza as president, and somehow stood straight in this post too, not once fooled or circumvented by the devious methods of the President and his group of flattering shadows.

And now it is December 1st, 1920, and here is General Obregon about to become President of Mexico, after spectacular events, and a series of stupendous tragic blunders on the part of the fleeing Carranza. At twelve o'clock at night provisional President de la Huerta is to give over his office to General Alvaro Obregon. Preparations are all very festive, for everybody shares in a fiesta in Mexico. The city is strange with the voices of foreign people—we hear the shrill American voice, the tinkling Mexican voice, the gurgling Indian vocables, a scattering volley of French, truncated British speech, Spanish spoken in twenty different accents, for the South Americans are here in force. Here are the city Mexicans, rancheros grandiose in buckskin charros and great embroidered sombreros, Indians with sandaled feet and softly woven blankets luminous with color. They are all fearfully alive, fearfully bent on getting somewhere—the narrow sidewalks will not do, everybody takes to the street center, and disputes rancorously for place with the outraged drivers of cars.

Plainly, Obregon becoming President has a definite interest for all parts of the world, each part nursing its particular interest, its personal hope.

Chapultepec Castle, Mexico City. This photograph and the following ones were published with Porter's "The New Man and The New Order." She may have composed the captions: "THE HOME OF MEXICO'S PRESIDENT. The Castle of Chapultepec (Aztec, meaning grasshopper hill) occupies the site of an Aztec temple and fortress in the old Chapultepec Park, once an island in the salt lake of Texcoco. The Emperor Moctezuma made a summer residence of the fortress, and established here his harem, baths, gardens and hunting lodges. The present castle was begun as a fortress in 1783 by a Spanish Don, with funds supplied by the Spanish Crown. Later it became a branch of the Mexican Military School. In 1866 Emperor Maximilian caused the castle to be renovated and decorated elaborately in the Italian style. With Empress Carlota, he made a beauty spot of the park. The empress planned the two lovely hill top gardens which are today attractive to visitors. It is now the official residence of the President of the Republic. The Military Academy—The West Point of Mexico—occupies the building immediately to the rear of the castle."

Mexico is a mine unexploited, and all the riches to be had here shout from the gray earth, speaking all tongues, heard and understood of all men. Here are soils fit to grow anything human beings can use. Here are silver and gold, coal and oil—the air is redolent with the sound of these unctuous words. Men mouth them lovingly, and stare at vague and varied horizons.

Beauty is here too—color of mountain and sky and green things rooted in earth. Beauty of copper colored human things not yet wholly corrupted by civilization. Those things are well enough in their way, but business first. And our immediate business is getting this new President inaugurated, and finding out what he means to do with all the power vested in him.

Hours before the time of taking the oath the Camara is filled. The boxes of the ambassadors blaze with gold lace and glinting ceremonious swords and the jewels around the necks of the women. Next door are the governors' boxes, not quite so impressive, but gay with the gowns of the governors' ladies. Below, the diputados come in, leisurely, one at a time, each man uniformed in black dress suit, gleaming white shirt front, imperturbable dignity of demeanor. On the right hand side the aristocrats seat themselves. You notice a great many long Bourbon faces, with hair rolled back from thin brows. They are men with several centuries of power back of them, and they love the accepted order of things. What they think of this occasion no one knows. For Alvaro Obregon's face is not in the least Bourbon. He is Mexican, and a soldier, and a farmer, and a business man. On the left wing one notes a curious assortment of folk, evidently there by right, and vastly interested in the proceedings. One of them is Soto y Gama, thorn in the side of the old government, a man of wide education and culture, who rode his native mountains for seven years with a copy of Karl Marx, and another of the Bible in his pocket. Near him sits a wiry little nervous man, with an intrepid face, eyes tilted a bit at the corners. He is trim in his magpie uniform. His fingers drum the arm of his chair. He shifts about impatiently and crosses his legs repeatedly. He is Luis Leon, educated for an agricultural engineer, who could not work with the Carranza government for his conscience's sake, and therefore became a bull fighter—one of the best in Mexico. When Obregon came in, Leon came in also, and was elected diputado. So we see him sitting there, his plain black and white a long step from the silver embroidered splendor of his torero's cloak. And a longer step still, from the time he fought nine black bulls in a pen in Vera Cruz for the benefit of Zapatista revolutionists who mistook him for a spy. He did not have a torero cloak that day. He killed bulls, one at a time until there were no more bulls to be killed, and the revolutionists were convinced of his vocation as he had declared it to them. They let him go, in order, as you see, that he might sit tonight with his wing collar chafing his chin, waiting for Obregon to come in and be made president. There is Felipe Carrillo, poet, friend of poets, champion of the Indians in Yucatan, who is also here on grave business.

There are others, on both sides of the house, who are worth watching. There is not an interest in all Mexico unrepresented by these seated men. They arrive in small groups, with the look of folk who have dined in peace and are now prepared carefully to consider the business of state. The diplomatic boxes and the governors' boxes are now rivaled by the society boxes, where ladies fling off great cloaks and sit bare shouldered in the chill spaces of the Camara. We in the Camara are growing a trifle nervous. Two minutes until midnight. One minute. Half Minute. "My God," murmurs a man sitting next, "Something must have happened!" They are so accustomed to things happening at inaugurations in Mexico, they doubt if even so civilized and dignified a procedure as this can pass without exciting and untoward events.

A blare of trumpets sounds in the streets. Nearer. A great muffled shout, a sustained mellow roar soaks through the walls of the Camara. Another and milder roar inside, as the people rise to their feet. The clock hands point straight to twelve. The main portal swings back ponderously, and two men in plain dress suits, one wearing a white and green and scarlet ribbon across his chest, enter. The man wearing the ribbon has only one arm. The other has been left by the wayside between the farm and the President's chair.

The top gallery folk shout "Viva Obregon! Viva de la Huerta!" while the others applaud. President de la Huerta walks a step ahead of General Obregon. Presently, in not more than three minutes, they go again, and this time President Obregon walks a step ahead of citizen de la Huerta. But before this Mr. de la Huerta steps forward and embraces the new President. It has every evidence of heartiness and good will. And the incident is remarkable for being only the second of its kind recorded here. The old and the new have not been distinguished for amiable relations to one another.

Once again Mexico has a duly installed constitutional government. Splendor, pomp, militarism, democracy, and internationalism have combined in one grand pageant to do honor to the new regime. It has begun with a thick surface layer of good will and gayety, a hopeful way for a new government to begin. The jubilation and applause was an indication of harmony at the moment at least—a sincere, deep down desire for a better and more livable Mexico; an obliterating psychological moment when personal desires, ambitions and private interests sink into the common weal and an unbreathed hope that this nation will take its rightful place in the commonwealth of the world.

Being part and parcel of this grand spectacle, yet removed in sort of an impersonal observant way, one is compelled to pause and wonder. What will history say of this new man? What symbolism will designate the new order upon the destiny of the nation—this conglomerate and but little understood people?

An unenviable position certainly is that of President Obregon. There are those who do envy, but surely from the point of personal ambition and aggrandizement and not from high minded service to country or as the solvent of the innumerable problems that hang over and wind about the presidential chair. He stands at the head of a nation that for a long time has been at utter discord with itself and its neighbors. Unharmonizing causes date back to the Spanish conquest and beyond. Republican form of government has never been successfully engrafted upon the Aztec and other primeval roots. There has been a steady oscillation between despotism and revolution. Constitutions have come and gone between volleys of musketry.

It has been well remarked that there never was a country for which God did more or man did less. Its very richness is its danger. Personal ambition and private self interest of those who constitute themselves the chosen few is rampant in Mexico today. It only exceeds the same virulent species of other nations in its tendency to subvert the ballot and the constitution by the rifle and the cannon, and by the richness of the prize sought. Neither does the exploitation by the arrogant few confine itself to Mexican citizenry. They are here from every point of the globe and the conflict for riches and prestige rage between race, color, and creed of every known angle and combination. There are plots for prestige, there are plots for political preference, there are plots for graft, great business interests are at stake, international problems of growing importance, an interweaving of selfish, private and governmental problems without end. Not hopeless to be true, unless the whole world is hopeless, for it may be truly said that for every problem of Mexico the rest of the world has a bigger one. Yet like the naughty boy in school, all eyes are on this turbulent one. For these great problems Destiny has handed the text book to President Obregon.

"Mexican Sovereignty must be kept inviolable." This is his answer to the first question on the first page. To this, every right thinking man of every nationality agrees. Only those who believe their own personal interest could be better served otherwise, can raise any objections to this and then only in whispered words in secret places. However the president has intimated by his public utterances that he does not consider sovereignty and provincialism as synonymous, that narrowness does not build a nation and that national rights as well as those of humans must work two ways, to the mutual best and equal division of interests and benefits—a sort of a national golden rule. If this policy is maintained as well as spoken, it will make the rest of the problems easy and many of them will disappear as corollary to the major premise.

Carrying for some years the title of General is the policy of the new man to be militaristic? Is the iron hand of Porfirio Diaz again to rule? The enormous mass of Mexican people, like all other nations, detest the tyranny of an army. The president's answer was given long ago. "I would rather teach the Mexican people the use of the tooth brush than to handle a rifle. I would rather see them in school than on battle fields. I prefer any day a good electrician, machinist, carpenter, or farmer to a soldier." A modern statement of "And their swords to plowshares beating, nations shall learn war no more." Yet this must not be taken for a high sounding platitude. President Obregon has his critics and severe ones but he is not accused of being unpractical and a dreamer of dreams for dreams' sake. He has method and is a disciplinarian—nerve if you please—as has been shown on many occasions. He hates and distrusts professional diplomacy and politics. He is a man of action primarily. He has a curious suddenness in action very disconcerting to the professional politician, accustomed to weaving situations deftly and slowly.

Granting he is right on the two great problems of sovereignty and citizenry the rest is comparatively easy. With a nation granting complete recognition of all rights legitimately acquired, it will soon be right with the other nations at issue whether to the North or more remote. With order, cleanliness, industry and labor established, Mexico with its riches would bound to the front. The capital of the world would come to its aid and capital is the one and only material need of this retarded, stunted and potential giant. With its great natural resources under development, debts would soon be paid, confidence restored, economic conditions adjusted, and bankruptcy turned to credit balances at the ports of the world. Being a farmer from the farm the land question should find easy solution at the president's hands.

To be right with his neighbors an individual must be right within himself. So it is with Nations. Possessed of brilliant mind, seasoned along the hard road of experience within his own land and broadened by travel without, President Obregon indicates by his words and actions that he has grasped the great principle of right dealing. At his first cabinet meeting he impressed most emphatically upon his collaborators the necessity of absolute morality in government. The English language employs the hard fibered word integrity, yet morality is broader and expresses the profundity of feeling of the new man for the desire to make the "Inner Chamber" of Mexico fit for the inspection of the world. Mr. Obregon knows, and the world will know, that he has enemies—many of them—strong and capable of deep hate, stopping at no thing to accomplish his downfall. Some will tell you he has done this or that discreditable thing in the past; others will say he will never stand to the end of his constitutional term. Yet strange to say none accuse him of stultifying official position to personal gain or placing personal ambition above his country's good. Close observation would lead one to the conclusion that he is the choice of a great majority of his people and that he is the strongest available man to

"PLAZA DE LA CONSTITUCION. This is also known as the Plaza Mayor. It was the exact center of the Aztec city Tenochtitlan. The cathedral facing the square is known as the Holy Metropolitan Church of Mexico, and occupies the former site of the first Aztec teocalli. It is also the site of the first Christian church built in New Spain. The present cathedral dates from 1573. In the towers are the three famous sweet toned bells, Santa Maria de Guadalupe, Santo Angel de la Guardia, and San Salvador. At the extreme right is a corner of the Palacio Nacional. In the center of the Plaza is the lovely little Zócalo planned by the Empress Carlota. Around it swirls the traffic of the city. Near by are many spots rich in historical interest—the Volador, or Thieves' Market; the flower market; Monte de Piedad, the national pawn shop; and a little further away the old University, center of culture in New Spain. The Plaza Mayor may be called the site of history in Mexico City."

fulfill their need and longing for peace. They want room for expansion of their business, freedom and opportunity to manage their own affairs in their own country, and in their own way. These rights they claim with a calmness of men standing on their own solid earth. The great majority, peace loving by nature, want that prosperity that comes from stable conditions and they see in their new president a man who sincerely and with only the personal interest of real service, desires that they have these rightful inheritances and their God given dominion. Others, only luke warm, wish him well for they too want peace and the other things that go with it. His antagonists, when asked to name a better man either admit it can not be done or by a national shrug of the shoulders refuse to nominate. Some go so far as to claim that with Mr. Obregon the last card has been played. If he can not bring about and maintain order in this troubled land, Mexico does not have a son capable of the task. This however, is only heard where zealous partisanship is strong or personal interest is involved.

"THE PALACIO NACIONAL. The facade of this interesting structure extends along the entire side east of Plaza Mayor. Here are located the office of the President of the Republic, the Senate, the minister of War, the stamp printing office, the Federal Treasury and the Public Archives. On the roof is the Central Meteorological Observatory. The National Museum has quarters on the north side of the building. The Palace was built first in 1530 by Cortes on a site occupied by the castle of Moctezuma. It was rebuilt in 1692, and renovated in 1908. The section in the extreme rear is practically untouched, and remains as Cortes built it. Over the center balcony hangs the Liberty Bell, rung by the patriot Miguel Hidalgo in the Dolores Church to call a meeting of revolutionists on the night of September 15, 1810. From this balcony the President of the Republic gives annually the Grito de Dolores on the night of September 15."

However two supremely important and terse questions arise and will not down wherever and whenever the possibility of failure from any source of Mr. Obregon's administration is discussed. These are the questions. Who? What?

Yet perhaps the new president's greatest distinction is in his knowledge that of his own self he can do nothing. He has frankly told his people this and given them the admonition that only by their co-operation could Mexico take its rightful place. He can guide, direct and counsel; give the most useful service, stamp out evil practices, and put down incipient revolutions, yet if the public conscience is not attuned, General Alvaro Obregon must bow before defeat unavoidable though undeserved.

So in its last analysis the new order which is beginning with every evidence of permanence and stability rests with all the people of Mexico, from president to peon, each responsible according to his own degree and station in the scheme of destiny.

No better words can be found than those used by Waddy Thompson, Envoy Extraordinary and Minister Plenipotentiary to Mexico, in a book written in 1846, which were as follows: "God grant them success, both on their own account as well as for the great cause in which they have so long struggled, and under circumstances so discouraging."

Where President Obregon Stands

As Shown by Acts and Words of Recent Months.

Peace and rehabilitation.

Inviolability of Mexican Sovereignty.

Friendliness for the United States.

Honorable relations with all nations of the world.

Foreigners to enjoy absolute guarantees of personal safety.

An invitation to all bona fide investors to join in the rebuilding of Mexico and sharing in its opportunities.

Absolute integrity in governmental matters from the presidential chair down to the lowest official.

No question pending between Mexico and the United States but what can be settled in a satisfactory manner.

The border between Mexico and the United States to be as peaceful and relations as pleasant as that between the United States and Canada.

An open door to men of culture and morality; a barred portal to the exploiters of the poor and ignorant, the fomenters of discord and the preachers of anarchy.

A prompt, direct and decisive hand against lawlessness, banditry, vice, graft, political discrimination, favoritism, and the various insidious practices that have kept Mexico in ceaseless fomentation for the past decade.

In a Mexican Patio

Magazine of Mexico (April 1921)

Since the Mexican government failed to back the *Magazine of Mexico*, the April issue was the second and last. We have not found a copy of this issue, but know that it contained "In a Mexican Patio" and Porter's complimentary essay on Luis Morones, whose photograph appears on the cover. Colonel Harvey Miller, head of Military Intelligence at the U.S. embassy in Mexico City, supplied this information to his superiors when asked about Porter. Two versions of the sketch exist among her papers, the second version cutting out a few passages from the first.

In this sketch Porter relates, from the time she awakes until she retires, a day in the life of her pension at 20 Calle Eliseo, next door to the Habermans' apartment. The account perforce concentrates on the women servants of the house, whose day extends beyond the narrator's waking and sleeping. The charm and humor of the sketch give way to her guilty perception of women who grow old before their time in the service of others, and finally to her own loneliness. The configuration of images, from the description of the patio to the narrator's fear of the dark, anticipates Laura's fears in "Flowering Judas."

Porter unsuccessfully tried to republish "In a Mexican Patio" in the United States. (Paul U. Kellogg, editor of the journal *Survey*, wrote her on April 23, 1924, that the piece "does not exactly fit us.") It deserves to be known.

In a Mexican Patio

Small sounds and smells filter up from the patio, and float vaguely through the grey net of my morning sleep. A delicate slapping together of hands, rhythmic and energetic, would be young Maria making tortillas. The splash of running water, plentiful as rain, would be Manuel washing the square brown paving stones of the driveway. The smell of roasting coffee and of carbon smoke means that Lupe the cook is fanning the charcoal blaze in the red-tiled brasero in the first balcony. The gentle conciliating whimper of a very young voice, with occasional commands in a very old rattling voice mean that Consuelo is having her hair brushed by her grandmother, Josefina the portress.

The latticed iron outer gates and the tall inner gate of carved wood are not yet opened. The enclosed garden is mottled with cold early shadows. The stagnant shallow fountain, where the tangled shrubberies weave green mats to the water's edge, has not a ripple. Lilies grow here, spreading pale leaves under a trellis weighted by an arrogant bougainvillea vine, whose fronds rise to my balcony, thrusting their purple through hospitable windows.

They give warmth to the frosty white room with the high ceilings and glass candelabras. The sunshine strikes across the bare floor thinly. In the afternoon it will be there again from the other side, thawing and yellowing the chill spaces. Now I stand in the strip of light while I dress, shivering.

I cross the inner balcony to breakfast. The red and delft blue tilings are slippery and damp from recent washings. This balcony extends around three sides of the patio, with blue plaster pots set in wrought iron containers fastened at intervals along the top of the railing. The pots nourish a miscellany of struggling vegetation, flowering in pink and scarlet. A roof bordered with a ribbon of iron cut and painted in a lace pattern protects one side of the house. Here the walls are nicely tinted in squares of rose and yellow and blue, with thin edgings of mustard colour. On the opposite side the surface is rainwashed, sunfaded, streaked in pallid pink and grey.

Near the door of the dining room, grave faced Heraclia hangs the bird cages of decorated wicker on the outer wall, where the gold coloured birds may bathe and spread their feathers in the vehement sunrays. Her long blue reboso falls back straightly almost to her feet as she stretches up her neck. The black bands of her hair bind her forehead and cheeks in a sleek curve. Her eyes are fixed with curious intensity on her simple task. A kitten sleeps on the threshold, where I step over him carefully.

A thin little boy, very brown, is already setting a plate for me at one corner of the long table. His head is thrust through a slit in his short green and yellow serape. His hair stands up all around, like the bristles of a horse brush. He has bread crumbs on his chin.

I sit and regard the light through window glass stained in orange and red and rose: greenish orange and purplish rose, done in relentless symmetry of pattern. I sniff the bitter fragrance of poppies sprawling in a blue bowl at my elbow. A mirror framed in a confusion of carved oak roses and bulbous Cupids over-sophisticated of eye and posture, reflects in its ravelled silver three dying annunciation lilies, shrivelled pale ochre at the edges.

I think calmly of death as I butter a roll and examine the lilies. Then I turn my eyes toward the pine tree with four planes of branches rising above the wall, drowned in prodigious blue distances, and feel immortal. It always pleases me to feel immortal at this hour of the day, while I drink my coffee. The muchacho brings the coffee in a pottery cup, capacious as a bowl. He holds it with extraordinary care, gripping the saucer with both hands. But he splashes it anyhow, on the cloth, on my plate, on my sleeve, and on his own thumb. He gives a strangled yelp of surprise and puts his thumb in his mouth. Thank heaven, that means the coffee is hot for once.

An Indian girl wearing huge brass hoops in her ears trots through the dining room carrying an immense tray of food on her head. Her hair is braided in a thick round coil on her crown, making a flat surface for carrying burdens. Her raised arms are curved as softly as the handles of a native jar. She disappears into the corridor leading to Doña Rosa's apartment.

Doña Rosa is the hostess, as the courteous phrase has it, of this guest house. She is large and leisurely and placid. She lives in rooms adjoining the kitchen, whence her two children, a son and a daughter, both as fat and wholesome looking as apple dumplings, emerge and disappear again at intervals. Doña Rosa herself rarely comes out. She sits inside and rings a bell which sounds in the rear hall. At the first jingle, a cook, a maid, and several of their children rush to answer it. In a moment they all rush back to the kitchen, where after some confusion and excited talk, they clatter again through the dining room, carrying a cup of chocolate and a plate of rice and a pitcher of hot water for Doña Rosa.

On rare occasions I have seen her, at the noon hour, returning from market. The cleanly brown skin of her face is unmarred by powder. Her smooth black hair is fastened with three flat jet pins. Her eyes are clear brown, her teeth strong and white. She is tall, and her ample black skirts sweep the floor, swinging handsomely over her opulent hips. A black reboso of heavy crinkled silk, fringed thickly and at great length, falls about her shoulders. She moves with extraordinary decision, turning her head slowly on her muscular neck, observing everything serenely. She is the widow of a general who was killed in a casual battle at the frayed end of some revolution, when her children were babies.

Now she wears mourning, and goes to church, and to market.

I take occasion to speak with Doña Rosa concerning the young coyote tethered to the water pipe on my roof. He is a pilgrim on his way to another fate; Heraclia's brother will take him to the country in a few days, and there, I hope, he will become the pet of an indulgent household. But in the meantime he grieves, and although I grieve with him, still I cannot devote all my time to it. Is it possible to have him removed to a far corner of the patio for the rest of his stay? He has an enormous voice for so young a creature.

With this question carefully assembled in Spanish from a phrase book, I enter the darkened room of Doña Rosa. Against the precision of the maroon coloured wall paper design hang pictures of obscure saints, their upturned eyes glazed with highly specialized agonies. A shrine lamp is blood colour before a pallid Virgin gazing into the mysteries of a paper-flower bouquet.

Doña Rosa sits in a vast bed overflowing with puffy quilts riotous with strange blossoms. Her daughter sits at one elbow, her son at another. The three of them wear dressing gowns of the same material. The tray is on her flattened knees. They are drinking hot milk flavoured with coffee, munching great sugared buns.

Daughter feeds a grey kitten. Son feeds a yellow kitten, and with difficulty persuades him not to drink from the family milk pitcher. A pair of slightly fevered, ill-humoured eyes and a moist, black lacquered nose burrowing under Doña Rosa's arm, belong to Pipo the naked Chihuahua dog. We have met only once before, but I remember him well. He was then painted a watermelon pink, and wore a blue ribbon on his tail. He was eating beans from an orange and red Oaxaca bowl, and it occurred to me then that I had never sufficiently understood the phrase "local colour." Pipo was It. Now, he struggles out a bit from his smother of blankets, and I see that his crepe de chine surface is tinted emerald green. No wonder his eyes are fevered.

Doña Rosa offers me a cup of coffee. Daughter gives me a roll. I sit on the billowing bedside, and we straighten out the coyote question with the utmost amiability, in snatches of three languages.

This is a house of respectable age merely, not antique. It was built during Emperor Maximilian's time, and therefore clings to doubtful grandeurs of the Italian type, such as stained glass windows, steps of streaked marble, and other steps painted to resemble marble. The floors are bare and rough from much scrubbing. The furnishings must be wedding presents of several generations, for carved walnut and horse hair share the same rooms with gilt chairs and sofas upholstered in rose brocaded satin, and slab settees in that deplorable style known as Mission. Plaster casts of smiling ladies, effulgent of bust and hair, are set about in corners that would otherwise be happily empty.

Doña Rosa takes no pleasure in her house, except in that one big overfilled room where she sits, and where her children love to play. She spends part of her afternoons in the shady garden beside the fountain where friends come for long visits. They sit here, gossiping over chocolate thick as soup, sipping slowly with long handled wooden spoons from little lacquered gourds.

The natural industry of the servants is reason enough for the general air of freshness and dampness that pervades the house. They mop and sweep and dust, talking softly all the time. There is no quarrelling, no dissension. La Cocinera is maybe a trifle brittle of temper at times, but she is an overworked, distracted woman with three children at her skirts. Life is a tragic business for her.

This morning when she came to my room with ten o'clock chocolate her smallest son came with her, and sat on my bed as we talked, his round grubby face as friendly as a little dog's. His mother shrieked. Her act of seizing and flinging him out of the room was done in one curving motion. I have never seen anything so finished. Then she examined the spot where he had been. There was the complete outline of his little shape, done neatly in charcoal dust. Her gesture of despair measured calamity. And these people face real calamity with perfect stoicism.

On the walls of the servants' quarters is painted a curious landscape: a tall castle in the middle distance, abnormally rotund domestic animals in the immediate foreground, and dying trees along the water's edge. It is acutely surprising to the eye when one first walks through the gate to see this painting, so utterly removed from anything resembling either life or art, down the hundred foot vista of patio. At its base the servants' children, Consuelo, her cousins and friends, play amid a confusion of brown cooking pots and baskets and mats. They are contented little people, who rarely weep and who are never punished. I have seen Consuelo busy for an hour, trying to bend a bit of wire into a shape that pleased her. It is a pity she must be a servant when she grows up. She is very beautiful, with finely formed hands and feet. In a decade, she will be like her mother, a seventeen year old girl already haggard, who works with a baby on her arm, wound in her reboso. In two decades she will resemble her grandmother, who cannot be older than forty years. But she has the look of something agelessly old, that was born old, that could never have been young.

Why not? One may have the complete use of a human being here for eight or ten pesos a month. They carry water in huge jars to the stone washing tubs, where they kneel at their work. They toil up and down endless flights of stairs: to the roof to hang linen, down again for another load, crossing long courts on hundreds of small errands. If I go to sleep at twelve, it is to the sound of their voices on the other side of the wall, still gathering together the ends of the day's labour. If I wake at six, they are pattering about, their bare feet clumping like pony hoofs.

My poor Gatito de Oro (Golden Kitten) has passed out attended by every circumstance of tragedy.

He did not come in for breakfast this morning, nor did he appear for his noon bowl of milk. I had begun to miss him seriously this afternoon, when the small brown child from the patio came up to tell me that poor Gatito was dead, in the garden, with blood on his arms and breast, and dried blood on his mouth.

I inquired no further into particulars, but she supplied them lavishly. They had found him lying twisted, so, with his head so,—and the ants were at him. His teeth were showing, and he seemed very angry. But he was not angry—of course not, he was only dead. Pobrecito!

Pobrecito indeed. He was a gentle, childlike beast, living by his affections. He was the first cat I ever saw who required to be loved. He came to my window one morning wailing aloud, his yellow fur standing up; I thought he was sick. But no, he wished only to be petted. When I stroked his head, he purred. When I stopped, he wailed. For weeks after he came, he went back to the patio kitchen for his food, and never for one moment could I accuse him of self interest in the matter of shelter. He was fat and thriving when he took up his abode with me.

He slept on my pillow at night, and sat on the window sill by day, washing his adolescent person carefully; or he followed me about, talking to himself, answering when I called. He understood my Spanish very well.

Pobrecito! The night before he died, the wind rattled the window latches, as though a hand was trying to unfasten them. Gatito de Oro stared at the window and listened, his eyes blackened with uneasiness. He growled in his throat forebodingly, like a little dog. Now he is not afraid of anything. It is too bad.

Five Indian men, their women and six children are on the roof of my neighbor's house this morning. They have come from Xochimilco to build her a thatched hut, which she means to use for a tea house. The men are setting up roughly hewn sapling trunks, and the women are tying the thatch together with thick strands of twisted maguey fibre. They have their food baskets, a collection of beautiful brown decorated pottery, and many blankets and mats. One of the women is building a charcoal fire on the cement paved roof. They will eat, sleep and build the hut up there for two days.

The babies roll about almost naked. One of them, a large child, is hanging at his mother's breast nursing, arms and legs clutching monkey-like, as she walks about unconcernedly with both hands free, arranging her household. The women are quite nice. Their blouses are embroidered in red and green, they wear very wide skirts wrapped about them, plain and smooth across their hips, pleated amply in front and bound with a woven girdle in many colours.

The hut is finished. It stands solemnly, the thatch droops around the edges like the brim of a dilapidated hat. It seems strangely different from those we saw in Xochimilco. But my neighbor, an American, regards it affectionately, and promises us tea in it. Her husband explains to the Indians that he means to call it the Hula Hula Hall because of the grass skirt. They smile politely.

I encounter at dinner today the young married couple. She is fat, with the fresh and blooming fatness of the happily married bride who apparently is living by the twin delights of food and love. If a thought ever ruffled that sleek brow, or darkened those full thick-lidded eyes, it left no trace. Wearing a pink silk pleated jacket, and thin green slippers on her white stockinged feet, she comes to dine with her husband, leaning on his arm. He is a portly, rather too-knowing young man, who scolds her and reproves her and slaps her resoundingly on the back, to the amazement of every one. She reacts like a devoted, slightly bewildered dog: she snaps when he scolds and fawns when he pats. Either response seems equally to amuse him.

When she dresses to go out, her hat is enormous, of fluffy black lace, strapped under her full chin. Her complexion is a chemical marvel of whiteness and smoothness, her lips a bleeding bow. Her light blue silk dress strains over her round high bosom, and she tilts forward perilously in her tight French slippers. Her husband admires her immensely at these times, and cannot take his eyes from the sight of all that magnificent femaleness.

He tells me his wife is clever, and does not wish to be idle merely because she is married. "A very modern girl," he pronounces in English. He allows her to have her voice trained. Ah, so it is she I have heard for the past four days, singing the Musetta Waltz, a half tone off key.

I will have dinner in my room this evening. It is brought to me by the sweet sentimental-eyed Dolores, who often helps in small ways, though she is cousin to Doña Rosa. The tray resembles the food-dream of a delirious person. There is a huge plate of rice, deliciously cooked with peppers and spices, very dry and rich. A dish of ground meat mingled with peppers and garlic, flooded with red sauce. Coarse spinach with onions. A croquette of frijoles. Two very red apples, a dish of zapote, the suave delicately flavoured black fruit pulp I like, and coffee. I eat heroically, because a failure to do so will bring the household about my ears, inquiring if I am sick.

Dolores seats herself with the air of one come for a visit, and sews on a dress which hung over her arm while she carried the tray. She is accompanied by Duquesa her little copper-coloured collie dog, who folds her paws and watches her mistress prayerfully.

Dolores applies the diminutive to everything. "Un momentito," she says, bringing her thumb and forefinger almost together, measuring the smallest possible fraction of time. "Pobrecita," she calls the prosperous Duquesa, everybody's pet. "Yo solita," she calls herself, her appealing black eyes floating suddenly in inexplicable tears. She sews as she talks, stitching lace on a dress that has even now too much lace. A blue reboso over her head, a black muslin dress with red ribbons showing in her embroidered chemise top, a hiatus of four inches of white cotton stockings between her skirts and her yellow topped shoes, she talks and smiles, her brown hands vague and groping among the folds of her material. When I see the sadness of her down drooping face, I know she is beginning to think of love. "Yo solita," she calls herself.

In the early evening, fragments of life quite different from those of the hurrying day drift through our street. I like to stand in my balcony and watch them. A wide hatted man drives a two wheeled cart, cumbrous and full of groans, the shafts too high for the struggling little mule, who wavers from side to side, his hoofs knocking against the wheels. An Indian boy carries a bundle of long handled feather dusters, used for sweeping the ceilings. He walks steadily, balancing the wicker poles, setting one foot exactly before the other. The feathers nod in time, and his vending cry shatters the silence. A very old woman with scanty grey hair drives a burdened burro; a tiny girl trots beside her, bent under a sack of corn. They are country Indians leaving town until another day. They all carry lighted candles set in deep cups of paper, and the pointed flames flutter delicately as birds' wings.

Others are also watching life pass by; I count the young girl heads at this moment nodding under high coiffures, discreetly visible at upper windows. There are two in my house, one on either side, and three in houses across the narrow street.

The girl in the balcony at my left hand is Dolores, only fifteen years old. Her hair is not yet pinned up, but falls in two thick braids to her knees. Darkness is here, and the heads in the windows are lost. Here and there a pale face glimmers for a moment in the framing blackness, and floats away. The girl on the right hand balcony is gone.

Dolores leans forward, her chin on the rail, and stares at a blotch, humanly shaped, defined against the fog grey of the wall of the opposite house. The flare of a match lights the face of a man whose eyes peer upward. His lighted cigarette moves and traces lines before him. The spark spins gently, in long curves, sudden down-jutting lines, circles. I read: "Yo te amo, Cielito Lindo . . ." and then three times over, "Dolores, Dolores, Dolores!"

Observing this, I ponder the finished technique of ardency required to form those burning words with so fragile a torch. How practised are those fingers, turning delicately on a steady wrist, scrivening in ash veiled flame upon a wall of air!

Dolores rises and leans over the wall. She kisses her fingers many times toward the spot of light. Her outstretched bared arm shudders to the shoulder with the agitation of her shaking hand.

Tonight, hurrying through the patio, with the moon not yet risen over the massed tree tops, I saw a man leaning against a pillar on the narrow driveway. A wide black hat blurred his face, a spectral black cloak swathed him. . . . In such a moment, one's conscious mind contracts, and cancels all engagements for this world. . . . But the nervous centers know better. They gather themselves and spring for safety, remembering for your help-less mind that tomorrow also will be sweet. From the top step I glanced back. He was gone. In the lower hall, I collided with Heraclia, wearing a white lace veil over her hair, and carrying a lighted candle. I leaned on her arm, shaking, my breath gone. "Don't go in the patio," I said. "Something is there."

Heraclia was very calm. She held the candle above her head, so it shone on both our faces, and smiled gently. "It is probably the ghost of the house," she explained in a low whisper. "He comes often. But he is harm-less. Do not be afraid. I will go with you up the stairway." She followed me to my door. "Buenas noches," she said, her grave eyes shining a little. "I assure you, you need not fear ghosts."

I listened to her footsteps down the stairs, across the hall, and from the patio her candle glimmered an instant, and was snuffed out. There were happy, confused little noises—a whisper, a rush of skirts, smothered laughter, feet running on tip toe. I am very much amused. She is two years older than poor little sister Dolores, and has managed to learn a great deal, it seems. Doña Rosa would take it out of the skin of Josefina the portera if she knew; but I am pleased that Heraclia will have her love messages by another medium than lighted cigarettes writing in cold air.

Josefina is not usually so hospitable, to ghosts or other shape of folk. Lying awake listening to noises, I hear insistently now near, now far, up and down the little Eliseo, the rat-tat-tat and thump-thump of late return-ing persons knocking at their barred gates. Getting into the house after ten o'clock is an achievement of no mean order.

Josefina sleeps soundly, without sympathy for those owlish ones who love the world by starlight. Two nights since a pilgrim entertained himself with rhythms for the better part of an hour, playing upon the knocker in waltz time, both slow and fast. He changed to the jota, and jingled away cheerfully. Then he experimented with the two-step, and not doing so well, he ended with a marvelous flourish, a soft shoe dance finale. At last he settled down for the night in doleful marching time, a steady proces-sional knock-knock-knock. In the midst of this, Josefina opened the door arguing shrilly. He replied with laughter, keeping a high good humour . . . to have got in was enough.

I danced the other night with a group of young Mexican boys and girls in an old square garden, paved with tiles and lined with rose bushes and palms. Jasmine and violets were sweet in shallow bowls. Two Indians from the country made melancholy music with fiddle and flute, and our feet followed the sad, gay pattern of rhythm. Now and then someone clicked his heels ringingly on the glassy tiles. There was no light except a late-rising moon, swung between stars like a plaque of white-gold beaten thin.

A man draws his thumb lightly across all the strings of his guitar . . . a sighing breeze of sound. He sings, mournfully, with a jolly face. . . . "What does he say?"

"He is singing about love, how it is cruel, because life devours us, a day at a time, and a dream at a time, until we are ended utterly. . . ."

He wails on and on, ecstatically.

We danced until the moon went down, and by candle light we danced until the morning. When we went home, the sky was grey and our faces were grey. . . . Sancha had drunk a little too much wine. She looked at us, as we silently stepped into motor cars and huddled silently together. She touched her own face. . . . "I am a ghost too!" she cried out in a high shocked voice. Her mouth became a turned down crescent moon. She began to cry. "I am a ghost, a ghost! I can never dance again!"

A woman in this house plays Chopin at two o'clock in the morning. I know it is a woman, because she plays very softly, with many mistakes, and for her, you understand plainly, the music takes the place of tears. Women always corrupt the music of Chopin with tears. It is like listening to one who weeps in a dream. In the sunlight one may laugh, and sniff the winds, but the night is crowded with thoughts darker than the sunless world.

Now I lean on my window ledge, wrapped in a shawl, shivering. The sky is empty, the patio is like a well. I listen to the Mexican woman who weeps Chopin through her sleepless nights. It is a group of Preludes . . . why be so stubborn, so intent on composure? I love them. I am thankful for her tears.

Xochimilco   *Christian Science Monitor* (May 31, 1921): 10

Children of Xochitl   (unpublished, ca. March 1921)

When Porter's friend Mary Doherty arrived in Mexico, she became a teacher of Indian children in Xochimilco, an occupation Porter gives Laura in "Flowering Judas." Xochimilco, located a few miles south of Mexico City, became the favorite weekend place of Porter, Doherty, and J. H. Retinger. One of those visits—probably in March 1921—became the inspiration for the two versions of the same sketch, included here. Nowhere in Porter's canon is there such a Rousseau-like response to the village's inhabitants who live close to the earth and spurn the "artificial world." One of the men could be a servant in a rich house, but, unlike the women of "In a Mexican Patio," he prizes his independence more. In "The Children of Xochitl," Porter created a mythological framework for her sketch by claiming that the inhabitants were children and worshippers of the legendary Xochitl, the goddess of pulque. (Although some Mexican Indians did worship earth goddesses in the form of the Christian Virgin, Xochitl—a literary invention of the seventeenth century—was not one of them.) When Porter submitted her sketch to the *Christian Science Monitor*, she eliminated all references to the pagan goddess, apparently so as not to offend its readers with her anti-Christian bias. In the process she made the sketch less pointed and less personal to the point of blandness. The editors much prefer the unpublished version.

Xochimilco

While we were still a mile distant from Xochimilco, a band of Indian lads clad in white cotton and prodigious straw sombreros, leaped howling upon the running board of the car. They besieged us with questions, and by listening attentively we managed to reduce it to one question, repeated endlessly in varying phrases: "Do you wish a canoa?"

We shook our heads, smiling, and shouting at the tops of our mingled voices, "No, muchas gracias!" for selecting your barge is one of the adventures of the day. They shouted also, insisting each one that his own canoa was the finest one on the canals. But we continued to refuse loudly with thanks, until we had dispersed all of them save one brown determined boy, who leaned into the car and regarded us fondly, as newfound personal property he had no idea of relinquishing.

"It is written," we said, "that we are to have a canoa, and it will be rowed by this boy." Wherewith we resigned ourselves, and hoped it would be a beautiful one. Several trips to the Xochimilco gardens had developed in us a discriminating taste in boat decoration.

We alight in a whirl of dust, at a point where the road ends and a path falls steeply to the bank of the canal. On either side the village is spread unevenly, the thatched huts with their peaked roofs heavily burdened with vines and drooping tree branches. Several Indian babies are trotting ahead of their mothers, babbling, their bare feet kicking up dust, their scanty garments swathed tightly about their middles. They are fat and cheerful and not to be detained for greetings, although we attempt to renew our slight acquaintance of the visit before this.

The earth is swept bare and spotless before the doors of the huts, built of sheaves of maize stalks, bound together flatly, thatched with dried maguey leaves, all burned golden and sweet in the generous sunshine. The low fences are also maguey stalks and maize, woven with hennequin fiber, dry and rattling in the slight winds.

We are in the midst of a spare forest of straight and tranquil poplars, lining the banks of the canals. The sunlight falls in long strips between the trees, and gardens grow abundantly in the midst of them. It is March, but the foliage is as profuse as in midsummer, glowing and drowsing in the benign air, the pansies and small, gold chrysanthemums dreaming on the green chinampas (islands) whence the canals flow away in a divergent network.

In all of the chinampas the Indians are working, gathering vegetables, making intricate bouquets of flowers in many colors. They seem a natural and gracious part of the earth they live in such close communion with, entirely removed from contact with the artificial world. They hardly lift their eyes from their task, unless it is to talk among themselves, and the visiting stranger does not feel alien because he is not noticed.

These Xochimilco Indians are a splendid remnant of the Aztec race; they have maintained an almost unbroken independence of passing governments, and live their simple lives in a voluntary detachment from the ruling race of their country. They build their homes with maize stalks grown in their own fields, with the trunks of poplars and cedars for foundation. They grow their own food, and flowers for the city markets. They load their garden fruits on great barges and follow the ancient waterways into Mexico City, where they sell them. The loveliest and freshest flowers in Mexico come from these chinampas—often called floating gardens, though they do not really float, being built and anchored firmly in the canals.

Our canoa proves to be a lovely one, and we go aboard at once, in order to avoid being kidnaped by the rivals of our boat boy. We are among the earliest visitors, and competition is keen at this hour. There is an Egyptian air about this long narrow, flat-bottomed barge, of hand sawed wood, with legends cut along the sides. The awning is supported by arches, and cedar branches are twined thickly about the foremost arch, with chrysanthemums woven in elaborate designs on the entire surface. There is a fine jungle air about it, too, when we get away from land, and our boy stands in the prow bent over his long oar, sweeping the waters heavily, disturbing the loosened floating flowers.

We recline on long benches on either side, and float out calmly into the main canal. The small boats of the women are still moored to stakes before the huts, and the women and children are washing and dressing themselves at the water's edge. They spread their long hair on the rocks to dry, their shy heads thrown back, faces turned away a little, eyes closed before the sunlight. A child is bathing his mother's feet, standing on a wet stone and scrubbing away valiantly with a mop of hennequin fiber. We pass near enough to touch her, and drop a few pansies beside her. She stares at us with gentle eyes the color of brown one sees in the native pottery. She is too amazed at our sudden appearance to pick up the pansies. She stands, with her head down, one foot drawn up like a water bird, wriggling in embarrassment.

Farther on, a tall girl is washing clothes, pounding them on a stone, scooping up fresh water with an Oaxaca bowl, decorated in splashes of blue and green and orange. Her blouse, short-sleeved and low in the neck, is embroidered with red, in an Aztec design. Her full, crimson skirts are looped up over bare ankles. Her braids, tied together in front, dip in the water when she bends forward.

The sun is beginning to blaze with a noonday fervor. The canals are filling rapidly with flower-decked barges. An enormous boat, broad and slow, overflowing with cabbages and onions, drifts out from a chinampa and floats downstream, guided by a man whose white cotton garments are rolled up at shoulders and knees, his hat shading him completely. He drags his pole through the water with a tremendous gesture, then rests, leaning upon the oar, and stares out across the islands, over the valley and skies. His face is massive, neither happy nor unhappy. He lives as a tree lives, rooted in earth, drinking in light and air.

Now the women come out in their tiny boats, just wide enough in the middle for them to kneel comfortably, pointed at prow and bow, so shallow that the rim is only a few inches above the water's edge. Some of them have charcoal braseros, and are busily fanning fires under cooking pots. They will be welcomed later by the visitors. Others have flowers, and each one of them paddles with a single light oar.

A girl wearing a gay pink reboso, with gold hoops in her ears, sits in a vast bouquet of pansies, white violets, sweet peas and delicate pale roses. She darts forward at our nod, her slender oar barely touching the water; her shallop runs along the side of our barge, and she seizes hold of the rail with one gleaming wet, brown hand.

Under the parted sleekness of her oiled, carbon-colored hair her pleasant face with round dark eyes is lifted inquiringly. We buy an armful of flowers, done into tight bouquets, bound with the inevitable hennequin fiber, with a long loop whereby one may trail them in the water occasionally to keep them fresh.

Another girl, her shallop brimming with lettuce and celery, rows swiftly up from a bye-canal. She kneels erectly, her wide, high-crowned hat shading her pointed face. The poplars rise tall and dark on either side the stream, the flowers crowd down to the very water. Her oar sends faint ripples out, lapping the bank and swaying the water lilies.

There strikes out from a dilapidated landing a boat about three feet long, very old, unpainted, with a mended oar. Carved along the sides we read, "La Fortuna de Juan Ortega." Juan himself stands in this ancient craft. A few heads of lettuce, a basket of tomatoes lie at his feet. Juan is small and shabby, his hat is a ruin, his shirt is negligible. But he smiles gayly at us as we pass, and we do not presume to feel pity for him. He makes it plain, in that smile, that he has freedom and fortune.

Juan could go into town and be a servant in a rich house, but depend upon it, he will not. This time next year he will be plying up and down the canals in the battered La Fortuna, an independent human being, vending his small wares, under a kindly sky, in company with the poplars.

Another boat, crowded with children in gay Sunday dresses, and their merry-making elders, bears the legend, "I was once a beautiful tree in the mountain of Cordoba, but a strong axman cut me down, and now I live to serve my friends." A small barge, festive with streaming awnings in red and white, bids us "Remember lovely Elena, with the sweet mouth and the green eyes." "For remembrance of dear Panchito," says the motto along the side of another. A medley of names, and dates and sentimental recollections adorn all of them, carved carefully in scripts as varied as handwriting.

We face a fleet of barges coming in from the side waterpaths. They are majestic and leisurely, grouped with charming effect, their arches as individual as human faces. One is slightly pointed, woven of yellow maize, studded with chrysanthemums and pale green stalks of cane. Another is made of purple dyed hennequin with small bouquets of jasmines set at intervals. Yet another is lovely with cornflowers and cedar. Each man has decorated his boat in the manner that pleases him, and one cannot choose which is the most beautiful.

We are about to pass under a low stone bridge, built before the days of Cortes in Mexico, and the fleet of boats approaching meets us here. In this narrow passage we are brought to a halt. One boat has come in already, and we are also under the shadow of the arch. It has the look of an imminent collision. One expects mutual recrimination, a crash of boat sides, much talk. Nothing of the sort occurs. Each boatman makes way for the other. Each steers carefully, running his craft almost into the bank in his effort to make room for the other.

"Have a care, comrade!" says one, when he is crowded a trifle too closely. "Pardon me!" says the other. And somehow in the midst of the work he finds a hand with which to doff his tattered sombrero, and to make a bow. The second one bows deeply also. They exchange felicities of the day and season. The occupants of the other boat smile at us as we glide through, and one of us throws flowers into the other boat. "Gracias," they call, and throw flowers in return. The waiting barges form a line and pass under the arch in a quiet procession, the awnings casting colored shadows into the clear water.

From the tangle of vines and rustic pavilions along the banks comes the sound of music. The guitar, mandolin, violin, flute unite in a series of orchestras, scattered along the shady banks, where people sit and talk, or dance. There are endless small tables and rustic chairs and swings for the children. A dozen gay tunes mingle in curious harmony, hardly distinguishable one from the other to us on the water. We have snatches of "La Adelita," "La Pajarera," "La Sandunga," and "La Nortena"—all of us hum the melody we prefer, at once, with extraordinary tonal results.

Young Indians, wearing white garments, their red or blue or green blankets draped grandly about them, lounge under the trees in groups. The town people are arriving in numbers, and horsemen from the country, wearing handsome charros, the native dress, are dismounting at the upper landing place, where we have now arrived.

We stop for a final look in the shade of a willow tree. Our boat boy seats himself cross-legged in the prow. He has the composure of a statue, his eyes slanted and meditative. His scarlet cotton sash is knotted twice and hangs with definite style. His feet are bound with thonged sandals of leather. We admire him immensely as he sits, eating peanuts in a lordly, detached way, placing the shells in the upcurving of his hat. A flower girl passing in a tiny boat throws him a bunch of purple and yellow pansies. He smiles, making a grandiose acknowledging gesture at the full length of his arm, and places the flowers in his hat brim also.

Then he stretches out on the mat, his face to the brilliant sky. The hat is by his side. He hums "Adelita" softly. It is a pity to disturb him, but we must be going.

Children of Xochitl

Xochimilco is an Indian village of formidable history, most of which I learned and have happily forgotten. It is situated near the city of Mexico, and is in danger of being taken up by rich tourists. Spared that fate, no doubt it will continue as it is for a dozen generations longer. The name Xochimilco means in Aztec "the place of flowers." In a way, the village is a namesake of Xochitl herself, the goddess of flowers and fruit.

There are flat roofed houses in it that have resisted destruction since the days of Cortes. The silver blue skyline is jagged with crosses and tiled domes of churches, for these Indians have suffered the benefits of Christianity to an unreasonable degree.

Some one tells me there are seventeen churches here—or more. A hospitable patriarch leads us into a small church dedicated to San Felipe, its portals open to the roadside, elbowing a pulque shop on the one side, and shows us a fiesta in progress, honoring the patron saint. The church is merely a quadrangle of walls, the roof having been blown off, whether by accident or design, in a revolution. They are collecting money for a new roof, and in the meantime a tent of white canvas clarifies the stone walls, dappled with mold and shell-powder. The lilies on the altar glitter like tinsel.

The saints support ponderous plush robes on their flattened chests, and the patron himself leans slightly to the wall. His face is yellowed with age and fatigue. They are all untouched, the man points out carefully, by the hail of bullets which swept the holy place. The patron is rich and generous, and moreover, the church is protected by four Virgins, the Virgin of Guadalupe, Our Lady of Lourdes, Our Lady of Pity and Our Lady of Help (de Los Remedios). If one Virgin did not answer a prayer, it was always simple to turn to another—and in this way it was often quite possible to get blessings from all four of them.

Quite incidentally he added, as we left, that the great Reina Xochitl was also a patroness of this church, and was often more abundant with her favors than all the others together. . . . Xochitl is the legendary Aztec goddess of the earth, of fruit, of abundance, who discovered pulque— especially the strawberry flavored kind!—and also made known the many other uses of the maguey plant, by which the Indians can live almost entirely.

"Xochitl?" we ask, for we cannot quite place her among this assembly. The Indian makes a slow gesture about the church; his pointed finger pauses a moment before each saint—"This one gives health after sickness, this one discovers lost things, this one is powerful to intercede for the Poor Souls (in Purgatory), this one helps us bear our sorrows—"

"What about Xochitl?" we must interrupt for eagerness.

He turned and flung his arm toward the wide portal, where the smell of the clean open world defied the grey mold of centuries prisoned in damp stones. "Xochitl sends rain. Xochitl makes the crops grow—the maguey and the maize and the sweet fruits and the pumpkins. Xochitl feeds us!"

He remembers that food is not spiritual. We see the thought in his face.

"She is a saint of the body," he adds, apologetically. "These are saints of the soul." We detect the inflection of piety. It is most annoying. It is a good heathen putting on a starched shirt. Unendurable!

Of all the great women deities from Mary to Diana, Dana of the Druids to Kwanyin of the Buddhists, this Xochitl has been endowed with the most cleanly, the most beneficent attributes. In a race where the women sowed and reaped, wove and span and cooked and brewed, it was natural that a goddess should be fruitful and strong. We looked with intense sympathy and interest at the decaying and alien stronghold where Xochitl had set her powerful foot, there to compete with usurping gods in caring for her strayed family. We did not contribute to the roof fund, fearing influences other than hers at work in this business.

My memory of Xochimilco is always a drowsy confusion of wet flowers on the chinampas, the taste of cold sweetened pulque flavored with strawberries, the sting of the sunshine scorching my neck, the silent Indian girl in the wide straw hat, working with her bees, lifting the tops of the hives to find me a comb of honey; an Indian baby, in shape resembling a pumpkin, wrapped in red fibre cloth, kicking up dust in the road ahead of me. . . . things of no importance whatever, except that I love them. The pumpkin shaped baby is joined by several others, all friendly as chipmunks and as alert, who will walk with you, and smile at you, but will not speak or come nearer than arm's length.

At a turn of the road a band of Indian boys clad in white cotton, wild heads crowned by prodigious straw hats, leap howling upon us. They clamor one question repeatedly. "Do you wish a canoa?" We do, but the choosing of it is the adventure of the day. It is not in our plan to be seized and propelled, with courteous finality, into just any sort of boat. A few visits to the gardens develop in one a discriminating taste in flower decoration. With smiles and dumb arm wavings and shouts above the shouting, we finally disperse all of them but one. There is a brown determined youth who lags along with us, his eyes fixed upon us hauntingly. He insists in low tones that his "canoa" is the most beautiful one in the gardens. It is also to be had for an absurdly small price.

We resign ourselves. It is written that we are to have a boat, and it will be rowed by this boy.

We are in the midst of a spare forest of straight tranquil poplars, lining the banks of the canals. The sunshine falls in long strips between these trees, and gardens grow luxuriously in the midst of them. It is March, but the foliage is lush as midsummer, the pansies and cabbages and chrysanthemums and lettuce glowing and drowsing in the benign air.

The earth is swept clean and bare before the thatched huts that line the waterside. They are contrived of sheaves of maize stalks bound together flatly, burned golden and sweet with year long sunshine. The leaning fences are also of maguey stalks and maize, woven with henequen fibre, dry and rattling in the slight winds.

In the enclosed places are placid children, playing inconsequently, without toys or invention, as instinctively as little animals. Women on their knees sweep their thresholds with a handful of split maguey leaves. Men sit, their legs straight before them, tinkering with boats or mending their rude farming implements.

Everywhere is a leisurely industry, a primitive cleanliness and rigor.

These Xochimilco Indians are a splendid remnant of the Aztecs. They are suspicious of strange peoples, with good reason. They have maintained an almost unbroken independence of passing governments, and live their simple lives in a voluntary detachment, not hostile, from the ruling race of their country. They get all material for their needs from the earth; vegetables and flowers from the chinampas are their wares offered to the outer world. The freshest pansies in Mexico are brought from the chinampas—a word that means an island with flowers. These islands do not float, but are moored substantially, girdled with woven branches.

Our "canoa" is decorated with chrysanthemums and cedar, the flowers woven into a flat background of the sweet smelling greenery. The awning is supported by arches of poplar, bowed while the wood was full of sap. We sit in benches along the sides, looping up the curtains back of us. There is something Egyptian, we decide, about this long, narrow barge of hand sawed wood, with legends carved along the sides. There is something darkly African about it, too with the boy standing in the prow, bending slowly as he rows, the long tapering pole sweeping through the water, disturbing the loosened blossoms floating with us.

It is early, and the small boats of the Indian women are still moored to stakes before the thatched huts, while the women and their children are washing and dressing at the water's edge. They are lovely creatures, the color of polished brown stone, very demure and modest. They spread their long hair on the rocks to dry, their heads thrown back, eyes closed before the light.

A child is bathing her feet, standing on a wet stone. We pass almost near enough to touch her. Mary throws her a few pansies. Her eyes are vague and gentle, the color of brown one sees in the native pottery. She is too amazed at the sight of us to pick up the pansies. She turns her head away, and blushes—arms, legs and curved neck suffuse. She stands fixed in a trance of instinctive modesty, one foot standing over the other, toes in.

The heat of the day rises in slow waves. Singly, the women come out in their tiny narrow boats, pointed at prow and bow, so shallow the rim is only a few inches above the water. They kneel before their braseros, small furnaces for burning charcoal, and cook their complicated foods, which they serve hot to the people in the be-flowered barges. In this limited space, the woman will keep her supplies, her cooked food and dishes. She will serve any number of customers, without haste or nervousness, in competent silence. Her face will be smooth and untroubled, her voice not edged. Primitive woman cooks the greater part of her time; she has made of it, if not a fine art, then a most exact craft. There are no neurotics among them. No strained lines of sleeplessness or worry mar their faces. It is their muscles, not their nerves, that give way in old age; when the body can no longer lift and strain and tug and bear, it is worn out, and sits in the sun a while, with the taste of tobacco in the mouth. It counsels and reminisces, and develops skill in tribal witchcraft. And dies. But the nerves did not kill it.

Nearly all the women in the boats are young; many of them adolescent girls. One of these wears a gay pink reboso, and thick gold hoops quiver in her ear lobes. She sits in the midst of a great bouquet of violets, pansies, sweet peas, and delicate pale roses. Her slender oar barely touches the water. She darts forward in response to our nod, her shallop runs along the barge, her brown hand, gleaming and wet, grips the rim. Under the parted sleekness of her carbon colored hair, her round innocent eyes speculate. We are openly pleased with her. She charges us twice the usual sum. We pay it, and receive an armload of flowers, done into tight little bouquets, bound with henequen fibre, arranged in long loops whereby one may trail them in the water to keep them fresh.

The sun is blazing with noonday fervor. The canals are alive with barges and the darting shallops, swift as swallows. A ponderous boat, overflowing with cabbages and celery and onions, drifts out and floats downstream guided casually by an old man whose white cotton garments are rolled up at shoulders and knees, his hat shading him as completely as an umbrella. He drags his pole through the water with a tremendous gesture, then rests leaning upon it, staring out across the chinampas, past the valley to the mountains. His face is massive, hugely wrinkled, not happy nor unhappy. He lives as a tree lives, rightly a part of the earth.

A tall girl washes clothes in a hollow of bushes matted into a shadowed cave. She rolls the garments on a slanted stone, and scoops up fresh water with a Oaxaca bowl splashed with blue and green and orange. Her blouse, almost sleeveless, is embroidered in an Aztec pattern. Her full crimson skirts are looped over bare ankles. Her braids, tied together in front, dip in the water when she leans forward. There is a trance like quality in her motions, an unconsciousness in her sharpened profile, as if she had never awakened from the prenatal dream.

"She should live for a century," says Michael, who is tormented with neuroses. "Fancy her inner repose!"

Another girl, her shallop brimming with lettuce and celery massed in fragile shades of cream color and pale green, rows swiftly down a side canal. She sits perfectly straight, her wide hat almost obscures her face, all save the pointed chin and calm, full lipped mouth.

Her oar sends faint ripples out to lap the banks and stir the broadleafed lilies. We read, cut along the curving side of weathered wood, "No me olvide, Lupita!" (Do not forget me, Lupita.) One imagines the giver, whittling and carving before his hut, making a pretty boat for Lupe to carry her vegetables in. He offers his work and his thought, but humanly cannot forbear his one request—"Do not forget me, Lupita!"

This sentimental discovery sets us on the watch for other like mottoes. At once we read this, carved in a cumbersome craft draped with willow branches—"I was once a beautiful tree in the mountains of Cordoba, but a strong axeman cut me down, and now I live to serve his friends." A strange, ironical cry out of captivity. It is the Indian who speaks. He tells a tragic story in a few words, without complaint. "Remember lovely Elena, with the sweet mouth and the green eyes," entreats another, passing to the laughter of young voices and the muted whine of mandolin strings. A line of boats keeps the eye busy searching for inscriptions. . . . "For remembrance of dear little Pancho," says one. "For the daughter of Pepe Gonzalez," reads another. A boat about four feet long, very old, unpainted, is christened "La Fortuna de Juan Ortega." Juan himself stands in this battered shell, plying up and down the canals with a few heads of lettuce, and cabbage, seeking that fortune, but without haste or greed. Juan is small and shabby, his shirt is faded, his hat is a ruin. He smiles at us, and offers lettuce, slightly wilted. He accepts our coin with a fine air of indifference, makes a grand bow, and is away. Juan could go to town and be a servant in a rich house, but depend upon it, he will not. It is the fashion among town people to go to the country for Indian servants. Many of them are docile and hardworking. But the Xochimilco Indians do not make good servants. They are apt to return on the second day to their chinampas, and finding them again is hard work.

We face a fleet of barges coming in from the side canals. They are majestic and leisurely, grouped with charming effect, their arches as individual as human faces. One is slightly pointed and woven of yellow maize, studded with chrysanthemums and pale green stalks of corn. Another is made of purple tinted henequen with small bouquets of jasmines set at intervals. Yet another is lovely with cornflowers and cedar. Each man has decorated his boat in the manner that pleases him and one cannot choose which is the most beautiful.

Under the awnings small parties of young Mexican people, attended by their chaperones, eat fruit and throw flowers to each other; in every second barge, it seems, there is a gifted youth with a guitar or mandolin, and they all strum in the careless manner of the true amateur of music. There are many types of Mexican youth and age—young school teachers and clerks, stenographers and shop keepers, with a scattering of the more wealthy folk; there is every type of girl from the modern young person in the flannel walking skirt, to the more reactionary type who wears a fluffy dress with a pretty scarf over her shoulders. It is the Mexico of industry and work and sober family virtues, the respectable, comfortably well off people whom we see here for the most part; all of them happy, bent on a day of leisure and recreation in their incomparable playground.

We are about to pass under a low stone bridge, built before the days of Cortes in Mexico, and the fleet of boats approaching meet us here in a narrow passageway where it will be a problem for two boats to pass each other. One barge has swung in under the bridge already, and we are also in the shadow of the arch. It has the look of an imminent collision. One expects mutual recrimination, a crash of boatsides, much talk.

Nothing of the sort, each boatman makes way. Each steers carefully, running his own boat almost into the bank in his effort to make room for the other. "Have a care, comrade!" says one, when he is crowded a little too closely. "Pardon me!" says the other, and somehow in the midst of the work he finds a hand with which to doff his shaggy hat, and to make a bow. The other bows in turn, good days are exchanged, the occupants of the boat smile at us as we glide through, and the flying garden of flowers fills the air between boats once more. The waiting barges form in a line and pass under the arch in a quiet procession, the awnings casting wavering shadows deep in the clear water.

From the shadowed recesses of the pavilions along the bank the native orchestras play gay tunes. Guitar, mandolin, violin, flute make scattered harmony. A medley of airs comes mingled to us on the water. "La Adelita," "La Pajarera," "La Sandunga," "La Norteña,"—all of us hum the music we prefer, with curious tonal results. The young people are dancing in the pavilions. Children play in the swings and rope trapezes. Parties sit at long tables in the shade, having luncheon festively. It all has the look of a huge special fiesta, though it is merely the usual Sunday holiday.

Toward the end of the main canal small boys run up and down the bank, or stand holding patient small horses, saddled disproportionately in leather contrivances very elaborate and heavy. The ponies are for hire by the hour, and the boys shout the attractions of their mounts. One of them leans fondly on the neck of his steed, and says, "Muy bonito, muy fuerte caballito," (Very pretty, very strong little horse!) stroking the ragged mane, while the small creature sleeps obliviously.

"Your pony looks cynical even in his sleep," we told the boy. "As though he doubted your motives."

"What does he expect?" asks the boy. "To be loved for himself alone? It does not happen in the world."

We decide not to ride the pony. "He will have his supper anyhow," says Mary. "He will lose nothing by it."

"What about me?" the owner wants to know.

"We cannot pity you—you are a philosopher!" Michael tells him.

We stop in the shade of a wide willow tree near the bank. Our boatboy seats himself crosslegged in the prow. He has the composure of a young idol, his eyes slanted and meditative. His scarlet cotton sash is knotted twice and hangs with a definite air of smartness. His feet are bound with thonged sandals of leather. We admire him immensely as he sits, eating peanuts in a remote, lordly way, placing the shells in the upcurving brim of his hat.

A flower girl passing in a slender boat throws him a bunch of purple and yellow pansies. He smiles, makes a grandiose acknowledging gesture the full length of his arm and places the flowers in his hat brim also.

He stretches on the mat, his face to the softening afternoon sky, arms under his head. The hat is by his side. He whistles "Adelita" gently, and smiles to himself. It is a pity to disturb him, but we must be going.

Trinidad

(unfinished story, 1921)

Porter never gave this uncompleted story a title, simply referring to it in her notes as "Trinidad's story to Felipe as he repeats it to me." There is no question that Porter and Felipe Carrillo Puerto saw a great deal of each other in 1921. Hank Lopez's *Conversations with Katherine Anne Porter* reports her assertion that the two frequented Mexico City's night spots where they danced the tango and all the latest dance steps. Among her papers are several descriptions of the sinking of their rowboat in the shallow lagoon of Chapultepec Park and a photograph inscribed "To my dear friend Catarina from Felipe."

"Trinidad's story" may have been part of Porter's "Mexican book" begun as early as 1921. In an apparently unsent letter dated September 8, 1921, Porter described the project, "to be done in the form of the Patio story" ["In a Mexican Patio"]. It was to have four parts; the third, "Four Portraits of Revolutionaries," proposed to depict Samuel Yúdico, Robert Haberman, Angel Gómez, and Felipe Carrillo Puerto. "Trinidad" is probably the Felipe Carrillo Puerto part of this proposed work. As the individual "portraits" were to be loosely interrelated, it is possible that the apparently confusing references to characters named "Steban" and "Soledad" in the story as published here would have been clear in the context of the entire book if Porter had completed it. It seems unlikely, because of the physical evidence of the manuscript, that Porter mistakenly misnamed the character Sebastian Guerrero "Steban" or misnamed Trinidad "Soledad."

We are sure that Porter set down Felipe's story in 1921, but unsure whether she worked on it later, for it is not a mere transcription but a calculated work of art, in which the "Felipe" figure is puzzled and frustrated by the mysterious behavior of Trinidad. In Porter's works, the female is often beyond the scope of male comprehension, as María Concepción proves to be to her husband Juan.

Trinidad

Incident of the Yucatan riots. The captain of the bandit forces [Sebastian Guerrero] who raided the convent and took Trinidad. Her story to Felipe, as he repeats it to the men. Her sleeplessness, her long fits of weeping, her silences that tortured him. . . . Many men after that first, her many escapes, her wanderings. . . . The captain gave her away to the second man. . . . She reached Mexico City, Felipe found and loved her.

His capture and punishment of the Captain . . . during a political battle . . . grilled him, and sent him out to walk into the desert. Set a guard around the town, many of them with field glasses. So long as those glasses could reach him he must be moving. To prevent him slipping back to the city. On his third day under the sun, in the sand, he had crawled back within shooting range. But they did not shoot him. He would get up and stagger, waving his arms, and advance and fall down, and rise and come a step forward. But they had orders not to shoot him . . . simply let him stay out there. . . .

"He lay down and did not get up again.

"So that night I kissed Trinidad, and sat by her, and said, 'It is cool here, and the wind blows. You will sleep tonight, my sweetheart.' I stroked her forehead, and her eyes closed, with that trembling of the lids that was only a part of the terrible small shiver in her whole body, which made me think of flesh with a knife newly thrust in it. . . .

"Then I told her what I had done. . . . Her breast tightened and hardened under my hand, her mouth gasped, gray white. She rose slowly in one movement, like a shadow rising when a light is turned down slowly. . . . I thought she was dying, for she kept feeling out for me her eyes black as if the pupils had scattered. I caught her softly, and held her . . . Oh my poor Trinidad! In that moment she was like my own child.

"'No, No, No,' she whispered strangely. My skin crawled. 'Did you do that? Is he there—now?'

"'He is there now,' I told her, trying to reassure her, to give reality to that revenge I had made for her. . . . 'He is there now, Trinidad of my soul, lying in the sand, with his ears and mouth and nostrils stuffed full of it, and there he will stay until the crows find him. Don't trouble any more, don't cry, don't suffer! He is out of the world. You can forget now, and sleep sweet.'

"And I went on rocking her in my arms, for she lay with her head fallen back over my shoulder, and her temples looked empty of blood, sunken like a dead woman's. Then I saw that I should have waited for another moment, this was not the time, she was too spent after the strain of those days of fighting. When I smoothed her braids back, and straightened her out in her bed, she lay perfectly still. I went to get some wine for her, and when I returned, she was weeping terribly, with a sound as if she was choking, her body would twist itself in spasms, her hands pressed over her mouth as if she meant to strangle herself. . . . I was frightened, then at once my heart gave a hard leap and began to kick on my ribs until my ears were deaf with the drumming—and I was in a rage with her.

"I seized her arms and dragged her up, shaking her until her face was purple. . . . 'Look you! What do you want? Have I not done what I could? And now, by God, you weep! I am sick of your tears! Stop them or I shall beat you! Hush! Hush!' I found myself shouting ludicrously like a boy shaking a dog! 'I give you half a minute to be quiet!' And I raised my fist over her ready to strike. But she had no spirit left in her. . . . She held to me, and reached up and closed her hand over my fist, and her lips moved over my arm in humble grieving kisses.

"'O, let me weep now! Let me weep.' She said, with an effort, not speaking clearly—'These are my last tears! They are for joy! I swear to you, Felipe.'

"And then she began to scream with laughter, high quick shrill cries that tripped over the one before it, her mouth turned up at the corners, with tears pouring down her face, a thin stream of tears that divided on her cheeks and ran into tiny branches, so that her face was melted with them.

"That is the punishment a man gets from love, my friends. There I sat, and she had forgotten me, and was away in some strange and awful secret place of her own soul, and I could not follow her, or draw her from it. Afterward, she was quiet, and even smiled at me, with eyes like I have seen in people after a long fever, but I could not feel the same. . . . I had lost her and I do not know how. She kept murmuring, 'Thank you, Thank you, my beloved generous Felipe!'

"I wanted to make her a low bow, and bitterly say, 'You are welcome, Trinidad! It was nothing, a mere diversion, I assure you!' But I could not wound her. No, I was utterly without courage of any kind where she was concerned. I know now I should have been harsh with her, have wrenched her out of her self-concentration. . . . How do I know? I say I know. But I don't. . . . I could only love her. That was my helplessness. . . . If I could have been easy in my mind about her: 'To the devil with you! After all, I picked you up one evening, and I shall drop you again one day on the same corner . . .' but it would have been a lie, and what would it serve? And she was so marvellously, strangely beautiful, like a woman one sees in a dream, moving just above the ground, with her whole body quivering in a strange light, and her black hair starting smooth and clean out of her temples and forehead like golden colored wax, and the blurred light on the outside of the arms where the flesh feels like a peach warmed in the sun. . . . A superstition used to come over me about her—that she was a witch woman of some kind, and that story she had told me was just a charm she used—a terrible, black charm which she spun out in words, and wove around me, winding my heart up tightly in pity, so that I could not bear to touch her rudely, or to speak sharply to her, or forget her sorrows for one minute. . . .

"Then I would come upon her asleep in her hammock, her head thrown back, looking like a marble woman in the moonlight, and I could stoop over, breathing softly so as not to disturb her, and I would see tears in the soft hollows of her eyes, and her mouth would look like a child's after it had been punished. I would forget everything. Sometimes I would go away, but in a minute I would be back, whispering her awake; she would deny that she had wept for anything. And we would talk the whole night. . . . She would cry, 'Ah, I will make you certain that I love you.'

"At these times, she seemed to melt into me, so that I didn't have simply the familiar feeling of a man who possesses a woman he cares for—a sense of power and triumph, of satisfied sensuality—no, no—she was part of me, and I of her, and we seemed mysteriously to be one body, and I did not have even a shade of hatred for her, or a feeling that she belonged to me. I was simply certain of her as I was of my own existence in that moment.

"But now mark you—after that day when she wept at my news every-thing changed. I would tell myself that I understood, that it was all very simple, that she was ill, and a hysterical woman does strange things. But she had never been hysterical—not in the ordinary way of women. . . . And afterward, she was different. . . . She would sit quite still in her long chair in the patio, with her head covered [with a] white lace scarf, so thin I [could] see her eyes with their dark shadows, and the faint red of her mouth. I could glimpse her face, you see, exactly as if it was a shell seen faintly through the veil of ferns over the fountain . . . and I couldn't get any closer to her thoughts than this, either. We drove together in the evening, and she always sat forward, bending her head a little side ways, the lace veil falling back from her cheeks, a tiny set smile in the corners of her lips, and she would bow to the line of soldiers on either side of the streets when they saluted as we passed through.

"<One evening I came back earlier than usual, and she was not in the patio. 'La Nina has gone to the cathedral,' explained one of the small serving maids. 'La Nina desired me to say to you she would return at seven o'clock.'

"I waited, out of patience, trying to put down my reasonless irritation at the thought of Trinidad kneeling in a church. She was above priests and religion, I told myself. It was my way of dividing her image in my thoughts from all other images, my attempt to separate her from a past in which I had no share: she slipped back, in those times, in my thoughts, into a small believing child, seized at her prayers and tumbled into Hell: that she could pray again seemed simple absurdity. In his zeal to test a soul, God had a trifle over reached himself.> She came in slowly with old Josefa trotting at her heels, a black shade against the darkness of the bougainvillea vine, her veil caught under the chin where her hand glimmered palely. Her eyes were hidden, and her skirts covered her feet. . . . I had a sudden terror of her, as if she was a holy thing that I had helped to desecrate. . . . I said to myself, 'But I have pleaded with her to marry me!' and then I laughed at myself, thinking how evil a thought to hold against her, and an excuse I was making for myself. . . . She was holy within herself, and she was at the core of my life. I could feel the presence of love shining inside of me like the beating of my own heart. That was all. She cast back her veil, and leaned on my arm silently. I felt the gentle weight of her, from head to foot, inclined toward me, the adorable even softness of her.

"'I have a little caprice that will amuse you,' she said. 'Tomorrow I shall have a mass said for the soul of an old friend—one who is so long dead I had almost forgotten him. . . .'

"'Him? Why could it not have been a woman, Trinidad? But then, I can't be jealous of the dead.'

"'I hope not of this dead, at all events,' she said softly.

"We walked with our arms around each other the whole length of the garden, then back again, and around the narrow path of the fountain. I remember everything: it is more clear to me now than this garden and these stars because for the first time since the day of Steban's death I was at peace—the sound of the small pebbles slipping under our feet, the calm rhythm of her body undulating with her long, even step that kept pace with mine, that strange stillness of the night that releases the heart from care and fills it with melancholy—I remember it all now, because it was the final hour of peace for me; my allotted joys were used up, and I thought them only at the beginning.

"Soledad was already gone to the church when I awakened, and I had scarcely taken my coffee when a boy from the barracks brought word from Captain [Sebastian] Prim: we knew there was the devil to pay in the business, and he had presented his bill a trifle precipitately. Could I come quietly at once to the barracks?

"The captain was in a fret; he walked about and cursed, stopping to examine his waxed mustachios in a small pocket mirror carried inside of his tunic, brandishing a cigarette, the very picture of an elegant gentleman disturbed at cards.

"'Shall I take my regiment? go out and attack before they arrive? I'm sick of having them clutter up the streets with their filthy carrion, besides my mother is nervous. I can't persuade her to go away to the lakes. Shall my mother's entire summer be spoiled by running gun battles under her very windows? Again, valgame de Dios, [today] is my dia de santo, and my novia expects me to dine at her house. Por Cristo, I shall put an end to this before night! If San Sebastian is a true warrior, he will collaborate with me in making his day a success!'"

[Felipe] paused, eyes fixed on his glass—he had the air of a man having finally to disclose a profound secret, hesitating, weighing.

"Sebastian! Trinidad had a mass said for [Sebastian Guerrero]!"

Then he gazed at me as if he expected me to understand the meaning of that disclosure without words—he conveyed to me in a single glance, a mortally shaken look, almost half asking me to share with him a little the anguish of that blow. We were silent a moment. He took a gulp of wine then spoke suddenly in a changed voice—

"You remember Prim, do you not, Vicente? A man well paid with himself, that's certain. He took his troops and went on his fool's errand into the country, and there came up Candido with twice the number of men, all fresh, and horses, and an army of soldaderas worse than the soldados. And Prim was shot through the head within ten minutes after Candido's first man fired from behind a maguey, and afterward his men came scattering back into town with the rebels at their heels and the summer was spoiled for Prim's mother and for his novia too.

"It was all one with me. I returned and got my ammunition, and joined my men."

[Felipe's] voice dipped again; he had come once more on the thing he wanted to tell. . . .

"But first I spoke to Trinidad. She came up instantly when I spoke to her, at a few steps away she seemed calm enough, but when I looked into her eyes I saw a deep blaze there, a spark of terrible excitement. 'Is this another battle? Oh, must you go again so soon?' I could hardly control myself.

"'Yes, I am going. . . . Well! will you say a mass for me on my dia de santo next spring?' I asked her hatefully. 'You'll fill the Holy calendar with your dead lovers.'

"A mask slipped down over her face, making it strange and dreadful, a strange gray look, as if she was withering there before my very eyes. If she had dropped into ashes before me I could not have been more struck.

"Then I shouted, 'I have been a fool too long, Trinidad! now you will tell me the truth, or I will kill you here, before I leave you! Did you have a mass said for Sebastian Guerrero?'

"Her eyes never faltered, never changed. They fixed themselves upon me without fear, without pleading, without any shade of love or hate. Her lips scarcely moved as she spoke. I bent my head and listened with an insane idea that I could not hear the word when it came.

"'Yes.'

"It was a tiny undulation of sound, like a deep sigh. It fixed me as if a ghost had breathed on me. Then all of the fury drained out of me, I wished to sit down. I felt very tired. 'Trinidad,' I whispered, humbly, not daring to come near her for fear she would think I meant really to harm her. 'Trinidad, I must know—then I was wrong all this time—you loved him?'

"'No.'

"'But you hated him—you are not religious—' It seemed necessary that I should reason it out aloud for us both. 'How did you remember him for so long, why did you weep that day I told you—?' She did not answer or move. Silence fell between us. In the quiet room the sound of the curtains blown in the wind flapped lightly in the air, a noise of firing in the street came. I felt that if we did not speak now, there would never be any speech between us afterward—words, yes but the simple coin of the heart would not be exchanged again. I had wasted it all, what was a mass, what was a memory? But why, then, had she told me she hated him, that she could not sleep until he was dead?

"'Ay Dios!' I said finally, despairing.

"She stood with her head inclined to one side, her eyes upon me, her lips sealed lightly, her hair curved flatly around her forehead and head, hiding her ears and temples, her fingers netted together before her. Unless I was willing to believe utterly, there was no hope for me. She would not help me . . . maybe she could not. I don't know—if I knew. I came over and touched her. Then I drew her toward me, and she came, unresistingly, passively. I kissed her lips. She began to tremble, and covered her face, shaking her head slowly.

"'Is a kiss so difficult for you as all that?' I said, and before I was conscious even of the impulse, I had flung her from me. She barely saved herself, an outflung arm steadied her on the window sill. She leaned against the opened casement, it gave way with her, and she stood against the wall, still and vigilant, not frightened, but on the defensive. Then truly, I wished to kill her. But I knew I would not, and twice I had threatened her without the courage to fulfill them. Manifestly, she despised me: into my frantic blurred thoughts, racing and stumbling and turning upon themselves, her voice broke clearly, measured and full of sorrow, deliberate and a little weary:

"'You have said you would kill me. If you knew how I wish to die, you would keep your promise!'

"'Then why do you not kill yourself? Must I have your death on my soul too?'

"'Ah, forgive me!' she answered, and for a moment I thought she would weep—'How badly I have endured my life!'

"She nodded her head, simply, with her whole face lighting up in an amazingly childlike smile, very slight, a mere lifting at the corners of her lovely mouth. But her expression was one of sudden comprehension, as if I had happened accidentally unknowingly upon the place where she had been hiding a secret. A shadow smoothed away from her face, she drooped a little, and recovered herself again. Then she stepped swiftly toward me, her face lifted and smiling still, a quick determination in her eyes. 'Felipe,' she said, and after her immobility, it seems to me she was all alive, warm, smoldering within, 'Let us not quarrel now. Go, goodbye, mi aforrado!' she uttered the foolish name she had called me before in playfulness, 'Aforrado de mi vida! You must not distress yourself about me any more. I am not worth it. O my love, you are better than I am, and more lovable. Now forget me as a good soldier should. If I were a man, I should go to war today!' She caught hold of my hand, gayly, and went with me down the steps, out along the path by the fountain, and to the closed gates. We stood there a moment. She seemed to be in a fever of excitement, now that she had fairly spoken. I had a feeling of something being finished, that in her own mind a question had settled itself, she was free from [it].

"She turned from me, running lightly between the tall blooming lilies, at the turn of the path she stopped and flung up her arm, fluttering her hand in another farewell. I saw her smiling, her eyes half closed against the sunlight, she waved me a light swift kiss—bewildered with the changes of her mood as ever, I stared uncertainly, waving back. I even took a step toward her, meaning to touch her again, to assure myself of her. It seemed futile. A witch woman. I had had of her what there was for me to have. If I went back, she would look at me with candid eyes in a mysterious closed face, and never give me the answer I waited for, oh, well. . . .

"I moved out into the street. Prim would be waiting."

*   *   *

dipping sugar in black coffee and nibbling it. His tastes in food were those of extreme youth—one might say childhood. And he was known for his perversities of sentiment, the diffusiveness of his affections . . . where women were concerned.

He tilted one eyebrow, so that the light picked up little streaks of gold in it, and in the long thick lashes that shaded his exceedingly blue eyes.

"Yes, I saw her twice—once at the Corrida de Covadonga, last year, when she stood up and applauded Mejias when he made the perfect [move]—and again I sat near her at the opera this spring. . . . There I was, you know how I loathe dark women—there I was, with this Trinidad on the one side, and the Ebony Venus on the other—their perfume overpowered me . . . fainting as I was I still had presence of mind enough to look at Trinidad's profile, and thought, Christ, what a pity she is not golden, but you know, to touch a black haired woman would make me positively nauseated—yes, it affects me like sea sickness—I can think of no other comparison. . . . But La Trinidad has 'grandeza'—you comprehend? a manner. But she is an unsmiling sort. . . . She hardly spoke or moved the entire evening . . . and [Felipe]. His case is hopeless. He is gone. They say he will marry her."

He finished with a perverse flickering of the eyelids, and sucked sugar with the air of one who had been very clever. . . .

"Ah, Narcissus!" jibed Prim, "if he were black, he could endure only ebony Venuses. When he falls in love, he wishes only to look into a little mirror!"

*　*　*

Note: He had choked her with a handful of dry hot sand scooped up from [the desert]. She spat frothy blood and bled at the nose for a long time afterward. He sat up with her and bathed her face afterward, she said, and made her drink a mouthful of tequila.

Don't tell all, too many details, hint here and there, in simple words, a terribly matter of fact way. . . .

His quarrels with her—threats—I will throw you to my soldiers . . . one night, horribly drunk, he does it. . . . She passes through the hands of several soldiers, a young lad takes pity on her, helps her to escape, goes with her, drags her over the mountainside trying to reach a village, when she is exhausted, carries her on his back. Pursued, they hide in a cave. Soldiers pass by.

Next day he ventures out for meat. She waits, in rain, shut in her cave. He does not come. Next morning driven out by hunger, she ventures out, slipping along behind trees close to the cliff's edge. . . . Comes upon the boy swinging to a limb over space—into the crevasse . . .

Her insistence on this point. How he looked, she would say the wind would not let him be still. His hair would flutter, and his hands would swing back and forth, and then there would be a slow wavering, and he would swing around, half way, and back again—and then his face, grimacing quite horribly, with his tongue thrust out as if some obscene impudence.

*　*　*

Newsboys shouting about the rebellion of Sebastian Guerrero and his successful defeat by Prim. The work also of [Felipe] the governor.

Begin with group in Cafe El Globo, with sketch of Josef, Christina, Gaona—only for atmosphere. [Felipe], Prim?, Jiminez, Hernandes together. Meeting place of certain of the younger revolutionists, idealists, intellectuals. Sebastian Prim is the only one of army tolerated by them. [Felipe], newly elected governor of a turbulent state to the south, drops in for a moment, they with Prim, discuss affairs going very badly at home. [Felipe] leaves almost at once.

Tell in first person. . . . Describe Prim, mannered and handsome, I doubt him, he takes trouble to appear important to humble little people. What is the trouble with [Felipe] nowadays? He is scarcely seen, only in conferences. . . . He comes once, twice to the chamber of labor.

Prim . . . that black girl he picked up in Guadalajara . . . she is a lady of moods, I think. She weeps, and [Felipe] obeys. An amazing business!

She is troubled with a past, I believe. Ladies with a past always weep! It is the proper thing!

Look you, when I said to [Felipe], now this row is settled, for the moment, let's go up to the capital and enjoy life for two weeks. . . . He refused in the gloomiest sort of way, without giving a reason . . . and two days after I arrive here, I see him in the paseo on Sunday morning, with La Santisima Trinidad sitting beside him looking very pale under a wide gray hat, and [Felipe] staring at her like a man in a fog—mind you! what horror—with the bosque full of ladies totally unknown to him, the poor lost soul sits and gazes at a woman who has lived in his own house for upward of two years.

God, how he has changed, the simpleton!

I turned to silent young Luis Hernandes, who was

*   *   *

of the state where [Felipe] is governor.

They moved away, and made their bows at other tables, stopping for a[while] with Christina the dancer. Head of the local land commission.

"A nest of puppies," pronounced Jiminez after them: "Without sentiment, without chivalry, without imagination. They have nothing but youth and good looks. . . . I envy them bitterly!" He turned and smiled at me sourly, his tangled black hair springing up from his low forehead and spreading into a fan, somewhat like the clipped tail of a pigeon in Guadalajara. "When I went to [Felipe]'s house last summer, I had not seen him since the elections. He was involved in the difficult business of arranging the affairs of a state that had been in disorder for four hundred years. I had heard he was doing it very well. . . ."

[Felipe] was the God-appointed man for that job . . . he came in there all braced for [a struggle].

They all insist she is gloomy, beset with [melancholy]. There was something bright and flashing about her, like a knife blade in the sunlight—not edged and hard—no, I don't mean that, but she had a great look of valor about her. . . . I said to her, "You are not all Spanish—surely there is Indian blood in you from somewhere."

"Oh, I think so—she said easily—[Felipe], you know, is four fifths Indian,—"

He tells about the rows between the army of Prim for the Federal government and the young rebel chief Sebastian Guerrero.

*   *   *

There before my very eyes, she began to take on the quality of a myth.

Her hellish, diabolical, maniacal physical and moral endurance. The look of her long legs moving like a story-book hero over that craggy and difficult landscape. . . .

Felipe's profound self-possession . . . soft spokenness . . . a complete dictator. . . . Indians come to him with all their possible combinations of sorrow and misfortune, their bitter grievances, their petty irritations. . . . The thing is settled then and there, by order, in the presence of Felipe and the complainant. No court, no jury. . . . He dictates an order to his secretary, and the man goes away with his affair arranged, or all prepared arrange them. . . .

A small soul, bent on scaling down all souls to his measure . . . he wants easily understood things, facile friendships, easy loves.

My contention was that for him it is better to know once for all the boundaries of his slavery. . . . He must work so many hours for his food, and afterward he may play: within this easily measured compass he may make an endurable life.

Notes on Teotihuacan

(unfinished essay, 1921–1922)

Perhaps in 1920 or early in 1921 Porter met Manuel Gamio while he was still working on the Teotihuacán project. With the publication of *Forjando Patria* in 1916, he is credited with launching social anthropology in Mexico. His monumental two volume *La Población del Valle de Teotihuacán* is a study of the ancient civilization and modern inhabitants of the region. In "Where Presidents Have No Friends," Porter praises his restoration of the pyramids and his study of the indigenous peoples of the area; the sole purpose of his study was identifying their needs and improving their lot. According to Mary Doherty, Porter never missed the opportunity to accompany Gamio to Teotihuacán and other places. He was by far her most knowledgeable and influential informant about Mexican culture. It was he who informed her about the legend of Xochitl.

As the title indicates, the sketch appears in early draft. Still in their present form, the notes reveal how Porter, with a sure eye, rapidly and vividly sketched in significant detail. Even the shorthand compilation of verbless nouns is stylistically effective. And Porter is sardonically eloquent here and elsewhere in the description of religious statues and paintings. Gamio, who reinforced Porter's anticlericalism, is the source of the quotation in this piece about the bloody cristos, "El mas sangriento, el mas milagriento" (the bloodier, the more miraculous). She later incorporated her brief description of St. Ignatius Loyola in "Flowering Judas."

Notes on Teotihuacan

The cottage at the foot of the Pyramid of the Sun. The cart, two wheeled, rattling. The high shouldered old horse, a study in pathological anatomy, his long under lip drooping. We call him the Philosopher.

The photographer. The interpreter. Myself. The look of the country, the lane cut through by an enterprising person, whereby invaluable stones, walls of ancient Aztec houses and temples were upturned in ruins to the sun, and used afterward to build the low scattered wall on either side of the road.

In the narrow road with the flecked shadows of the Pirú tree, the bars of cactus and organa shade. Our cart takes up the road. We entice a wee Indian maid to have her picture taken. She stands, with a still, painful dignity at the wheel, her eyes not meeting ours. We regret having embarrassed her so.

In the meantime, a cart full of Indians, with mules. They cannot pass us. They pull up the cart with good natured laughter, and the leader shouts, "Silencio, ranas! que va a cantar el sapo!" This does not lend itself to perfect translation, but it means, "Silence, frogs! The bullfrog is going to sing!" An ironical acknowledgement that their business must be held up while our pictures were being taken in the highway.

Their saying that the shade of the Pirú (corruption of Perú) causes one to sleep at church was brought from Perú by Viceroy Antonio de Mendoza. La Purificación, a tall church in conventional Spanish style, built in [the sixteenth century]. A cemetery, with old and new graves. The new concrete tombs look garish beside the grey old square stones of the older dead.

Atmosphere everywhere—lizards on the stones and walls, butterflies in the vines. The time of roses in bloom. The small uncultivated rose trees bloom with a desperate fecundity—every branch thick with stunted blooms.

The small boy with a crooked stick driving sheep. Others driving laden burros, great mounds of green grass or wood.

San Juan the Parochial church. The doors, the look of the roof and heavy headed trees over the wall. The doors open. A youth, wearing a charro of blue drill, with an embroidered hat, stands quietly, leaning on a double barrelled shot gun. He handles the gun with easy familiarity. During our walk together it was not once out of his hand. His frank eyes, and

The Pyramid of the Sun at Teotihuacán, one of the restored Aztec temples described by Porter in "Two Ancient Mexican Pyramids— the Core of a City Unknown until a Few Years Ago." Sergei Eisenstein Collection, Lilly Library, Indiana University.

beautiful face. His manners, which would have been good manners anywhere in the world. The exquisite small patio, with the grouped arches of which one never tires. Ruined, a quiet, warm drowsy ruin of weeds and stones. The old drain runs through it, the water clear and cold from a spring which begins under the high altar. Out of it, through the baptistery, the cold damp dirt floors, the beautiful, tesselated railings, across a small field to the lake—artificial lake, deep blue and purple water in which small trout move without disturbing the stillness, the bottom fringed with pale green weeds and fern. This grot clear on one side, with a prodigious wall rising beyond, of weathered grey stone, and a forest of trees beyond is noisy with the song of birds. This convent older than the church itself. Founded by the Franciscans, the books of baptism and of the affairs of the convent date from 1632. We went first into the new part of the chapel— shining and modern, with gilt on the altar instead of gold leaf, and glossy black and grey tilings instead of the reddish tezontle stone of the older part. Clean, empty, with light streaming in rays like the haloes of the saints from round windows high up under the eaves. And over the altar, a flutter of birds' wings and their high sweet singing. The sound in this stillness linked seven centuries together since the time Saint Francis preached to the birds, and again to his last moment, when he died singing the praises of Sister Death to the scandal of blue nosed ecclesiastic formality, and when he drew his last breath, outside a multitude of larks burst into a canticle. (Birds over altar gorriones.)

And here on the ugly shiny altar of one who hated altars and roofs and the gestures of religion, birds flocked and sang. A straight line of centuries, seven hundred years linked together, an avenue of singing birds.

The statues in the old church. The Lady of Consolation. Lady of Sorrows. The Christ. (Get all pictures and describe.) The birds, who doubtless believe the church was built for their shelter, have knocked askew the black cope of young Saint Aloysius. He is delightfully attractive thus: many of the saints garbed in cloth. No carven garments. His cope over his eye, his humorless expression of piety. Saint Anthony, probably brought from Spain, is carven in wood, with the splendid overlay of gold leaf and paint in brocade pattern which was one of the loveliest arts of the 15th century Church. His robe is carved subtly in a suggestion of the fashion of Spain in 1500. His face is that of a Spanish aristocrat of the period. Drab Saint Anthony, patron of lost things, saint of the bereaved, is here a poetically ascetic young aristocrat; even his shaven poll manages to be a thing of beauty.

Maria la Soledad—Mary of the Sorrows, Solitude?—is in black plush embroidered in spears of silver wheat. Her black plush headdress arranged like the veil of a nun, falls to her feet, a gorgeous golden coronet makes rays around her face. Inconsolable clasped hands and lonely forsaken brows. La Soledad! All the sorrows of the world, of the poor, of the desolate, of the terrible believers of the world, have been brought to those prim feet. Have been held up to those unseeing eyes turned forever upon her own griefs.

Saint Francis himself, in whose name this church was wrung from the blood of the poor, himself a lover of holy poverty, gentlest and most blessed spirit of the Middle Ages, has only a small statue in his image. Beautiful ascetic body, thin and draped with the coarse wool robe of his order, his face a trifle severe. The stigmata in his hands bleed a little. Not the Saint Francis of the early joyful times, but the starved and emaciated creature of his later days, when the crystal mind was muddied with the tortures of the body, when the lovely radiant heart was darkened with the cruelties of his faith.

Everywhere the awful, pallid blood streaked mask of the dying Man. Note. Study of this preoccupation with the physical torment of Christ and the saints. Saying of the Indians, "El mas sangriento, el mas milagriento" (slang). Their belief that a saint has no power unless he is covered with blood. The statues of the Spanish church in Mexico are endowed with a peculiar horror. The statues of the Christ, his body a mass of bloody suppurating wounds, raised in great welts upon his flesh. Streaked with the scourge, dripping from the hands and feet, pouring thickly from a gash over his heart, thin rivulets of blood upon his face. Not so bad in Spain, though the insistence there also is upon wounds and terrors. The Spaniards accentuated the blood because of the fact that the Aztecs at that time made blood sacrifice upon their altars. In order to compete with their rituals, the Spaniards must have a god as bloody. The so-called cannibalism of the Aztecs was this: the body was beheaded and thrown down, and parts of it were eaten by the priests as a sacrament. This objective ritual cannibalism must be supplanted by the subjective [ritual] cannibalism of the Christian faith—that is, the body and blood [were] eaten under a symbol of bread and wine. This body and blood [are part] of nearly all faiths in some form or other.

In order to do this, the Spaniards increased the wounds of Christ from the sacred five to as many as the human body could sustain and still be recognizable. A simple meeting of an emergency such as all new faiths must practice—the early changing of the pagan feasts into Christian ones, by the simple changing of the name and observances, while the idea and the date remained the same. Birds, gorriones, golondrinas, etc. Baptismal font, carved in one huge piece. <Beautiful holy water bowl of prodigious size, carved in one piece. Perched on rim, next to the decorated cross painted in fruit and leaf designs in green, red and black, very old, a human skull with two bones laid cross wise—an old skull, scaly, brown and leprous, as you dip your fingers into the water, you look into the eye sockets of the skull. It is meant to be terrifying. One feels as if a child had leaped at you and said, "Boo!"> The great trees. The incident of "su pobre casa." The boy, when we bade him good bye, in Spanish, "Good bye, Senora, whenever you return to Teotihuacan, have this for your poor house, su pobre casa." I said in my halting Spanish, "I thank you. But it is a very great and beautiful house." He replied, "It is not too good for you. If you wish to take my word, be assured that this is, without condition, your poor house."

The curious stateliness, the very sensitive perceptions. The shadow of something touched to the quick that went over his face at the little laugh of the interpreter; I could cheerfully have strangled the creature for his bad manners.

As we came through the narrow passageway from the main church to the main patio, he showed us charred walls and broken stones and a deep pit in the earth. Here was where the Zapatistas stabled their horses in the revolutions of 1915. Church used as quarters for the troops.

The hacienda of Santa Catarina. A survival and development of the feudal system brought here by the Spaniards. The high battlemented walls, round as castle turrets, of red brick. White cobble stone entrance, great open patio, with a low platform strewn with hay and grass, where horses, mules, pigs, sheep, and chickens and turkeys mingled. The red tiled Spanish roofs. The swallows singing and flurrying under the eaves. Shelter for horses and mules.

*　*　*

Brown face under yellow shawl, her orange skirt faded and melting into the warm color symphony. Baked earth and muddy puddles of water where gauzy winged flies cluster.

The chapel of this hacienda is very old, dedicated to Santa Catarina. The small musty interior is old and shabby, covered with dust almost ready to sprout small spears of weeds. Gone into unimaginable decay. Altar mean and poor in its blue paint peeling off in streaks. Only Santa Catarina, a very fine statue carved in wood and brocaded with gold leaf, glimmers like a dying star in the gloom. She regards the mouldering ceiling with eyes of unfading blue, and holds her cruel iron wheel with the pale fingers curved delicately, unrememberingly over the instrument on which she suffered death.

In this chapel also there is a small oil painting, very good, of a madonna and child, it is in the Italian fashion. They could not tell me its history. Ask Gamio.

This chapel is to be refurbished and opened again to the Indians on September next. Here their starved souls are to be fed again on the pale bread of an alien faith.

Beside the story of the churches—get history of the Spanish occupation. The life of the Indians. Get translation for picture of Indian complaint to the King. Stories of good and bad priests, their work. Pictures of any.

*　*　*

San Martin of the Pyramides. Dead recumbent Christ. Into the priest's house, the screaming parrots, the hot odor of flowers wilting in the sunshine. A tiny boy opens the door.

Here St. Ignatius Loyola with chaste lace-trimmed trousers showing beneath his black cassock. St. Martin a bishop. Painting of him depicting what seems to have been the outstanding charitable act of his life. His fame seems to rest securely on the fact that once, as he rode magnificently garbed, on a great shining horse, he met a beggar, whom the painting represents as in a state of almost entire nudity. St. Martin, touched to tears, no doubt, cut with his sword his scarlet cloak in half, and gave the handsome remnant to the unclothed one, who is depicted as describing contortions of gratitude at the stirrups of the saint. . . . Several paintings immortalize this scene of the saint severing his coattails, in what seems to me the most incomplete act of charity any.

In one he is a splendid mailed cavalier with a wide flowing hat— painting dated 1791. [In] another dated 1795 he is represented in the dress of a conquistador, embroidered doublet, flowing cloak, a small feathered hat and rigid neckruff framing the face of a Bourbon prince. Still another shows him in the dress of the Italian Renaissance. There are restorations in this church, as ever very bad ones.

San Lorenzo. Over interminable roads, between walls of organa surrounding fields of maguey and cactus blooming and flaming in orange and red and yellow, everywhere the singing of birds.

Poverty of church contrasted with the altar of gold leaf on wood. Chief interest a large painting in very bad style, tablet of the blessed souls. Three layers—God at the top, garbed as a benevolent pope. The saints interceding in the center, headed by the Man on one side, the Virgin on the other, all kneeling. In the pit, souls in the uncomfortable process of being purified. Saint Michael is the guard.

* * *

battling and building and dying, irrevocably bound by their very navel cords to the past.

In Mexico this was true for many epochs. In all the ruins uncovered, superimposed layer upon layer, there is kinship of spirit and ideal from one to the other, the old bequeathing to the new some part of itself, the new accepting unconsciously, as it should be. . . .

In the Valley of Teotihuacan the whole history of human kind is discovered in miniature. Long ago in this valley, in what age no man knows, so cleanly has each succeeding conqueror done his work of destruction—a great race of builders made themselves a city, and endured for a span. Another race more warlike and less cultured came and built their city over the old one, and flourished and made themselves great, and worshipped their own gods, and all that was left of the old culture came under the dominion of the usurpers.

Whether by fire or by flood or by earthquake, or by hosts of invaders no one knows, but these people also vanished, and time hid their houses and their bones and idols of their temples under hills of earth. Their gods vanished mysteriously also, as gods do when their devotees are menaced. And still a third race of people, who built less magnificently but who still were splendid, raised their houses, and temples, where they sacrificed to fierce gods.

Yet these races were akin in many things, and each age wears a family resemblance to the others, until the Spanish came, and broke the line of ancestry with new religions and new customs and strange ideals alien and unassimilable, and the race, in its integrity, perished.

The Spanish, after the manner of invaders, killed many of the people and enslaved the rest, and destroyed their temples. And over each temple they set a church of their own, and said, "Here at last is the true faith. Worship here, and forget your heathen superstitions."

And afterward they taught the Indians that statues could work charms, and relics could make magic; that Virgins painted on cloth could speak, and little figures of wood could cure their sicknesses, and a man in a black dress could free their souls from sin.

The class of people who had been slaves under the Aztecs were slaves again under the Spaniards, and those who had been princes among the Aztecs were slaves also, and all the heads of the people were bowed in preparation to descend into the earth with their epoch, for their time was finished.

In Acolman, in the valley of Teotihuacan, in the very spot where the first man was created from the spent arrow of a god, the Spaniards built one of their first churches in the new world. I saw it, sunk into the earth for the distance of the height of a man, stained and mildewed, shadowed and stooping with years, bowed in preparation to descend into the grave with its epoch. Scientific men of the country are beginning hastily to enclose these churches, and to restore them, and to place their relics in museums, in order that the next age will know what it has freed itself from. And they have not begun a day too soon, for already there have been men ahead of them who have stabled their horses there during wars, and stripped the altars of the soft gold leaf, and tore the robes of the saints because the souls of men were once in slavery to a belief in God. Now they will level the churches with the earth, and make barracks of the altars. In this way they will free themselves.

But what of the residue of that race who built these churches under the arms of the invader? It was not only to see churches that I went to Teotihuacan. Indians live there, uncorrupted by one drop of white blood. I wished to see what four centuries of civilization had done for them.

The Dove of Chapacalco

(unfinished story, 1922)

After leaving Mexico in late August 1921, Porter settled in Fort Worth, Texas, where she began but never finished "The Dove of Chapacalco," her first Mexican fiction. The typescript goes on for twenty-nine pages of clean copy and then breaks off. There are also three fragments in rough draft and, fortunately, a page of plot outline. If Porter had continued at the pace of the completed section, she would have written her first novel. The story is interesting for her choice of subject matter and for the way she attempted to bring together different experiences of 1920–1921. Although the setting is supposed to be the southern state of Chiapas, which she never visited, it really is the demoralized, priest-ridden area of Teotihuacán; her description of the Virgin of Soledad is lifted from "Notes on Teotihuacan." The archbishop of Chapacalco is based on Archbishop Francisco Orozco y Jiménez of Jalisco, who had been bishop of Chiapas. An arch-conservative who opposed land distribution, he gained a private audience with President Obregón, who was trying to mend fences with the Church. The archbishop would have come to Porter's attention at that time. In her notes she writes, "If he had not been a priest, he would have been an excellent bandit of the old style. In Chiapas he armed his Indians with lances and arrows against a village that refused to pay him extortionate contributions to the church. . . ." The description of the president's cabinet in Mexico City is based on her own description of it in "The Mexico Trinity," where she also reports an eruption in the chamber of deputies over a bloody confrontation between Catholics and Socialists, in which Angel Gómez was involved. He was a Spanish anarchist, a member of a Mexico City union, and indeed a bomb-thrower. Porter describes him as such in her notes and didn't bother to change his name in her fiction. Since the government sought to deport him, he may very well have hidden in the Habermans' home, as the fictional Gomez hides in the Liebemanns' home on Calle del Cielo, changed from Calle Eliseo, where Porter and the Habermans had lived. The use of Gómez as a character also connects this story to Porter's 1921 plans to write a "Mexican book."

Vicenta, the dove of Chapacalco, is Porter's invention. Like Nayagta of "The Shattered Star," taken captive by the demon-archbishop, she learns all his magic until he has no will over her. With the help of Angel Gomez, she overthrows him, and when Angel attempts to exercise his will over her, she walks away from him. "The Dove of Chapacalco" could be considered a dress rehearsal for "María Concepción," whose setting is also borrowed from Teotihuacán and whose heroine is also an Indian woman who subjugates her husband to her will. The triumph of María Concepción is less spectacular than that of Vicenta but a triumph nevertheless.

The Dove of Chapacalco

[Porter's plot outline of the story]

Vicenta, mistress of the archbishop. Gomez, revolutionary, dynamiter. Archbishop, extorter of money from the Indians. Takes Vicenta at fourteen. Six years as mistress, develops mind, reads, thinks.

Gomez, spending his time in church on knees as devotee, looking for chance to plan a dynamiting of the holy statue which is chief source of fame and revenue to church. Vicenta here much also on knees. Sees Vicenta, loves her.

Tries dynamiting, fails. Plot brings out great revolt of Indians who gather at church, frightened, to pray and avert wrath of God, gather at archbishop's palace to have him reassure them. He is away. Vicenta comes on balcony, explains. Gomez, in crowd of Indians, sees her, learns who she is—little sister of the archbishop, or daughter of vieja who keeps house for bishop. Haunts church afterward, meets Vicenta at altar. She also falls in love with him, a little. He tries to tell her about revolution.

About freedom, about liberty, about the freeing of the enslaved Indians. Her sympathies are aroused. She plans with him destruction of palace, murder of the archbishop, general uprising of the Indians. Plans are carried out. Gomez, in patio of wrecked palace, tells Vicenta to follow him—he will marry her. The judge will marry them. She says she is free, too, and she does not want marriage or children. This freedom is only for men, then? It is, he tells her, for she must be a slave to his love.

She goes.

[*The story*]

I

It was the time of the Easter festivals, and the Archbishop of Chapacalco was making the rounds of the smaller villages in the southern edge of the state, collecting his yearly tithes, administering discipline among the Indians, and stimulating zeal for soul saving in his country priests.

His mistress Vicenta welcomed his absence. She loved the freedom of the slow moving days with no duties to perform, no Latin lessons to read. It was better to think her own thoughts, to kneel in the Cathedral and say her rosary endlessly before the altar of Maria La Soledad. Or she would feed her doves in the smaller patio, and distribute her bounties to the peones who lived in the compound adjoining the palace, removed, yet on Church property, and an important part of it.

Vicenta was Indian from the far southern border, nineteen years old in this, her fifth year in the palace of the Archbishop. Five Easter times had passed since the Archbishop, travelling in his old carriage drawn by four white mules, surrounded by his body guard armed with bows and arrows, had lodged for the night in La Merced convent, in the village where Vicenta was born.

She had been taken into the convent by the Spanish sisters, who reclaimed with Inquisitorial rigor the dark souls of the natives by means of threats, persuasions, food, prayer and the setting of heavy tasks on wild shoulders.

They taught Vicenta to kneel with her arms spread in the form of a cross when she was at mass, to bind her black braids to her head with hair pins, to scrub paving stones clean, to sit properly upon a chair and say "Ave Maria, gratia plena . . ." in a singsong fashion. Maria Immaculata, the mother superior, hoped the girl would discover a vocation, and become a lay sister. The convent was badly in need of skilled servants. There was no dependence possible on the Indian girls unless they took the veil.

They would go away and live with men in filthy jacales, and forget God entirely.

For this reason, Mother Superior was deeply vexed when the Archbishop, entering the convent patio, was forced almost to step over Vicenta, who was cleaning the stone walk with a mop of henequen fibre. She lifted her eyes a trifle sullenly, and hitched her knees out of the way. "Soft and warmly colored as a ripe mango," thought the Archbishop, who loved food. And other appetites recurred to him in the simile.

After some talk with the nun of affairs in the village, of the impossibility of making collections from the Indians who spent their yearly gain for fermented liquors, the Archbishop said casually, "My housekeeper needs a girl child for a servant. That brown one with the strong arms will do, if she has not passed the age of innocence. I want no Magdalenas in my house."

"She is fourteen, and not willful, but she is all Indian and therefore stupid," answered Maria Immaculata, blushing and not daring to meet the eye of her old friend the Archbishop. She had known him when he was a humble cura of this village, and she had reason to believe all of the tales she had heard of him since that time. Her heart thumped hotly under her holy linen. Her hands gripped together in her white sleeves. "She needs more training, Your Grace."

"She will get it from old Antonia without fail," said the Archbishop, his sallow dark face twisting a little as if under some deep inner excitement, "That good vieja allows herself only the one worldly indulgence of beating her servants, and she does that, by her own word, to the eternal glory of God!" He smiled kindly at the round faced nun. "She grows feebler, Pobrecita! Would you deny her? She has been like a mother to me. I shall take this kitten home for her to amuse herself with."

Vicenta found herself being turned about in the hands of several sisters who seemed very frightened and nervous. They gave her a clean dress and a package of food, and a new cotton reboso. She was told to bathe her bare feet in the fountain where the lambs and hens and pigeons drank, and to be ready to go when they called for her. She sat on the stones after she had dried her feet and held her bundle, and wondered what would happen to her.

It was almost dark when Sister Maria de la Paz, an Indian lay sister from Guatemala, led Vicenta through the patio and under the dark arch of stones that separated the convent from the world. The nun wept. "Be a little servant of God," she kept saying over and over as if pronouncing a charm. "Pray for me," responded Vicenta, because she had been taught to say it.

She was not frightened but she did not understand anything. She gazed around at the bare inner court, now almost dark. The tops of the walls lay perfectly straight except for that corner where the steeple of the church rose and pointed like a hand with a cross in its fingers.

She climbed into the far corner of the carriage, crossing her feet on the deep leather cushions. The interior smelled strangely of leather, of tobacco, of wine like the breath of Mother Immaculata. The panes of glass in the sides, rattling when the mules stirred, were thick and dim, full of silver bubbles.

The Archbishop came out, with a young priest; a mozo followed with his bags. Cotton clad Indians, lying at full length along the wall, rose, gathered up their bows that were taller than themselves, and swung their heavy quivers of arrows over their shoulders. They formed about the carriage in a straggling casual line, mute as wraiths.

While the mozo arranged the bags in the front of the carriage, the Archbishop stood with his hand on the door, blinking a little in the light of the lantern swinging at the side. "Now, you know what you must do," he repeated to the cura, an unhappy looking young mestizo in a greasy cassock. "If you need more bows and arrows, I can send you two hundred. But see that the Poor Box is not empty this May Day. Las Flechas de Dios! The arrows of God, eh?" He laughed. The cura bowed, trying to smile. He kissed the ring of the Archbishop on a hard fist, thrust suddenly under his nose. The Archbishop snarled. He made the sign of the cross over the cura's head, and it was like a blow.

"What, on the seat? To the floor with you, Nina!" He spoke to Vicenta. She slid on her knees to the bottom of the carriage, covering her face in her reboso. The weight of the Archbishop bent the springs as he stepped in, his great feet fumbled among the rugs and threatened to crush her legs, but she dared not move.

The forward jerk of the carriage, as the mozos swung their whips over the mules, unbalanced her, threw her over the spread feet. The mules galloped away, and through the dim panes, the shock heads and the bow tips of the Indians swam steadily, in that long swinging gait of theirs. Out of the village, the pace settled into a steady trot, to an obligato of small bells strung on the harness.

Vicenta crouched as far in her corner as she could, and dared to glance at the silent man above her. His black cloak was drawn up to his chin, he glared at something beyond the reaches of her imagination, his face a brown blur slashed with black frowns. She feared him vaguely, impersonally, as she feared God. Not as she had trembled before another priest whose hand she used to kiss, and who turned back her warm palm to find the centavito hidden there, at those times when she would forget to drop it in the poor box.

She fell asleep with the soft breathing of a very young animal curled into the rough blankets. The Archbishop, rousing out of his thoughts, leaned forward and studied her face attentively. Indian, all through. Not a taint of Spanish blood in her. He, a mestizo with the arrogance of a Castilian grandee, loathed that part of himself which claimed kinship with these earth stained people. Yet the women drew him with a ferocious desire. This one was charming, a soft reddish color all over, like a painted clay jar; round arms set strongly on broad shoulders netted with firm flat muscles. Her head thrown back left her throat naked—sharply modelled under the chin, swelling a little at the base, a round deep hollow accenting the line above the sloping wing like collar bones. The slanted eyes seemed smiling in sleep, though they were grave and timid when awake. A pretty soft girl, an obedient child who would not trouble him. The Archbishop crushed his hard fingers over her knee, drawn up to her breast.

Vicenta opened her eyes, with a sharp intake of breath and sat perfectly still, trying not to tremble. The voice of the Archbishop terrified her. A wolf nuzzling her and growling his friendship.

"Ah well, Paloma! You need not be afraid. It was all a lie I told our good friend Immaculata. You shall never be a servant in my house. La Vieja shall never beat you. Be assured, only do not turn your head away from me. What is your name, child?"

She whispered it. "That is very good," said His Grace. "I am weary of Marias. Come up here, patroncita del Alma, little hostess of my soul, give me a kiss for good luck."

The Archbishop was now almost fifty years old. For several years his distaste for life had increased. He believed himself to be dying of impotence, his Indians were growing restive, his political enemies were yearly gaining upon him. Every revolution for the past seven years had eaten away some part of his privilege, had changed the spirit of the people insidiously. Twice within twelve months two of his captains had played the traitor making a revolt among his army of Indians. True, he had executed them both, had solemnly pronounced against them from the altar of the Cathedral, but the soldiers remembered them as heroes. From his palace he ruled, but with less severity from year to year. His troops had dwindled until, at the time of the Easter collections, the palace was left in the care of a half dozen servants and a guard of ten soldiers. And the heads of the government, who had once sent him detachments from the regular army to help in quelling riots, now sent commissions to inquire after causes. A republic of peones for peones. Pah!

Now he forgot his rages in the touch of this child who slept at his feet. He became young again, sweetened, renewed. Mysterious springs of power were loosed in him. He had been cruel to many women, but he felt no cruelty toward this one. He laughed delightedly at the breath of her terror, labored and short, against his face when he held her with both powerful arms, implacable as his desire. "Poor little dove! Here, put up your mouth. Learn to kiss me!"

II

A sixteenth century Spanish king, muddled of head and soft of heart, dominated by spiral-shaped germs in his brain that twisted his thoughts in unaccountably fantastic directions, made, for his soul's health, a curious renunciation of power.

He gave back to the Indians of his far-off empire all their lands taken by his people of an earlier day. He revoked the land grants given to nobles by his predecessors; with a fine sweep of authority, he caused parchment documents and deeds to be drawn, sealed with his seal, which returned to the Indians, their heirs and assigns forever, the native earth under their footsoles.

This done, he fell upon his knees and wept, "Oh, Holy Father, I have made this restitution, and yet my head is still full of spiders that crawl continually and will not let me sleep!" But it did not occur to him to take back his gift.

The parchments were sent to the New World, where they were read publicly with solemnity: and smiled over in private by the grandees who had got their land grants as inheritance from their fathers. The Indians, not aware their properties were now restored to them, continued as servants in the houses and fields of the Spaniards. And the Spaniards, well enough aware that possession is the sole necessary point of law, continued to build a Little Spain of church and monastery and municipal palace in the dark new country.

Three hundred years later the half-Spanish Archbishop of Chapacalco and the Indian girl Vicenta were living in the palace adjoining the Cathedral built by the first Archbishop in 1580. In the capital city of the republic a harried and fallible group of men, mestizos and Indians, half idealistic, half petty politician, had set up, after appropriate and necessary bloodshed, a proletarian government. It was their intention, after they had executed enough enemies and malcontents to silence the opposition, to put into immediate practise the theories of justice, liberty, equality, fraternity, land division, freedom for all and forever. And the chief beneficiary of these changes should be the downtrodden feeblest brother, the Indian.

As injustice goes, three centuries is not a long time. But the latest set of saviors recalled that, in their country, the average life of a man is twenty-four years. Thirteen generations of agony were long enough for any people to suffer. They would change it all. Not that suffering should be entirely abolished. No. But there would be a shifting of miseries, and they, themselves, would administer justice where it would taste bitterest, would distribute pain among those who truly deserved it.

The edict of the Spanish king should be carried out. The foreign holders of the land should be banished, informally and instantly. The Indian should be given his share of the earth, with seed to sow and animals and implements for working the soil. An Indian member of the chamber of deputies rose at this point of the deliberations and added that each man must also have, furnished by the government, a rifle and five hundred rounds of ammunition for the defense of his property.

This brought on a handsome disturbance in the chamber. The Bourbon side of the house attacked the Indian side with words, loose chairs and fists. The city fire department went down and set the fire hose, wide open, upon the scene through the broken windows.

The President and the Cabinet, disgusted with everything, called a meeting and talked bitterly for seven hours. They had committed themselves to the cause of the oppressed, and the oppressed were demanding special emergency legislation in favor of bread makers, candy makers, lottery ticket sellers, street car conductors, munition workers. They were calling strikes that left the city without light, without water, without telephone service, because the walking delegate of the serape weavers union had been refused a personal audience with the President at four o'clock Wednesday afternoon—the very time, unhappily, that the President was in the east border of the republic trying to reason with a group of ranch owners engaged in burning their own villages as a protest against land partition.

The Indians in the chamber encouraged the anarchists to set off dynamite under Church property. This gave the people's government a bad name with the socialists who were against violence of all kinds. But if they suppressed the anarchists, the bandits in Torela would rise again, in spite of the splendid estates lately parceled out among them. The bandits loved the anarchists, and the anarchists depended on the bandits for food and shelter in their intervals of bombing and dynamiting. . . . Most exasperating of all, were those free lances who took jobs with the government, learned more than was good for them to learn, and passed on the information to their friends on the outside. And these friends were usually bandits, anarchists, or communists. Quite often they were counterrevolutionists to the north. They were, in fact, apt to be any one of a number of unendurable things, all of them inimicable to the best ends of the government.

The Cabinet considered rightly that its hands were full. Of the eight, five voted radical, three voted conservative. But if the radicals threw the conservatives out, as they longed to do, it would make a scandal that possibly could not be concealed within the home borders; and beside, it chilled radical leaders to their marrows to think of three outraged and vengeful Cabinet members walking out carrying a bagful of diplomatic, financial and personal secrets with them.

The point was to get something definite done, at once. At this very moment, fragmentary messages of violence filtered up to headquarters from the Hot Lands. The Archbishop of Chapacalco had again attacked a village of his state with his army of bow and arrow fighters. The Indians had been forced to give up their whole year's increase as a thank offering to the miraculous image, Maria La Soledad, who had averted a plague of the Rotting Fever from the cathedral town. Other villages nearby had suffered decimation. But La Soledad showed her old partiality for the children nearest her: and the children farthest away must give thanks with the rest.

The Cabinet voted as one man on this question: They must send a commission to investigate the business, to take the land and repartition it among the natives, to give the Archbishop a warning that the old days were past, and to confiscate his collection of Church jewels, old documents and books, and instruments of the Inquisition, in case he proved incorrigible.

This appeared to be an inspired move. The state was far removed from the political center. The Archbishop had enemies even within the Church who would not grieve to see him set down. It would probably save the scandal of seeing the Cathedral dynamited by the anarchist Gomez, who was leaving a trail of bombing exploits in the republic. And it would please that member of the Cabinet who was also the curator of Church relics for the Museum. He had long coveted the Archbishop's collection.

The Cabinet meeting broke up at four o'clock of one morning. The next morning at the same hour, a carefully chosen group of men, with

Blanco Miramonte at the head, left by special train for Chapacalco. They were well armed and accompanied by two carloads of regular soldiers, with Juan Valdeo as Captain.

III

Angel Gomez lay on a tumbled bed in the closely shuttered back room of a house in the Calle del Cielo. Liebemann, the Austrian Jew, had been sheltering him ever since his attempt to blow up the National Palace, a week previous. Liebemann was a socialist with a love of the spectacular. He desired to be a respectable part of a respectable proletarian government, but a fantastical twist in his mind craved the feverish importance of intrigue.

He would sit on the bedside and talk for hours with wordy, mouthy bitterness, of "the workers, their wrongs and betrayals." He brought food and cigarettes and newspapers to the refugee, who thought him a good sort of fool, not intelligent enough to be dangerous.

He was waiting for the hour set for the special train of the commission. Having business of his own with the Indians in Chapacalco, he chose this moment as the happy one to travel thither without expense or anxiety. His good friend Juan Valdeo was Captain of the troops.

His head ached. He could not sleep. He turned on the light and read Amado Nervo's poetry, and tried to concentrate again on Karl Marx's verbose and windy paragraphs. Revolutionary theory always put him to sleep. It was his favorite boast. He shut his eyes and listened a moment to Liebemann quarrelling with his Gentile wife, who was not a revolutionist. She was a high voiced shrew suffering from eroticism, and Gomez decided that Liebemann should beat her once a week until she learned a woman's place in life.

The monotonous, bitter voices grinding away in an interminable duet sickened him. To drown the noise he read aloud a Sonatina of Ruben Dario: evoking with the easy song of the words, his own picture of the blonde princess, pale, sighing through her little strawberry mouth, sitting in her golden chair, dreaming of love . . . longing to be a swallow or a butterfly, to flutter out and find love . . . ah. . . . Gomez sighed, sat up, looked at his watch. Time to go. He rose thankfully. God knew why those European idiots chose to sit up all night and hurl curses at each other, but it was none of his affair. Action again. He hoped to sneak out and escape their farewells.

He dressed, slipped the volume of poetry in his shirt pocket, wrote a good bye note to Liebemann, and smiled ironically at his reflection in the mirror of the door. He wore the white cotton shirt and drawers of the peon. His shock of black hair was brushed up carelessly to protrude through the holes of his prodigious straw hat. His feet slapped softly in half worn guaraches, leather thonged sandals. A red handkerchief wrapped his other scant clothing.

A moment later, he was in the street, his feet flapping over the cobble-stones on the way to the station.

In that part of the town where the corner lights were gray, the door-ways deep, and the houses tumbled over each other on a fixed attitude of chaos, Gomez took to the center of the street and ran silently as a hallucination.

The station was outlined by intermittent lanterns swinging from posts about the terrace, and the flicker of small fires where the soldiers were lying about their stacked arms, waiting for their wives to prepare and serve them food.

The smell of coffee smote Gomez. His stomach ached with chill and sud-den hunger. He slunk into the warming circle of a brasero fire, looking for the captain. "Buenos dias, Companero," he said gently to a lolling man.

The man turned on his side, supported his head on his elbow and eyed the stranger indifferently. His uniform was new, his mustache was waxed stiffly, his boots hardly creased as yet. As he gazed, his eyebrows began to flicker. His mouth raised a trifle at one corner. He seemed deeply pleased. "Thou, Companero?" he whispered in a voice so low it scarcely carried. Gomez came nearer, sat quietly, resting himself on his bundle.

"So, Valdeo, you are captain in the army now. That is amusing!"

"Si, it is simpler. I watch many things with a free eye, Angelito. . . . You are going with us?"

Gomez nodded. "With your help."

The soldier grinned with satisfaction. "I can help, amigo. There is much work. . . . The commission is in there," he jerked his head toward the closed waiting room. "Talking. Talking—words about peace, and freedom for the Indian, and how to control the left wing of the chamber of depu-ties, and what the foreigners will do if we cannot keep order when every man has his own plan for making over the country . . . and what they will do to the Archbishop when they get him . . . and how Estrada must be shot for one kind of treason and Rodriquez for another before we can have peace. . . . And so on. . . . Talk, talk. . . ." The soldier stopped and cursed roundly, deeply, awfully, smacking his lips over the filthy double meanings of his phrases. "Si, hombre! they puke words as if they had eaten green fruit of ideas. But they cannot make an end of the things that cause their sickness. They turn the color of a pumpkin when a man of decision puts dynamite under the places where this rottenness festers, and they say, 'God's name! More treason—more complicity!'"

"In Chapacalco," said Gomez, "I will do the work the commission should do. But in my way, eh, Hermano?"

"In your way, Brother. . . ." He turned his head and spoke gently to some one in the shadow. "Paz, Patroncita, give coffee and food to my comrade."

A small bundle stirred soundlessly, a young woman rose to her knees, leaned forward and laid a sleeping baby on the stones beside her, throwing her reboso over her bared breast, wet with milk and the clinging mouth.

She fanned the fire under the earthen pots, and odorous steam came up. Gomez ate and drank. Paz sat back and gathered up the child. Gomez glanced at her, without speculation. He was pure Spanish lately banished from Barcelona, accustomed to chattering spitfires; these mute and humble creatures could not touch the imagination of a man in love with Revolution and Dario's blonde princess.

He was in love with his own dreams of destruction. His own ecstasies nibbled at his nerve ends deliciously. Better than love was a long night of lying awake, blazing with his desire to destroy, with his own hands, every church, every miraculous image, and every monastery in the republic. That was to be his glorious achievement, his unanswerable argument to the awful faith of the peones. "See, friends!" he would cry in his imaginings. "Here is your wonder working plaster image with painted eyes. I, Gomez, a man like yourselves, take it in my hands, so, and set a little flame to it . . . pouf! Where is your god now?" Ah, he would cleanse a whole race of superstition, he would awaken the minds of ten million enslaved peoples! He, Gomez, a little pale Spaniard from Barcelona, who slept in jacales with fleas gnawing him, who ate food where it was given to him, who hid for his life from funny little men, like these, going importantly on commissions guarded by soldiers. They would give land to the Indians! Oh, imbeciles! What a man needs first is freedom of the spirit, and he will take his land for himself! These fat little men, afraid to go alone. Afraid of the Archbishop of Chapacalco. Afraid of the government. Afraid of each other. Trusting to their soldiers, with Juan Valdeo, anarchist, for Captain.

He was sweating with his thoughts. He laughed aloud, shutting his lips over the sound so sharply that his teeth clicked. Juan smiled widely, as if he understood. "So, Companero! Yes—it is amusing!"

A consumptive whistle from the decrepit engine announced the hour of leaving. The inert forms on the terrace assumed upright shapes, their guns struck together as they were unstacked. The doors of the waiting room opened and released a square of light full of circles and streaks of dark. Blanco Miramonte, fat, round, head like a block, heavy clipped mustaches over his thick lips, stepped out first, looking about over his chest, frowning under his wide gray felt hat. His party of seven and the special guard entered the center coach, distinguished from the others by a new shiny coat of paint. The common soldiers and their women rode in the first and third coaches. In the last, Gomez took his place, sitting on the floor in a welter of food baskets, women and babies who reeked of grease and milk and sweat, men who sprawled sleeping heads on knapsacks.

He turned a misty lantern a trifle more toward him, opened his book of poetry and read again . . . about the pale princess, adorable vision of gold, roses and ivory, more beautiful than April's self. . . .

IV

Old Antonia awakened her adored Dona Vicenta by pulling softly at the heaped coverlids, timidly as a dog, gently as a nurse. "Wilt thou waken, little Dove, and drink the good hot coffee and eat the new-baked cakes I have brought you?" she crooned, her old face twisted in a smile that tied her wrinkles in tight knots.

The girl sat up, opened her eyes, instantly fell into incomprehensible depression of spirit. What made this day unhappy, when the thirteen days past had been so serene? Ah, yes . . . she remembered. "His Grace returns today, no?" she said aloud, hoping for denial, as Antonia's dry hands rattled over her hair, smoothed it, and rubbed her face with a soft cloth dipped in warm water. "Si, little Dove, he comes. Why not?"

"And those desgraciados from the capital are here to pick a quarrel with him." Vicenta remembered other visits of the kind. "With their talk of land for the Indian. How can a peon have the land owned by the great families and consecrated to the church? Madmen. But they make trouble in this house, and in this country. Dios! why am I so tired, Antonia?"

The old woman calculated shrewdly. "You are nineteen, His Grace the Archbishop is fifty-five. You are tired because the image of love in your heart has the face of an old man. . . ."

Vicenta stepped out of bed. "Silence, vieja! Impudent!" she paused and smiled warmly at her old servant. "My indiscreet old macaw! Now we must go to church for our sins."

She slipped off her white linen chemise before a tall, mottled old mirror framed in black carved wood. Her bare feet burrowed for warmth in a rug of woven wool. The faded red curtains of her high testered bed gloomed against the darkened embossed wall paper, relic of French taste imposed by some frivolous woman of the mid-nineteenth century. There were no windows, the outer wall was flush with the street in this wing, and only a wide double door led into the court above the patio.

Antonia sponged off the golden tinted, narrow hipped body with warm water scented with jasmine oil. Vicenta laughed and shivered with the morning chill, then sat, wrapped in a padded robe while Antonia brushed her hair, braided it sleekly, and wound it around the small ears with big gold pins.

"You are pale, poor Dove. Your face is colorless like the skin of a Gachupina (Spanish woman). Make your cheeks red for the Archbishop!"

Vicenta touched her lips, ear lobes and cheek bones lightly with a thick red juice made from the ripe figs of cactus, and powdered over it thickly. Then she examined her face closely, and sighed with satisfaction. "Oh, Antonia, how I love being beautiful!"

She slipped her feet into the softly woven straw sandals she wore in preference to the French shoes that filled her closets. Over her long, full green skirt she flung her wide, green and black reboso of hand woven silk. Energy possessed her, a feverish desire to have done with one small task and hurry on to another. Yet there would be nothing to do all day. She could go to church, walk in the garden, visit the compound, sit in the sunshine. "Oh, Dios!" she sighed again, and stretched up her arms violently.

The door next to hers opened on the sleeping room of the Archbishop, which he used also at times for a study. It was near Vicenta, and here he heard her lessons, made her read aloud to him, and allowed her to go to sleep on a hassock at his feet, her head curled down on his knee.

Vicenta paused at this door, and touched the prodigious hand wrought bar of iron that closed it from the outside. This side of the palace had once been dedicated to the use of distinguished visitors, liable to awaken and find themselves unable to leave their apartments, for reasons best known to themselves and the host. The hinges and hasps were buried like fangs in the worm eaten wood. Her morning languor fell away from her entirely, in her sudden desire to feel her young strength lifting and sliding back the bar.

Antonia reproved her. "Ah, the clean hands! Have a care. Let me call for Pedro—why soil yourself with rust?"

But Vicenta had already wrenched the iron. With a thump and a jangle it slid back, the door swung outward. A musty cold atmosphere followed, full of the dead odors of old wood and varnish and leathers.

"His Grace must come home to a well aired apartment," said Vicenta, with pretty civilised severity. "Have servants up here with mops and water. Let him see he is expected, and is welcome."

She regarded the place with dislike. The walls were covered with red plush faded in spots to brown the color of dried blood. Fat yellowish Cupids smeared obscenity over the room from the four corners of the ceiling. Their draperies leered, their eyes, painted askew with technical regard for perspective that did not exist, gazed down with eighteenth century sophistication. The great bed was covered with ancient lace set in yellowed linen. A crucifix of ivory on onyx, the figure almost life size, a treasure of his collection, dominated the tawdry, gilded panels facing the bed.

Books in Latin and Old Spanish, done in parchment, hand illumined, were set in rows above a desk brought from Spain in the sixteenth century. The Archbishop loved Horace, Suetonius, Tertullian in the original. A small ivory miniature of Vicenta, made by a visiting artist when she was fifteen, sat on the table near the bed, along with a night lamp of hammered copper, its spout blackened with burnt oil. In his way, the Archbishop was an esthete, who loved the subtle flavored essences of beauty a little decayed, mingled with the rancid taste of his powers and cruelties.

It was this confusion of aromas that pleased him most in his love for Vicenta . . . the soft handed Indian girl who could read Latin, who clawed him like a tiger kitten in her brief angers, who went to Mass fresh from his arms and said her rosary devoutly.

Vicenta, with her cleanly savage instincts, was oppressed by this atmosphere. She had come into the palace a pitiable, bewildered child afraid even to weep, and within a year she had cleared the rooms of priests who disliked her; she had brought in new servants who had no privileges except those she allowed them. The entire palace was in her hands, emptied of every one except her allies. . . . She did not know why she possessed this power. She was sure only of one thing: the Archbishop loved her, and so long as he loved her, she would be powerful. And she was careful to nourish the secret sources of her influence. To the Archbishop she was youth, the clean fire at which he warmed his failing, chilling body. . . .

Vicenta turned away from the door, Antonia following, and walked slowly around the upper enclosed balcony that ran the entire circle of the palace. The inner walls were gilded in the high spots, the gilt dulled and mildewed. White lace and silk hangings were hastily looped over the open windows, gray with dust and stained with rain. Over all the palace there brooded a silent decay, a creeping death, the tatters of grandeur waiting for the final blow of time.

The wide marble stairway writhed in one slow inevitable curve to the flag paved court, always chilled and damp with the running fountain. At the base, a gigantic brass dragon, added in God knows what period of perversity, enacted a monotonous pantomime of terror, a dead gesture of fear overlaid with cobwebs and verdigris. Servants were everywhere, always dusting and cleaning futilely, never making the place clean. They lived as easily as they could under a heaven that seemingly bore them a special grudge of poverty.

"Oh, Antonia, let us go faster, to your side of the house—I wish to feel sunshine. Is there a blue sky above this prison?" Antonia recognised the tone. It was a muffled desperation, a frantic despair that overtook the girl on those days when His Grace was returning.

She said nothing. They passed now under a double arch way and entered a long bare passage, floored with wide boards, lighted by square windows set inaccessibly high. The gray stones wept continuously, the creeping water left glistening tracks like tears on the cheeks of age.

Vicenta turned again into a small black door, and ran up a small secret winding stair, out again into an ancient square house, bare and clean and silent, flooded with light, half furnished, once a recreation hall for monks, now the apartment of Antonia.

Another patio was the core of this house, full of potted blooms, an old tiled washing fountain splashing in the center.

Vicenta sat in her favorite place, a low bench near the railing. She leaned forward on her elbow in the vehement sunlight, watching Mariposa dipping and whirling and wringing the clothes in the water. Mariposa sat back on her heels a moment, and raised her eyes shyly. She waited for the Archbishop's lady to recognise her presence, then bowed with incomparable gravity and humbleness.

The thoughts that wreathed themselves continually in slow dark circles closed in on the girl at the railing, circles of thunderous darkness that had nothing to do with the bright day, nor the simmer of joy in her veins, nor the smell of hay and warm breathing animals from the stables over the next wall, nor the gentle biting and mumbling of her fat puppy at her bare instep.

"I am Indian, too, Antonia, like yourself," she spoke suddenly aloud, voicing an old thought for the first time, "like Mariposita there, washing clothes. But for the Archbishop, I should be at the fountain, lifting burdens until my arms were numb."

Antonia, squatted at her side, sucked her harsh old lips and raised her hands, gnarled and twisted as the branches of a stunted Pirú tree. "Si, Paloma. You have had good fortune by the grace of God."

"But I feel as if I had died, or gone to sleep, and all my life is a dolorous dream." Vicenta turned her head restlessly, the gold hoops of her earrings swaying against her cheeks, "I am tired . . . too much softness. . . . I should like to be a soldadera, like those women in the cuartel . . . to shoulder my pack and march ahead of an army. I should like to be free, Antonia, in a storm. To wrap my reboso around my face and sleep in a little dark place in the side of a mountain."

"You dream, Nina. Pretty words. You read those things in your books, maybe, and that is not good for anybody. Hunger is not happiness, and a soldadera carries her pack on her back and her cub inside of her, and is beaten by whatever man she belongs to, and eats what is left after the man and sleeps when he is done with her, and life is a long trouble. . . . I know, Paloma!"

"Maybe I want love."

"Ah, love . . . well, love or hate, it all comes to the same thing. The beginning of love is one kind of sorrow, and the ending of it is another, and here you sit, easy and happy, wishing for griefs that will end only with your last day. Ay de mi, foolish child!"

"Ay de mi!" echoed Vicenta unhappily. "Come with me to the church. I am sick of this sunlight."

v

The gentlemen of the land commission, finding the Archbishop away on his own affairs, improved their time by calling in a body on the chief of police. He was a revolutionary mestizo who admitted blood kinship only with the Indian, and who wrote poetry in his odd moments, which were few of late. He greeted his brother revolutionaries in the grand manner, gave them the city with a single outward sweep of his spread palm, and promised all the support they might require in the difficult business of giving back to the peon his lost properties.

Then they got down to business. The chief had how many police, how many soldiers, how many guns, how many rounds of ammunition? Enough, he swore, for anything. They were good enough soldiers, except that the malditos were in the habit of selling their equipment, even to their water canteens, for [ten] pesos entire, and turning up at the cuartel a day later naked to the hide, and paralysed with liquor.

And how many soldiers had the gentlemen of the commission with them? Enough, they declared, to rout the primitive arm of the Archbishop, unaided. The chief almost interrupted them at this moment to inform them that His Grace had only a third of his regular army in the city, and there was open rebellion among them since they slept about in the compounds with the peones and often developed a sense of brotherhood with them. It was believed the Archbishop could be defeated in any sort of pitched battle, as between soldier and soldier; it was the peones themselves, unfortunates who could not be counted on. . . . They would jump to that side of the fence where the field looked greenest.

The trick then would be, decided the commission members, to enlist the Indian at once, with presents of money and food, in the course of explaining to him the new social regime.

Exactly. . . . "We are determined to do this work justly, and above all, peacefully," declared Miramonte, with sincerity. He did not add, "and as quickly as possible, for I am bored beyond words."

"Assuredly," said the chief of police, with a beam of humorous understanding upon his compatriot. Miramonte grew warm with outraged dignity. The other one thought he was in jest about wanting peace. He would see.

The party, with their soldiers, took a position in the public plaza, closed in after the old Spanish plan governing the arrangement of cities, a market on one side, the municipal building on another, the church on the third, the fourth a network of streets into the town. Here they announced themselves with speeches, preliminary to reading the new proclamation. A listless crowd gathered slowly, drifting in on the bloodless impetus of a curiosity long since divided from faith in the possibility of a change for the better. Men in soiled white cotton garments stopped their two wheeled ox drawn carts loaded with vegetables meant for the market, listened a while without comprehension and moved on again. Women shouldered their babies with a swing, and stood, so burdened, staring upward, their eyes empty of even the wish to understand. Then remembering their immitigable sorrows, they would trot across the plaza and go to pray at the altar of Maria La Soledad.

Blanco Miramonte and his associates shook their heads, filled their pockets with silver coins and set out around the city, personal apostles of good will, to persuade the Indian to accept the blessings they brought. They dared not return to the capital until they had first re-partitioned the land. So, cursing their luck, they went to work.

VI

The town, like all the older towns of this country, was a tomb; burial place of a lost race. The flat topped adobe houses plastered over with secretive barred windows, hid old griefs. The iron bars, once painted red or blue, were now eaten away to rust color. Beyond, colonies of small huts, contrived of dried maguey leaves and twigs, thatched and laced together airily, lay brown and torpid, sheltering their miseries in silence. Hump-backed pigs roamed in the uneven streets, snouting into puddles of water where gauzy winged flies clustered, greenish iridescence glinting with the vibrations of their wings. Over all, the pervasive clumps of the Pirú tree leaned, fluffy green foliage casting a feathery shade. In this shade, men lay motionless and slept, weary before their day was begun.

The enormous distances were full of shifting purples, the hot indigo sky dived down behind the mountains with the swift soundless violence of a dream.

Back of the palace, low walls enclosed the compound of the peones. Almost two kilometers of roofs ran about the hollow square cultivated as a vegetable garden. A series of small cages with a single door, darkened and silent, a single stroke dividing the clean blaze of the sun from the interior gloom heavy with fetid smells.

Babies with large stomachs and emaciated heads crawled about mutely on the hot baked earth, women stooped over fires and stirred in their cooking jars, or patted tortillas between their palms, all wordless, all as still of feature as if they were not yet awakened from the prenatal oblivion.

Angel Gomez stepped from one of these doorways, stood a moment looking about him, swept off his hat and bowed before one of the stoop-ing women. "Many humble thanks, Senora, to you and your husband for your hospitality." The woman nodded, without expression. "When the land is divided among us today, I wish for you a great share of it."

The woman crossed herself, thoroughly, completely, her eyes closed. She crossed her body, then her forehead, her lips, her breast, a rapid suc-cession of little crosses over her heart, and again an all-embracing sign of the cross from forehead to stomach and each shoulder.

"Jesus and Mary forbid!" she cried aloud, "I am not a thief. For the great of the earth whom God has appointed to rule over us, riches. For me, my prayers! No, hombre—do not tempt us with dreams. The cura has told me if I accept this land, I am a thief and my soul shall not see God! No, hombre! Away with you!"

Angel moved away. Then he turned back and called aloud, "Maria La Soledad is only a plaster image with glass eyes, and a little lighted match would set her ablaze! Yet you pray with reverence to a thing no more miraculous than your cooking pots! Oh, simple woman!"

"Blasphemer!" shrilled the woman, rising and shaking her fist at him. "Away! The good God will strike you dead!"

Angel laughed sharply. "Watch how safely I shall go," he taunted her. But she refused to look, bending over her pots again.

Gomez picked a path through the garden, rich with green foods, lettuce, beans, cabbage, onions, the walks bordered with stunted rose bushes in profuse and extravagant bloom. A woman worked there, the bow of her back naked where her shirt had slipped up as she leaned over, her face shaded by a ragged hat, her feet cracked and seamed to rawness in the loose mold of the beds.

Gomez stopped, took off his hat. "Senora, in the name of God, may I pick a few roses for Maria La Soledad?"

The woman drew herself half erect with a long sigh. Her eyes fixed themselves on him dimly. "In the name of God," she answered, "I cannot give away the thing that is not mine. But surely if you pick a rose for La Soledad in all this forest of roses God will forgive you."

He picked here and there until he had gathered a small cluster. "Thanks to God, then, senora," he said, and passed on.

The sight of the Cathedral, with its great doors swinging wide, moved him strangely. He stopped in the cool shade and stared up at the heavy headed trees bowed somnolently over the bulbous roof, at the many swallows singing and flurrying under the eaves. There were so many, and he, Gomez, was only one man to destroy them all. Yet here was his work, his love. This house, built from the infinite labor of men dead and gone for the enslavement of the human soul, should be utterly removed, forgotten, as if it was a little straw jacal caught in a blaze!

A youth, wearing a charro of blue drill, his slanted Otomí eyes shaded by a wide embroidered hat, stood guard at the entrance, leaning amicably on his long barrelled gun. A cartridge belt wrapped his lank curving waist, and circled over his shoulders. His hand went up in salute, he bowed with a manner that would have been good manners any where in the world.

Angel bowed also, and stepped aside to make way for a tall young Indian girl followed by an old servant. Her elbow, forming an angle for the folds of her green silk reboso, brushed him lightly. She glanced at him, an aloof, clear gaze of uptilted black eyes, without challenge, without arrogance. Her cheek bones were warmly flushed as ripe cactus figs. Her mouth was sweet in the corners, like the mouth of a young child.

"Perdoneme, por Dios, Senorita!"

"Por nada, Senor!"

She passed under the grouped arches framing vistas of light, of mysterious pointed altars hung with brocade stuffs, lighted deeply with the stains of sunlight falling through jewel colored glass.

Angel could not take his eyes from her. Delight flowed warmly all through him, the feel of her beauty surged in him softly as a river moving slowly between hot drowsy banks. The boy, leaning on his rifle, watched him steadily, his eyelids sheltering a remote, significant smile. Angel snared the look. Something caught him sharply under the breast bone. He wished desperately not to ask the question, but it came on the instant:

"She is the famous beauty of the town, eh?" with a struggle to infuse in his tone the right note of curiosity and impersonal respect.

The eyes smiled openly. "Maybe so. Yes, maybe she is beautiful. She lives in the palace there. . . ." A pause, a light nod of the head, a lifted brow. . . . "She is called the niece of the Archbishop, you understand? the Dove of Chapacalco!"

Angel said nothing. The boy struck an attitude, knee crooked, hat on one side, and took out his paper pack of cigarettes with the air of a man of the world. Match in hand, swiftly an old superstition overtook him, breaking down his pose. Involuntarily, he turned his head and spat. Angel, moved by an unknown, a surprising impulse, spat also.

They laughed together then, with knowing leers and down turned mouths. But Angel did it only to establish a man's understanding with the boy. Then he walked swiftly into the cathedral, carrying his roses.

VII

At the right hand of the high altar, in a niche of carved wood covered with hammered gold leaf, laid on thick as cream, stood the miraculous image of Maria La Soledad. Old wooden rosaries, faded ribbons and flower wreaths hung from her pallid hands, perpetual reminders of gratitude from her devotees, humbly importunate bribes for further blessings. Cheap glass and pottery vases were set about her, filled always with fresh flowers. A bronze candle bowl glimmered from Easter to Easter, the pointed flames casting off their little flickering prayers.

The rudely carved wooden limbs of the idol were concealed under ample black plush robes, stiff with silver embroidered sprays of wheat, sterile image of fe[rtility]. Over her long veil a golden coronet cast a wreath of [shining] rays, dagger-sharp about her face.

La Soledad! All the sorrows of the poor, the ineffectual, the sick, the desolate believers of the world had been brought to those primly covered feet, had been held up before those inconsolable clasped hands and lonely forsaken brows. All day the step of her shrine was dark with the shawled forms of women, the air heavy with the breath of their murmurings. . . .

Surcease from sorrow, oh sweet little Mother Mary! Ease us of our pain, give us rest and light! Oh, lonely and stricken Lady, pray for us!

Oh, Mother Mary, a pain gnaws in my stomach like a hot coal, and my legs are swollen! Help me! Oh, dear Holy Virgin, my man is in jail and my baby is dead unbaptised . . . save them for me! Oh, adorable Queen Mother of Mercy, my man beats me until I am not able to work. There is not enough food for us all, and my teeth are aching, and there is something the matter with my Rosita's eyes! Oh remember your lost child, pitiful little Mother of God!

For three centuries Maria La Soledad had stood in her niche, her agate eyes gazing upward, lighted by day and night with the pale fires of devotion. Dust lay in the folds of her gown, on her fingers, on her head. Dust.

Vicenta knelt in her pew, kissed her amber and gold rosary, once treasured by a lady of the fourteenth century Spanish court. Now and then, while praying, she would warm the beads in her hands, and sniff them delicately. She cared nothing for Maria La Soledad. She knew by what agency those hands lowered themselves in benediction on the first day of May. She knew what miracle brought tears of blood to those agate eyes at three o'clock every Good Friday. She liked to kneel and float in a pleasant revery, murmur her prayers in acceptable Latin, the smell of amber and lilies and incense curling into her nostrils like suave opiates.

*   *   *

[*Fragment of scene between Archbishop and Miramonte*]

Miramonte's face, swollen darkly with resentment now turned the color of dirty candle wax.

"The land will be repartitioned among the Indians this afternoon, late, and if Your Grace resists, or fosters resistance among your people, we will confiscate this property together with your collections, and imprison Your Grace. It is very simple."

The Archbishop stood. "My troops are not all here, but the strength of God is in their arms. If you want battle, gentlemen, that also is very simple." Facing one another, the two men became acutely aware of the grandiose hypocrisy of their words and attitudes. Miramonte, bored with the performance of a duty he did not believe in, now was bent only on the payment of a personal debt to the Archbishop. The Archbishop, who saw his power crumbling, felt only impatience to be done with the scene, to get the vermin out of his house, and to find Vicenta, who had betrayed him.

There would be the usual result of these conferences—a casual row in the streets between Indians and troops, and a peon or two would get under foot and be crushed, there would be talk of retaliation on both sides, and peace again until next year.

Yet where were his soldiers set to guard the gate? Why were these men accompanied by their soldiers against his orders? A dark annoyance possessed him.

"I should say, senores, that the best trial of strength is to go into the street and begin your attack. It is your intention I take it?"

*　*　*

[*Fragment of scene of storming of the palace*]

To strain at other men's burdens? To sweat for a master? To gouge in the earth to bring out food and gold for the rich? To give salutation to priests? Here is your earth, and your fields full of good grain and fruit that you gather to make fat bellies for other men! Tierra y Libre! Adelante! Burn—kill, level these churches and palaces! Take the earth! It is yours!"

His voice was no longer an individual sound but a single note of frenzy in a cataclysm of noise that rose, towered, made outlines and patterns of sound against the sky, that battered itself against walls and was cast back in enormous distortion of clamor. The blotches resolved into men, the men suddenly had faces, each one cast in its own mold of hatred, of horror, of destruction.

Bodies solid yet ever changing fell against him, over him, mouths belching hot breath shouted in his face, eyes met his for a moment, glaring like the eyes of men remembering their brutehood; and a single frightful purpose created itself from this chaos.

"Fire! Torches? To the church. A torch to warm Maria la Soledad—Lead us—lead us! Thou first, Gomez, deliverer! Jesucristo, guide us! Thou first, Gomez, hermanito! Limpia de curas! Lead us, Gomez, angel of God!"

Under the wall of the palace they rose and vomited howls like a beast sickened to death. Flares burned up and showered sparks upon heads bristling like the shoulders of dogs.

*　*　*

[*Fragment of scene between Vicenta and Angel Gomez,*
probably after the destruction of the palace.]

"They will not build [an]other, Vicenta—they will turn the gods afoot in the open field, and even Xochitl will not have any magic except for songs and poetry. . . . The fields will be open to any man who sows his grain, and every man shall make his house with his own hands, and every woman shall have milk enough for her children; those who have corn shall give to the man who has fruit, and they shall all exchange the labor of their hands, and no man shall put another in prison for theft, and no man shall kill another for money—and they will be free!"

"Si, Angel, then they will be free. . . ."

A Letter from Mexico and the
Gleam of Montezuma's Golden Roofs

Christian Science Monitor (June 5, 1922): 22

✴ In March 1922, J. H. Retinger sent Porter a telegram, informing her that the government had appointed her American organizer of the Mexican Art Exhibition at a salary of $3000 plus expenses, and that her immediate presence in Mexico was "indispensable." She arrived on April 5 and remained approximately two months, working intensely on a monograph that would accompany the exhibition to the United States. Her letter from Mexico, incorporated into an article by George Sill Leonard, communicates her enthusiastic appreciation for the objects of Indian folk art and for the work of Diego Rivera, who at the time was completing his mural *Creation* in the Anfiteatro Bolívar of the Escuela Nacional Preparatoria. Porter visited Rivera in his studio and dined with him and his vivacious model and later wife, Lupe Marín, who influenced the creation of María Concepción. In "The Martyr," Porter gives a less flattering view of Rivera and Marín.

A Letter from Mexico and the Gleam of
Montezuma's Golden Roofs

New York, June 3

I have met men of estimable character, though perhaps not given to great flights of imagination, who have assured me that they considered an art career a sheer waste of time and I at least have understood their point of view. Art is rarely mentioned in the market quotations. I have met others who have acknowledged art to be a legitimate activity but one to be classed as a luxury, and I have appreciated their attitude. A man can do without art as he can without religion—for a time. But when I meet those who intimate that they are too concerned with the larger issues of the world's progress to bother with art I can only be silent and wonder. For in art is written the history of man from the stone age to the present day, history in its most attractive, synthetic and penetrative form.

Here, on beaten bronze and incised bone, in columned temple and carven wall, in chiseled marble and painted cloth, are perpetuated the trials, the triumphs and the deepest actuating emotions of race after race who have passed from one to another through the long centuries the ever-burning torch of human aspiration. There is no age, no quarter of the globe, but has its yield of revelation for the student of art. Here's perspective for any mind.

But even the best of perspectives tend to get smaller and smaller until something happens to open your eyes. Something of this kind occurred the other day when I received a letter from an American woman who is assembling in Mexico City the national art exhibition which is soon to be brought to the United States. And as I read the Grecian temples and Egyptian columns which had been bounding my art horizon faded out and far away I caught the gleam of Montezuma's golden roofs.

"I spend my time in an old house of the seventeenth century," I read, "in an immense hall littered with beauty and great windows opening on the patio garden. Diego Rivera comes there at times, and Best, and Vasconcelos, and Toledano. Indians from the country help to assort pottery and painted boxes and serapes more beautiful than ever I imagined serapes could be, and great silver embroidered saddles and spurs that glitter like jewels. The stirrups are of dark blue polished steel encrusted with silver flowers and leaves and birds. A horseman's dream of saddles and stirrups!

"There is pottery from Puebla, done in the old style, Chinese blue on cream color, dragons and birds and leaves. In other colors, too, pale yellow and orange and green with that dark blue. It touches the heart to see how these people have persisted in their instinctive need to create beauty, and how they have taken the humble materials of their own earth at their very doorsteps, and have contrived lovely things that make you remember all beauty.

"In Guadalajara they make another kind of pottery, with most delicate and fantastic designs brushed on in thin exquisite lines, quieter colors on a background of gray or black or clay-red. Common brown cooking pots will have a pattern on them in thick opaque white so fine that at a little distance it looks like embroidery.

"In Aguas Calientes they make sturdy little straight chairs, painted black first and decorated with gay flowers frosted over with gold or silver dust, with hand woven seats of red fiber. I mean to have a half dozen of them. Baskets woven fine as cloth, with geometric designs, come from a dozen places, each with its own designs. In all these things I have never seen two objects that bore the identical pattern. Every man makes a thing with his own hands, after his own thought.

"Serapes are from almost everywhere, from the gorgeous black and green and red ones of Oaxaca to the beautiful blue and white and black ones of Texcoco.

"From Tehuantepec we have brought embroidered dresses and lace headdresses worn by the women there, with fine gold and silver filigree jewels, necklaces, earrings and bracelets. The Oaxaca women make their shirts from coarse white cotton embroidered in bead patterns more lovely than any other embroidery I ever saw. The Indians there do not speak Spanish, but the old classic Mixteca language, called by the Spaniards the richest language in Mexico at the time of the conquest.

"Everything that touches the life of the Indian, from head to foot, in all his household and his work, every object created for his daily use, he makes as beautiful as he can, in his own incorruptible fashion. The thing is his own.

"Rivera, whose paintings we are bringing, I think is one of the great artists of the world, though he has had to live down the fact that he founded Cubism, and gave the first Cubist exhibition in Paris ever so long ago. But now he is simple and splendid and paints like a god in a mood of repentance for the hurts he has given his creatures.

"When I first went to see his Indian fresco, still half finished, in the National University here, I was struck with the certainty that I was in the presence of an immortal thing. And as I stood before two enormous clasped hands, on paper, pinned in place over the charcoal outline on the wall, I was touched with the same feeling I had when I was 12 years old and saw for the first time the "Praying Hands" of Dürer. I felt like weeping with pity for struggling, suffering, human life.

"And we are bringing some of Best's wonderful decorative designs, based on the real Aztec designs, which bring back so vividly that rare and mysterious art and culture which remains to us only in archaeological remains, and which is the real inherited inspiration of the native Mexican art today.

"I must stop now and go to Diego's studio—an old ruined church—to select drawings. There are gardenias in my room and two bright green baby parrots are quarreling amiably over their breakfast of banana. It is early morning and summer in Mexico."

So ended the letter. As I read it was for me, too, early morning in and summer in Mexico. The book on Cézanne, which I had been reading, lay neglected.

Strange how little the world has concerned itself with the art of the ancient Americas, of ancient Mexico and Peru. It has dug down through thousands of feet of earth and rock to find traces of early man. It has toiled for years through sand and lava to expose the buried structures of Pompeii and Karnak. The smallest Chinese village and farthest South Sea Island has fallen under the avid eyes of the collectors. But in America so little has been done to unearth and study the remains of two great races and more than two great cultures.

And what art today offers more opportunity for fascinating speculation? Who were the nomad race who descended into Mexico from the plains of Utah and Montana and who, in the time of conquest, received the Spaniards in great cities with walls of carven stone, where opened great courts covered with colored awnings upheld by richly engraved pillars of scented woods, and where gold-covered roofs flashed in the sunlight? Were they of Asiatic origin, as their art seems to imply? Then who were the Toltecs, whose relics of advanced culture the Aztecs found in Mexico when they arrived? And who the Mayas, whose period of artistic and social ascendance probably antedated the Toltecs and surely influenced them? But, whatever their origin, they have left treasures of an archaeology to which the world has begun to awaken in the last few years.

Then, too, we forget the art of modern Mexico. Here, since the days of the Spanish invasion, has swayed the influence of Murillo and Velasquez. Here, for a period of nearly 200 years, have been imported great quantities of some of the best Spanish art. Notably Titian's "Entombment" which up to a few years ago stayed in a squalid little Indian village. What has happened to all these?

Here, too, in this period were developed a school of local artists of no mean talent, among them such men as Echave, and Correa, and the Zapoteca Indian, Miguel Cabrera. But how often do we find these names in books on art. And in late years have been developed the modern work of such men as Best and Rivera, fresh in inspiration, which will be seen in the coming Mexican show in the United States.

Art has seemed to be a much more zestful subject in these days since I received that letter. There are new currents stirring. Perhaps the art world is beginning to break away from the traditions of Greece and Rome.

G.S.L.

Outline of Mexican Popular Arts and Crafts

Mexico City: S. I. C. y T.; Los Angeles: Young & McCallister, 1922

The enthusiasm of Porter's "A Letter from Mexico" informs her *Outline*. Her acknowledgments record the books she consulted and her companions from whose expert opinion she drew. Porter returned to Mexico at the height of the Mexican mural renaissance, whose artists shared a keen appreciation of the history of the Mexican Indian and his art. In the first section, she drew from Manuel Gamio's ideas about the Aztec woman and from Best-Maugard's identification of seven motifs in pre-Columbian art. Porter modified Best's ideas to develop an art theory of her own. In the second section, she drew from Dr. Atl's *Las Artes Populares en México*, which stresses the indigenous artist's assimilative powers. Her statement that the native people are of a "race that expresses itself simply and inevitably in terms of beauty" captures the spirit of her response to the Indians of Xochimilco. In these two works they are not the "silent and reproachful figures in rags, bowed face to face with the earth" she had depicted in "The Fiesta of Guadalupe" and "The Mexican Trinity" and was to depict in "Hacienda."

Editing this previously published work proved a difficult challenge because Porter had expressed her dissatisfaction with it. A letter of January 1, 1923, to Porter from Xavier Guerrero, the art director of the exhibit for which the *Outline* served as catalog, apparently responded to a letter from Porter in which she had expressed dismay over the number of errors in the text. She had been unable to read proof before it was printed in Los Angeles. Guerrero had sent Porter 500 copies of the *Outline* about December 25, 1922. Guerrero's January 1 letter further suggested that he could have an errata page inserted if she desired. No copy with such a page of errata has been located.

Most of the errors in the text as published are relatively inconsequential: typographical errors, misplacement or omission of punctuation or diacritical marks, and inconsistency in the employment of British spelling practice. Others are more consequential. The names of three of the historians mentioned in the second paragraph of the "Acknowledgment," Bandelier, Riva Palacio, and Revilla, are misspelled. There are examples of faulty agreement of subject and verb (pp. 142 and 185). All of these except the faulty agreement have been corrected in the text that follows.

Two specific sentences are especially problematical. In the discussion of the pottery of Oaxaca state (p. 173), the published *Outline* states, "Second to the pottery of Guadalajara, the earthenware most prized by the Mexican is the thick yellow pottery made in the Tonalá village." The reference to Tonalá, a village in the state of Jalisco, clearly must be an error, because later in the monograph (p. 175), Porter discusses the earthenware industry of that town. Surely Porter must have intended Atzompa (or Asompa as it is spelled in an illustration caption). Another confusing error appears in the discussion of the charro costume (p. 185). The sentence beginning "Stirrups and saddles . . ." contains at least two errors: lack of agreement of subject and verb, and "Andeleon." One possible reading for this sentence is "Stirrups and saddles are made in several towns, but Amozoc in Puebla and León in Guanajuato are easily in the lead." Neither of these two errors is corrected in our version of the text.

For a complete list of the editors' corrections and emendations, see p. 277 of the Notes on Texts.

Outline of Mexican Popular Arts and Crafts

Upon the occasion of the Traveling Mexican Popular Arts Exposition in the United States of North America, under the auspices of the Ministry of Industry, Commerce and Labor of Mexico, Don Xavier Guerrero, being the Art Director, has caused this book to be published. It contains a study by Miss Katherine Anne Porter, of the Popular Arts and Crafts of Mexico.

My search for the sources and meanings of Mexican folk art has been a richly rewarded adventure among intelligences and devotions. Artists and scientists who have given many years to the work of recreating ancient Mexico from her historical remains, students who have brought enthusiasms as fresh and recent as my own, all have generously given me aid and counsel, have been swift to remove barriers of race and language and tradition that lay between me and the Mexican.

To avoid an accumulation of footnotes in the text, let me here set down that I have read such widely divergent historians as Prescott, Alexander von Humboldt, Bandelier, Madame Calderon de la Barca, Bancroft, Riva Palacio, Revilla, Nicolas Leon; such entirely opposing contemporaneous writers as Dr. Atl, authority on modern popular arts in Mexico; Licenciado Ramon Mena, whose studies of recent archaeological excavations have been of much value; and Don Manuel Gamio, whose theories of ethnology are sound and of deep interest.

Thanks to the initiative and energy of Don Miguel Alessio Robles, Minister of Commerce and Industry, the actual work of preparing this exposition has been accomplished, with the personal collaboration of his department.

For invaluable aid in gathering, classifying and interpreting the materials for this outline, I am happy to express my gratitude to Licenciado Jose Vasconcelos, Minister of Education and Fine Arts; to Licenciado Vicente Lombardo Toledano, director of the Preparatory School of the National University; to Señor Jorge Enciso, of the National Museum, collector and restorer of examples of early Colonial art, connoisseur of Mexican jade and Aztec design; to Licenciado Ramon Mena and his associate Mr. William Niven, the indefatigable digger who has brought out of the earth an extraordinary volume of relics from buried cities.

The group of men immediately concerned in organizing this Exposition have been especially generous with their aid, Señor Alfonso Caso, private secretary to the Minister of Commerce and Industry; Dr. J. H. Retinger; and the Mexican painters, Diego Rivera, Adolfo Best-Maugard, and Xavier Guerrero, all have contributed the fruits of their studies to my understanding of Mexican art, have helped me to form my point of view and to place my sympathies.

This simple outline of a profound subject is offered as an introduction to the arts of the Mexican people, on the occasion when they are sending for the first time an exhibition of their work to a foreign country. Virtually

Decorated Jar—Tonalá, Jalisco. *Outline of Mexican Popular Arts and Crafts*, p. 3. All illustrations for this work courtesy of Rare Books & Literary Manuscripts Department, University of Maryland at College Park Libraries.

no special preparations were made for this exhibit in the way of manufacturing wares. The examples shown here were gathered from the little country villages, from the common shops and street markets, where the native brings his goods to sell them to his own people. They are personal, authentic creations, by the peasant craftsmen of a race that expresses itself simply and inevitably in terms of beauty.

THE AUTHOR.

Mexico, D. F., May, Nineteen Hundred Twenty-two.

It is a unique truth that to trace the origin of Mexican popular art as it exists today, it is necessary to consult first the archaeologists and scientists. In this country the past is interwoven visibly with the present, living and potent. The latter day life of the native is an anachronism. To account for him, archaeology and ethnology must combine in what appears to be an ill-rewarded search for beginnings. It is not possible to settle the question of the ancient races of Mexico, to close the book and pronounce clearly on a dead civilization, as in other countries where the earth is giving up her entombed cities.

The descendants of the early Mexicans have survived the buried temples of their culture and are here, almost pure in strain, spiritually remote, stubbornly individual after centuries of alien domination.

They have given way before foreign conquest with reservations. They outwardly conformed to a religion imposed upon them, and mingled ancient significances with its new rituals.

They patiently wrought in the arts after the design of the strangers, and continued thereby an almost unbroken record of their own racial soul. Here is an art, almost unknown in the world today, a survival from internal wars, conquests, many fusions; an actual thing of full breathing vitality and meaning. Always the foreign influences have been assimilated and transformed slowly into something incorruptibly Mexican, personal to the race.

The first concern of the scientist is to discover the origin, the first impulse of the artist is to apprehend the spirit. If the artist has more nearly achieved his aim, it is maybe because his task is simpler. He perceives and accepts the fundamental kinship of all human beings on the plane of natural emotion.

They are agreed in this essential: the problem of the native is the problem of Mexico today. His future is invaluable, and must be secured. Modern sentiment of humanity and economic wisdom alike declare that the Indio has in the life of today his rights, his uses and his destiny.

For this it is necessary to arrive at an understanding of him. The one approach to such an eventuality is by way of comprehending first his contribution to society . . . and his contribution is beauty. A strange thing, sufficiently marvelous, of miraculous import. While we are attempting to explain him, he fulfills himself in his desert silences, unaware that he is enigma.

Scientific theory regarding the origin of the Mexican is at once less sure and more dogmatic than the artistic. One may say with all high regard to the devoted and serious research of the students and historians of Mexico, that each man has an individual theory, compounded of many fallible ingredients. He is committed to faith in his works with an intensity once the property of religious fanaticism. This Sphynx of countries, which for every fragment of authentic history yields two riddles, is an enormous field of travail for the enthusiast who will die in defense of his facts. Each of them proves his contention by his own illumined faith, defended by his carefully gathered and rigidly arranged group of theories beginning where all theories of origins must begin: on hypothesis.

This lends to their conclusions that quality of fantasy, of speculation and myth creativeness that has always marked the ideas of man pitiably eager to explain himself to himself, to open eternity with the key of his human imagination. But their work has this permanent value; they have brought out of the earth records in stone, unaccountable things in the main, but lasting documents for further study.

A certain student will tell you there were five successive civilizations in Mexico; it is true he has collected five curiously unrelated types of masks and faces modelled in clay from several cities and from varying depths. The doubter may go to these cities and dig them out for himself.

Another declares, and will show you charts to make it clear, that only two distinct types of culture existed here: the Maya and the Nahoa, so-called. Still others maintain that the races of ancient Mexico derived from the Chinese in the very dawn of time, and would raise the Atlantis to make a footpath for the migratory tribes across the sea. This last body of believers is almost large enough to found a school of archaeology and ethnology of its own.

They point to slant eyes, to anatomical character, to a gold colored skin surviving in the several tribes, in the Otomís, in the Mixtecas, in the early Maya. In effect, their contention is based on religious faith; it is not possible that in old time there were rival gods, each creating after his own fashion. The obscure monotheism in the soul of modern man declares the early man in the valley of Anahuac must be in some way blood brother to the human beings cradled in Mother Asia.

They seek to account for this common Asiatic origin by comparison of hieroglyphics, motifs of design, by feature and customs and dress. They restore that vanished pathway of islands across the sea, which, if they did not form a complete bridge, created channels narrow enough for peoples to navigate them in small boats. This was, they admit, in the dawn; if they came so early as that, their kinship with the east is a remote thing, a mere sharing of common humanity.

Analogies founded on comparisons so general have proved misleading. Those individuals who have studied origins in Egypt first find in the Mexican culture startling resemblances to the architecture and art motifs of the Early Egyptians. Scientists declare that virtually every culture of ancient Europe and Asia reveal some circuitous kinship with the inhabitants of Mexico.

These resemblances appertain to the humanity of all races. The fixed dates of the Mexican culture vary from the Glacial epoch of the extremists to the five centuries B. C. of the conservatives. Science is hopelessly divided in point of time; but whatever the period of their emergence into civilization, they followed the natural process of growth. They may have been parallel with the same development in Europe and Asia, or they may have progressed in a slower rhythm, governed by different climatic conditions and their insurmountable isolation from the rest of the world.

In important details they differ entirely. These differences give significance and depth to their culture. The resemblances are casual.

A study of early design, for example, shows us that circles and wavy lines, labyrinths, swastikas and angles existed as basic motifs among those peoples whom we are accustomed to call primitive. I submit that they existed as the simple universal expressions of emotions and perceptions that animated the awakening soul of man, the natural idiom of primary understanding. The individual use of these perceptions were developed differently by the growth of human personality limited and directed by its environment.

A child of today, fragrant of civilization that he is, yet sees his world first with the eyes of innocence. He draws by instinct a straight line. A wavy line is water, a round circle serves variously to express his feelings for a flower, a head, a moon. He draws these things because they are the first planes and outlines the human eye apprehends.

In his terrors the child is primitive man. He fears flood, fire, lightning, the mysterious and awful portents of nature. He creates superstitions about his birth, his emotions, his sex. I submit that these instinctive gropings make all men akin, and that they derive from within the individual. A race in China and a race in Mexico, emerging into the adolescence of civilization, would do similar things because those are the things all the men in the world did in the beginning.

Since conclusions as to the history of the early races of Mexico must be based on choice of sources of information guided by personal faith and

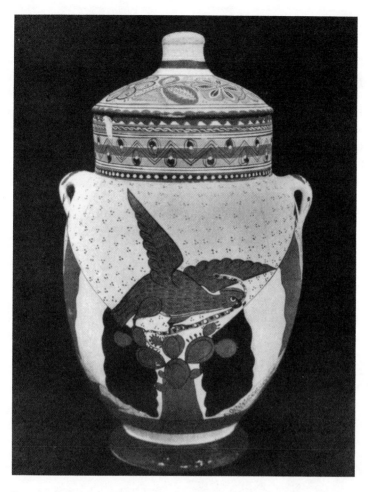

Decorated Clay Jar—Tonalá, Jalisco. *Outline of Mexican Popular Arts and Crafts*, p. 7.

judgment, I have contrived the following mosaic of selected theories and data from many writers, offering it not as dogma, but merely as one possible combination on which to base further study.

Three distinct race-groups formed the early civilizations of Mexico: the Otomí, the Maya and the Nahoa. Of these the Otomí is believed to have been the oldest, the most migratory and warlike. Their exact rôle in the history of primitive Mexico is so ill defined it would not be profitable to attempt even the most nebulous outline here.

Of the Mayas much is surmised. They came probably from North America in a migration that covered several centuries. The year of Our Lord 162 is the date assigned for the beginning of this pilgrimage of a race.

At the close of the second century following, they were settled in Yucatán, with territories including parts of Chiapas and Tabasco, possessed of a splendid culture that dominated Honduras, Guatemala, Peru, parts of North and Central America.

The Nahoa influence at about the same period embraced nearly all the valley of Anahuac, the central mesa of Mexico. At the time of the Conquest, the Mayas had long since vanished, while the Nahoa civilization had reached its final growth about the year 1400, and was in a gradual decline. The Aztecs, a migratory and aggressive tribe who came to the valley of Anahuac about the end of the thirteenth century, were responsible for the breaking down of the gentler Nahoa culture. The Aztecs assimilated the Nahoa arts as the Romans did those of the Greeks, adding the vigor and solidity of their military organization to the body of Nahoa culture, investing the arts of the decaying peoples with a harsher outline.

The true foundation of Mexican art is, however, a combination of these two primary cultures, the Maya and the Nahoa. Throughout the states of Oaxaca and Jalisco today, this influence is still astonishingly pure and powerful.

They were at first two totally different types of art. The practical difference was in method. All Maya stone carving was in bas-relief, marked by a finished nervous style and exquisite detail of design. The Nahoa sculpture was three dimensional, less fantastic, bolder in execution. The spiritual differences were expressed as freely: the Maya was devotional and religious, the Nahoa vividly objective and personal.

If it is not possible to fix dates and descents with certainty, we have unlimited opportunity to study the remains of their architecture and kindred art forms, the infallible signs whereby we may discover the temper and intellectual level of a race.

In this study, the important fact to consider is a psychological one. The early peoples of Mexico were dominated by the idea and practice of religion. In every tribe, at every stage of their racial progress and decay, faith in their gods was the compelling impulse of their lives. Priests were the guardians of the national spirit, the instructors of the young, the final authorities who governed the people in all matters of moral conduct even to the smallest personal details of daily living.

Among the Aztecs even to the early part of the sixteenth century there were thirteen principal deities, and more than two hundred inferior gods.

They ranked in importance from the War God Huitzilopochtli to the humble little household deity charged with the responsibility of bringing daily good fortune and happiness to the family under whose roof he was a guest.

Five thousand priests waited on the will of these gods, serving at altars which reflected their holiest idea of beauty, in temples set stone upon stone by the hands of unquestioning faith.

The nature of any art is determined by the medium of expression. The medium of the early Mexican was stone. If they had song and poetry and musical instruments, there is little to record that they were considered as important forms. A few songs have survived, notably those of the last Emperor of Texcoco, but he was comparatively of modern times. The Nahoas made picture writing and carved panels to tell of their wars, their feasts, their games, their victories and religious ceremonies. They expressed themselves primarily in sculpture as the Celts did in great songs and legends. The old Irish people were like the Jews in this: they describe their gods and praise them in words. The Mexicans carved the images of their deities in stone, and left them for us to see and touch and wonder at, and to make our own legends about them.

From this concern, this preoccupation with the will of the gods, there sprang a strange and terrible beauty, destined to remain as the sole record of a splendid race. The sculpture, the architecture, the decorations of the Nahoas and Mayas are symbols of the racial mind, and that mind was, above all, religious.

In the simplicity of the attitudes of these images, we understand that the worship of the Mexican was a completely honest thing. Keeping their gods alive and appeased was the difficult work of men bent on surviving in a world filled with hostile forces. They shared this fear of the unknown with all races of men fated to experiment with the incalculable mysteries for the first time, with no guide except human curiosity, no weapon except human valor.

The cruelties of their faith, so much discussed and theorized about, were then only the cruelties shared with a terror-stricken world of men. They would have discovered, finally, that the sun would rise even though no victim was sacrificed on their altars. Not hatred of humanity, but love of their gods prompted them to their ritual sacrifices. The intimate and precious possession of life was the ideal offering to their gods for the well-being of the race. The merely physical cruelties were incidental and necessary. Moral cruelty was unknown. It came later in other races, through different dogmas, with the decadence of the religious spirit.

With this in mind, we will examine their sculptured images.

The Maya civilization was the most advanced and important of all the old social structures of Mexico. They seem to have vanished mysteriously at the height of their beauty, for a sustained perfection of form marks their art from the first known example to the end.

The early bas-relief panels in the temples at Palenque, of which the best known are the tablets of the Foliated Cross, are sophisticated and delicate in design. The later image of Chac-Mool (called first the Maya Bacchus, now identified as the Tiger King) is as restrained, as classic and cool in modelling as only a race old in culture, or young and supremely innocent, can produce. But always it is civilized—the exaggerations of savagery are unknown.

The Nahoas followed a more natural process, upbuilding to a pinnacle of beauty and declining into over-ripeness.

To a fantastic degree they possessed the grotesque sense at once the property of very primitive and very decadent minds. In art, we begin with distortions of beauty and we end with them. But the grotesqueries differ in precisely the degree of separation between innocence and decaying wisdom.

In their sculpture we encounter these several phases of development. We find at first an innocent, artless animality, the crude efforts of a child to portray the human form, the shapes of beasts and birds and imaginary creatures, done with particularity and frankness.

The gods are monsters, the modelled portraits of men are masks with holes gouged to represent eyes and mouths. The figures squat with enormous hands dangling between knees upraised in the primitive seated position.

A period followed in which the Nahoas produced a caste of builders and artists so advanced their generic name has been mistakenly applied to the entire nation: the Toltecs. They created stylized, chaste and lovely images in crystal, in jade and in stone. The architecture of this period was massive, with an abundance of bas-relief carving in stone, more severe in design than that of the Mayas, and of great depth in cutting. The Toltecs had no iron nor steel tools for this work; they used only tempered copper and the flint-like volcanic glass called obsidian.

In this epoch began the growth of a desire and necessity for beauty not wholly religious in meaning. Purely decorative objects sold in the public markets took the form of carved amulets meant more for adornments than to ward off evil; masks for festivals, beads of jade and jadeite skilfully cut and polished, jewels of gold and copper, girdles and headdresses, all came into use for the sake of their own beauty rather than because of religious symbolism.

Human portraits in stone and clay, many of them gorgeously colored have been found in profusion in every buried city of ancient Mexico. In the middle period of the Nahoa culture an aristocratic and civilized beauty marks these faces modelled clearly and delicately under splendid head-dresses. Balance and proportion, sanity and graciousness mark the work of this epoch. It was the high point of Nahoa culture. The century was that of Our Lord 1200, yet it all seems as far away as the Flood itself. The Nahoa heroes of that time, the later poet King of Texcoco, seem to be one with the spacious myths of antiquity, akin to Dana and Pan and the warriors Homer sung. Mexico was the final stronghold of the great pagan gods, and even to the very day of the beginning of the Conquest there still clings about them the atmosphere of legendary remoteness.

A familiar flavor of the miraculous is in the religious accounts of the later times, as recorded by the first Spanish priests. Whether these are authentic myths, or a corruption of them due to the decline of the race at the time of the Spanish invasion, or imperfect translations by the historians new to the Mexican languages, we cannot be certain.

The myth of the god Quetzalcoatl, who was once a man, and became the culture deity of the Nahoas, runs like this: Chimalma, a holy woman of the Nahoas, swallowed a small stone of jadeite, and later was delivered of a son, conceived thus immaculately, who was very wise and good and gentle from his childhood. When he grew up, he taught the people the wisdom and beauty of holy living, besides the crafts of weaving and metal work, and the sowing of the fields. He incurred the wrath of the wicked among his people, and went away by the sea in a skiff of magic serpent skins. For this reason he has become associated in a mysterious, half-spoken legend, with the waves of the sea, and with a feathered serpent: In what way it is impossible to discover from the endless versions I have read. He vowed to the people that he would return, and charged them to receive him as a god at his second coming.

This legend so influenced the minds of the Nahoas, and later the Aztecs, it opened the way for that tragic and mistaken reception of Cortés and his soldiers, who came by way of the sea in the precise manner Quetzalcoatl had foretold.

Another legend concerned with the immaculate mortal conception of Immortals is told of Huitzilopochtli, the god of war, who wears on his left foot the feathers of the hummingbird. His mother saw rolling before her in the wind a bundle of brightly colored feathers. She placed them in her bosom, and a short while after discovered herself to be pregnant of a god. He was born full grown, with war dress and shield and helmet of green plumes.

This may or may not be an authentic Mexican myth. But the legend of the creation of man is unique, original, austere as a Nahoa god in stone, unmarred by evidences of modern revision. A young god stood in the valley of Anahuac, near a place now called Acolman, and shot an arrow of obsidian toward the noonday sun. It soared and descended, and when it touched the earth, it sprang up again a living man. Though it may be told in two lines, it is the most innocent and splendid legend I have found in any mythology.

It is above all a happy legend. There is no death nor sin in it. Man is created in a blaze of light, his being compounded of sun warmth and clean arrow point, touching earth and receiving there the divine essential energy of life. Not even among the Norse peoples have I found a legend more epically simple and great than this.

This version of creation gives us a glimpse of another soul than the dark and ritualistic one discovered in the old codices representing sacrifices, and in the tales told by the Spaniards. We have become habited to think of these people as being always a stern and terrible race, fixed and immalleable of soul as their idols, with ponderous headdresses crushing their frowning brows.

Those headdresses were contrived of paper and plumes and flowers, and the wearers of them loved color as the Israelites loved perfumes and spices. Their houses and robes, their votive cups, their temples and their gods were all splashed with the most vivid hues. Examine any insignificant clay figure today, recovered from the earth, not yet broken from its mold, and you find it brilliant with stains, sulphurous reds and yellows, burning blues and greens. This use of color is found alike in the remains of Azcapotzalco, in Teotihuacán near the Pyramides, in Yucatán, and in the Tarascan figurines of terra cotta, found in Cheran. Strange designs of animals, flowers and birds give life and rhythm to color in vases and flowers and pots.

In the arts of dyeing, the Nahoas surpassed the others. They had mineral and vegetable and animal color, and after the Conquest their dye secrets became very valuable to the world.

Their special discovery was a small insect which yielded a fine quality of purple and red dye, now called cochineal. A thick lusterless white made from calcined stones was also originated by the Nahoas, and is still used by the Mexicans in decorating certain kinds of pottery. We shall see how their use of primary color has survived in other ways also.

Engels and other scientists have been pleased to classify the early peoples of Mexico as semi-barbarous because of their lack of domestic animals. I believe they have overlooked the essential fact: they had no beasts of burden nor domesticated milk-giving animals because such beasts were not indigenous here. Their habit was to make pets of small creatures, chiefly monkeys, a species of diminutive leopard called *ocelotl*, and that strange breed of hairless dog, the *itzcuintli*, of which it is recorded they could not bark until taught the art by imported European dogs.

It is true that here devolved on human beings that burden of physical labor shared between man and beasts in other lands. But the attitude of the Mexicans toward animals and slaves was that of a race abreast with the civilization of their epoch. Men were not more enslaved for this lack of beasts than they were in countries that possessed both species of burden-bearing animals.

Their system of measuring time was original and distinctive. We have the symmetrical and beautiful Calendar stone of the Aztecs as enduring testimony to the perfection of their calculations. When the Spaniards arrived in Mexico, they discovered that the Aztec Calendar was only five hours late by the sun, while the Christian Calendar of Pope Leo the Great failed of precision by eleven days. Prescott gives an exact account of their measurement of time:

". . . The Aztecs adjusted their civil year by the solar. They divided it into eighteen months of twenty days each. Both months and days were expressed by peculiar hieroglyphics, those of the former intimating the season of the year, like the French months at the period of the Revolution. Five complementary days, as in Egypt, were added to make up the full number of three hundred sixty-five. They belonged to no month, and were regarded as peculiarly unlucky. A month was divided into four weeks, of five days each, on the last of which was the public fair or market day. This arrangement, different from that of the nations of the Old Continent, has the advantage of giving an equal number of days to each month, and of comprehending entire weeks, without a fraction, both in the months and in the year.

"As the year is composed of nearly six hours more than three hundred and sixty-five days, there still remains an excess, which, like other nations who have framed a calendar, they provided for by intercalation; not indeed, every fourth year, as the Europeans, but at longer intervals, like some of the Asiatics. They waited until the expiration of fifty-two vague years, when they interposed twelve days, or rather, twelve and a half, this being the number that had fallen in arrear. Had they inserted thirteen, it would have been too much, since the annual excess over three hundred sixty-five is about eleven minutes less than six hours . . ." (Conquest of Mexico: Prescott: Vol. I, Page 73). They had, in a word, calculated with such minute precision that more than five centuries must elapse before the loss of an entire day.

Their system of numerals has been explained by Riva Palacio in contrast to the Hindu and Aryan systems. Whereas, in the latter methods of computation, the essential numeral is five, and the perfect number 100, in the Nahoa system (which served all Mexico) the essential numeral was four, and the perfect number was eighty, arrived at thus: four plus one equals five; five times four equals twenty; and twenty times four equals eighty.

Their religious symbolism is equally distinct. Though the Nahoas employed characters similar to those of the Asiatics and Aryans, they differed in spirit. Their sign of the cross, for example, found designed on the walls of temples, or carved in stone, was their symbol of the four cardinal points of the compass; more simply still, of the four winds of heaven.

Various explanations have been offered of this mystical sign. Religious writers have woven legends of primitive saints, who were even prophesied in Revelations, who came to Mexico in the early Christian era. Scientists have sought to identify it with its phallic significance in the secret rituals of primitive peoples.

Their great feathered serpent was likewise free from the secret meaning of other ancients, and was a familiar symbol of godhead. The serpent and the sun are mysteriously related in Mexican mythology, probably with some distant association of ideas between the life-giving sun and fruitfulness, but there is no definite surviving legend explaining these things.

Their social customs were marked by one tremendously important difference from the world of their time. The position of women was that of a completely civilized race. The legal or religious bondage of women was unknown. They served with honor as priestesses, and had a responsible share in the education of the children. Every evidence is that they enjoyed a cleanly human equality in society utterly foreign to the ideals that governed the relations between men and women of the European and Asiatic races.

Their sense of rhythm in design was, and remains, unique. The basis of Greek design, for example, is the crossed line. There existed no crossed line in all Maya or Nahoa art. Even to this day it does not appear in the pure designs used by the Mexican craftsmen. When it is used at all, it is foreign, added since the sixteenth century.

Jardinier Talavera—City of Puebla. *Outline of Mexican Popular Arts and Crafts*, p. 15.

Their line of beauty is the bold flaring circle, the uninterrupted whirling of a leaf in the wind. This is why a design on a Guadalajara jug today gives the impression of one unbroken harmonious line from top to bottom.

In architecture, they had no arch, that fundamental outline in all construction of Europe and the Orient. A square topped portal, or two beams contrived to form a shallow inverted angle, was their conception of a doorway. A pointed arch without a keystone was to them an ideal expression of beauty. In this method perfect examples exist in the ruins of Mitla

Serape (Woolen Blanket)—San Miguel Allende, Hidalgo. *Outline of Mexican Popular Arts and Crafts*, p. 18.

and Chichén Itzá, of which the arch of Labná, in Yucatán, is the most beautiful.

As we have seen, these peoples resembled their human brothers in all elemental ideals. Students and scientists pronounce on the vessels of aragonite, the cloudy Mexican onyx, found in the Isle of Sacrificios, near Vera Cruz. They say they are Greek in feeling and line. They say the Maya art is Babylonish; that the headdresses of the old Nahoas are Egyptian; that the character writing on the walls of the Pyramides in Teotihuacán are Chinese. . . .

All these things do veritably have a surface resemblance to the art creations of all races. But in their profound, racial significance they were spontaneous and original. In nothing more than their early arts do they resolve themselves into a people whose developed psychology followed patterns unknown to both Europe and Asia.

Part II: Colonial Art

When the Spaniards came to Mexico in the year 1519, the Mayas had long since abandoned their splendid cities and were building no others of like beauty. The Pyramides at Teotihuacán were mounds of earth which the strangers regarded incuriously as natural hills. Nahoa civilization had reached its height two centuries before and declined with the death of the poet King Nezahualcoyotl of Texcoco. From thence it was gradually absorbed by the Aztec dynasty, and the city of Tenochtitlán became the center of wealth, power and culture of the race.

The Zapotecas and Mixtecas, ancient allies, occupied the present state of Oaxaca; they were divided in language, the customs and arts that once were one had diverged slightly, the Zapotecas toward the Aztec, the Mixtecas toward the Maya. Though both nations possessed the richest languages and picture writing in Mexico at this time, the Mixtecas were superior in civilized arts. They were settled in the South and West of the state, a gentle and tranquil people given to cultural development. The Zapotecas were objective, warlike, militaristic; they helped the Mixtecas to conquer the Isthmus of Tehuantepec, and held their ground by force of arms. In spite of this, it is the Mixteca spirit in art that survives in the state of Oaxaca today.

It was with the newer, intensely warlike Aztec in the city of Tenochtitlán that the invaders were to deal. The Conqueror has always the first word. Centuries must elapse before the defeated peoples can find a hearing for themselves. According to the Spanish writers, they found here a race curiously civilized, but atrociously savage in war; lovers of beauty, worshippers of mystical gods, in spiritual and physical bondage to a religion founded on ritual sacrifice. Nearly all of the historians that followed accepted without question the Spanish point of view that the benefits of civilization had been righteously bestowed upon barbarians by the bitter charity of the sword. Having achieved a substitution by force of their ideals over those of the Mexican, they rested in arrogant certainty of their right to impose their own half-developed culture, derived from a mixture of Europe and the Orient, upon a people whose blood was pure, and whose culture was grown evenly in one soil.

There ensued a collision of antipathies shocking to the imagination. It must have been as if two alien planets struck and fused. The story has been told many times, by makers of legends, by later historians groping among confused and conflicting legends. Yet they somehow achieve unity when considered as a whole. It seems that only a day elapses between that half-legendary ancient world of the Nahoa and the Maya, to the founding of New Spain that suddenly identifies Mexico with the modern world.

One steps from the half light of the centuries before the Conquest into the year 1519, and thereafter we have a record of events insufficient, fragmentary, but comparatively clear. However obscured with personal and religious and political motives, distorted occasionally with belief in the miraculous, seen through the eyes of prejudices incomprehensible to us now, since we are bound by different prejudices, the story still has form and outline; it lends itself to the truth.

After the shock of conquest there began the making of a new nation in Mexico, a slow series of rebirths, a gradual absorption of colors and fibres from many sources; Mexico became New Spain, a nation torn from its old gods and inborn visions, thereafter to take on the forms of faith of the conqueror, the laws of an alien world, the customs of strangers.

Teocallis were razed, and churches set over the places where they had been. New arts were added to the old, and were amalgamated with them. These arts came by way of the Spanish crown, but they were borrowed from the greater and older nations of France and Italy. . . .

The Mexican arts amazed and delighted the strangers, who praised them in their chronicles—those extravagant documents that are such curious blendings of religious fervor, curiosity, appreciation and rapacity—and long descriptions of the native crafts remain as the pleasantest stories brought out of that dolorous period.

They tell of the goldsmiths of Azcapotzalco, who wrought in gold and silver filigree, chains and necklaces and earrings and bracelets, in feathery and lace-like designs as minute and painstaking as those of the Chinese. It is as different from Chinese filigree as the Chinese is distinct from the Neapolitan silver work. The potters of Cholula were then renowned for making vases in a form resembling the classical Greek urn, but decorated with designs in that thick, vivid, unmixed paint they invented and used so perfectly.

The painters of Texcoco, the mat makers of Cuauhtitlán, the stone cutters from Tenajocan, all brought their wares to the markets of the throne city of the Aztecs. The florists of Xochimilco fashioned flowers into decorative shapes with a long patience of execution which is still the most remarkable thing about the flower arrangement of the Mexican.

Plume work, a special craft developed by these people to the dignity of a fine art, was then in its fullest beauty. Entire mantles were contrived of feathers woven in color compositions and patterns intricate as tapestry. On their simple hand looms they wove exquisite cloth in cotton and a finely spun fibre made from the maguey or henequen plant. Garments and curtains were made of this material, as well as their breastplates, tightly woven and quilted, a stout and durable armor against their own weapons, but not, as Prescott reminds us, proof against the musketry of the Spaniards.

Temples and houses were ablaze with light and color, curtained with woven feathers and dyed cloth, their temples adorned with carved panels and the images of their gods. Even while they praised the beauty of the new country and its social structure, the fanaticism that accompanied the spirit of conquest conspired in the minds of the Spaniards, and prompted them to blot out invaluable records and monuments. They were not interested in the subtleties of research among peoples whom they considered merely as advanced savages, inhabiting a rich and desirable territory.

Their purpose was to exterminate the rebellious, establish the church and the power of Spain, and to amass wealth for the Spanish crown. Art was left to grow or perish of itself.

Silently, ceaselessly, the Mexican spirit renewed and expressed itself in the making of beauty. It ran like a dark flood of dreams into all channels of Colonial life. It stained every idea, every physical manifestation of the slowly changing Mexican race.

The churches were the first and most important imported expressions of art in New Spain. They were designed, in the main, by Italian and French architects, built and decorated by native artists. Whereupon strangely they are Mexican; because an Aztec ground the colors and executed the designs, and carved the wood and the stone, and made the tiles for the domed roofs. His inalienable beauty-wisdom had the final triumph.

Writers of that period are accustomed to declare that civilization progressed in Mexico more rapidly within the first eighty years of the Spanish occupation than in any other country of North America or Europe during the same period.

It is true that they brought their crafts, taught them to the natives, utilized and commercialized them with modern practical thoroughness. A book was printed for the first time in Mexico City in 1536. The printer was Juan Paoli from Brescia, Italy. He was brought here to publish ecclesiastical works, and his press flourished. The first University in America was founded by the Jesuits in Mexico City in the year 1533, a building now used as a Preparatory School to the National University.

Weaving and ceramics were developed rapidly. In Puebla and Oaxaca splendid silks and wools were woven from raw materials got from the markets of Asia, and exported in great quantities. Wool was introduced in Mexico by the Spaniards, and took the place of the fine hair of rabbits, and plumage which the Aztecs had hitherto used for weaving warm garments.

An immediate and perfect use was found by the native for the more substantial wool of the sheep. He wove serapes and rugs in orderly, geometric patterns after the old style, that gave to them a classical permanence of value. The first ones were sober and dark, but gradually they grew into brilliance, with designs of birds and flowers and stylized figures of animals.

They developed a genius for leatherwork, especially in saddle making, a craft essentially Spanish, since the Mexicans had no horses previous to the Conquest. Under their hands, the saddle and all appurtenances of horsemanship became elaborated beyond anything known in Spain, and today the Mexican saddle is a marvel of costly workmanship in tooled leather and chased silver.

The characteristic Mexican faculty to imitation of design and method, combined with an entirely alien feeling for color and execution brought about a subtle shifting of surface expression. His ability to adapt and use strange forms, under curious conditions, was the foundation for his new art, destined to become racial and genuinely expressive.

The primary use of his imitative faculty was commercial. The native, out of his soul's necessity, made his wares first things of beauty. But he must also use them, and sell them. They must be beautiful and useful objects, not costly, for the use of an impoverished people. In a very limited way, they worked in bronze, silver, gold and stone, but mostly they wrought in clay and wood. They transposed and recreated everything that came to their notice, from whatever source and in whatever material it might appear.

Out of the influences that surrounded them they selected those things most in accord with their own ideals of beauty, those designs not too violently opposed to their own conception of form, in effect those patterns that resembled their own previously accepted motifs. For three centuries the Mexican was influenced by art expressions from Spain, through Spain from the Moors, from the Orient; from Japan, Persia, the Philippines, above all, China.

The results are happily still apparent in designs wherein are commingled, in a strange harmony, pomegranates, lacy leaves from Spain, peacocks from Persia and mandarins from China, traced on jicaras, bowls and pots. In the Puebla pottery of that period, and on the painted and lacquered chests, knights on horseback, ladies in enormous skirts, birds as large as the trees they perch in, strange animals from the weird other-worlds of the Oriental imagination, foregather amiably with an effect of loveliness.

That sense of the grotesque which we have noticed took hold of these foreign emblems. In the religious sculpture executed by the first Christianized Mexicans, distorted Aztec Christs bleed from wounds, not the legendary sacred five, but from as many as a human form can support and still be recognizable. In Manú, Yucatán, there exists an outdoor shrine, a

Candle Sticks and Plate—Talavera Ware—Puebla. *Outline of Mexican Popular Arts and Crafts*, p. 20.

Decorated Wooden Box—Olinalá, Guerrero. *Outline of Mexican Popular Arts and Crafts*, p. 21.

cross roughly hewn from stone, and the hanging figure is wholly Aztec, resembling images found in the older ruins.

The grotesqueries began changing in form, but they were still distinct, still quite other in feeling than the demons and gargoyles of Europe, far removed from the squat, sly humor of the Chinese figures.

Those sixteenth century merchant crafts plying between China and Mexico brought not only merchandise, but ideas. Lacquer, black and red, and blue porcelain jars were left here by the sailors, and immediately the Mexican began making boxes lacquered in all colors, encrusted, or painted in flat designs over the smooth foundation.

In Puebla, then a newly founded city, the making of a certain kind of pottery became the chief industry. The first Potter's Guild in New Spain was chartered there: an organization of pure Indian and Spanish craftsmen, with a strict clause declaring that no negro or person of mixed blood could be a member. Puebla Talavera ware was during the sixteenth and seventeenth centuries a synonym for excellent pottery.

The story of Puebla pottery has happily been written, and serves as an example of the methods used by the Spaniards in introducing their crafts and arts to the Mexican. Puebla de los Angeles was founded about the year 1532, and the first account of the new industry centered there was given by Fray Gerónimo de Mendieta in his "Historia Ecclesiastica Indiana." I quote from the translation given in "Maiolica of Mexico" by Edwin Atlee Barber:

"After they (the Mexicans) became Christians and saw our images from Flanders and Italy, there is no altar ornament or image, however beautiful it may be, that they will not reproduce and imitate. There were artisans in pottery and vessels for eating and drinking purposes, and these were very well made although the workmen did not know how to glaze them. But they soon learned from the first craftsman who came over from Spain in spite of all he could do to guard and hide the secret from them. And finally this may be understood as a general rule, that nearly all the curious and beautiful works of every class of trades and arts are now (1596) being carried forward in the Indies (at least in New Spain or Mexico) are being done and finished by the Indians."

Who this ungenerous craftsman was no one seems to remember. But sometime within the first half century of the new regime, it is certain that a small group of friars from a Dominican monastery in Talavera de los Reyes (Spain) came out to join their brethren in Puebla and instructed the natives in the making of the famous Talavera ware. This pottery had its

Decorated Chairs—City of Aguascalientes. *Outline of Mexican Popular Arts and Crafts*, p. 24.

Equipales (Leather, Wood and Bamboo)—Jamay, Jalisco. *Outline of Mexican Popular Arts and Crafts*, p. 25.

first inspiration from Persia through the Moors, and later from China: transplanted to Mexico, it followed the same line of development until the end of the seventeenth century, when the Italian influence crept in, and changed small details of design and color.

The Mexicans absorbed everything, and grew slowly away from their teachers. The transition in this particular instance was slow. Almost two hundred years elapsed before the Puebla ware became a completely Mexican thing. Gradually, the flowers and foliage became bolder, the designs were taken from native plants; the blue coloring became heavier, the patterns were raised in high relief, and the tattooed effect now so familiar came into popularity. The shapes reverted slightly to the primitive, and from simple blue and white the native potters used their own varied and exuberant schemes of color. A Puebla bowl now often rivals a batea (wooden painted tray) from Tehuantepec for gayety and vividness.

The history of Puebla tiles is not so well known, but they probably date from about 1550. They were called Azulejos, from a word meaning blue, and were at first literally blue tiles. They changed in character rapidly, and were for two hundred years a most characteristic form of decoration for houses and chapels, fountains and patio pavements. In many old houses there are large panels relating legends in the manner of European tapestry, picturing episodes in the lives of saints and warriors, or used simply as decorative motifs filled with birds and animals and figures imitating the Aztec designs.

Until the beginning of the nineteenth century these tiles were used lavishly all over Mexico. The most famous examples of tile work are the Casa de los Azulejos in Mexico City, the Holy Well in the Chapel at Guadalupe, the Tepozotlán Convent in the State of Mexico, and several churches in Guanajuato, especially the exquisite small church called La Compañia, as well as the Church of San Francisco de Acatepec near Puebla.

The imported forms of architecture became, in the hands of the Mexicans, a separate creation. The early churches of Mexico are full of this Aztec strength and heaviness. Even roses and Cupids and emasculated saints become virile and significant—they are not the roses and saints and Cupids of Spain. Later, the Mexican-born Spaniards who designed in all the arts, guided by some vague tradition of classical proportion, produced merely another Barroco style, coincidental with a similar decadence in the old country. But whereas in Europe two white and civilized forms merged and decayed, in Mexico the fusion was Spanish and Indian: and Mexican Barroco, "the Churrigueresco," amazingly genuine and alive, is the curious result.

Bead Work Child's Dress—Puebla. *Outline of Mexican Popular Arts and Crafts*, p. 26.

The only vivid and quick artistic impulse of this country grew in the soul of the native. The Spanish artist who maintained the foreign traditions painted merely after the style of his own country, imitating without adapting, lacking inspiration of his own, growing each generation farther away from his sources, until at the close of the eighteenth century the so-called aristocratic art was a puerile childish copy of the European seventeenth century manner.

Aside from this academic school, however, a national spirit was developing among the Mexican-born Spaniards, and a tremendously increasing class of Spanish-Indios who were genuinely Mexican in feeling. During the later Colonial times, they called themselves Mexicans and followed

Thread Lace—San Luis Potosí. *Outline of Mexican Popular Arts and Crafts*, p. 27.

native customs as a patriotic duty. This period was fruitful in the production of the native crafts. Everybody made use of the rugs and bateas and serapes, the painted boxes and furniture, the saddles and potteries. They adopted a highly individualized native costume entirely Spanish in design, called the Charro. It was usually made of finely dressed leather, embroidered in silver and colors. The hats and saddles designed to complete this horseman's equipment were splendid and very costly.

The dresses for the women, especially the country costumes, were of gaily dyed silks weighted with bead embroideries and native lace. The most beautiful of these dresses originated in Puebla and was called the China Poblana. It has latterly passed into disuse, but is still seen during fiestas and in the Mexican theatre. As early as 1840 Madame Calderon de la Barca noticed that it was no longer used by ladies of the better society—a pity, for it is most graciously feminine and becoming.

After the Independence of Mexico from Spain was established, the national psychology shifted, and it became once more the fashion to imitate Europe. All architecture and aristocratic art since 1825 degenerated into the European manner, and that manner mostly second rate French. The epoch of Maximilian completed the havoc, with wholesale importations of French furnishings and styles at the lowest period of taste known since the decadence of Greece. Mexican art disappeared from popularity, a thing admired only by students and collectors, and used only by the Indio.

During these changes, political and social, the native has remained racially and spiritually static. In common with all peasantry, he derived his ideas from the fine arts—not only the imported and foreign arts, but from his own magnificent traditions, filtered them through his own understanding, translated them into his common speech: the result is a thing of superb beauty and strength. He grew each generation a step further away from the object he had imitated—like the Mexican-born Spaniard who copied the methods of Spain—but with this difference, that the native added always more and more of his own feeling and psychic reaction, until at once the thing was his own, an interpretation of beauty, national, personal—even more, absolutely individual.

For he works after his own fashion, and creates each smallest object as a unique thing, and does nothing twice alike. Each object has its own incorruptible character, even to the pattern on the jug in which he draws his water, the serape which serves him both as cloak and bed.

Part III: The Present

There is virtually no bibliography of Mexican modern art. The student will have difficulty in finding definite essays, either on the history or the meaning of this vivid and natural expression of a race. From time to time individual writers have included a casual chapter on general culture in their political and psychological studies of Mexico; and the special departments of ceramics and architecture have been dealt with attentively by authorities in these subjects, in a limited number of handbooks that never reach general circulation.

Unfortunately, those few artists who have attempted either definition or criticism of the wide field of Mexican art have remained within the enclosure of an academic tradition. This is in a special manner true of the Mexican writers and painters of the past century, whose ideals and technique were formed by the Spanish or Italian, or worst of all, the French schools.

This is the rigid attitude of those who have written in English, at all events: They maintain, almost to a man, that Mexican art began well under

Baskets and Coin Purses, Palm Leaf and Hemp—Oaxaca. *Outline of Mexican Popular Arts and Crafts*, p. 30.

Lacquered Wooden Tray—Patzcuaro, Michoacán. *Outline of Mexican Popular Arts and Crafts*, p. 31.

the foreign influences, but that it is now degenerated into a mere meaningless peasant art.

They seem inexplicably to have missed the point. A peasant art: this is precisely what it is, what it should be. The alien, aristocratic influence was a catastrophe that threatened the vitals of the Mexican race, and diverted its natural expression to strange, superficial methods over a long period. Yet, once released, and only a little maimed, it settled back to its calm level, and persisted after its own way.

It is not possible successfully to comprehend Mexican art from any other angle. Seen thus, harmoniously adjusted to its native background and its history, we discover it to be an invaluable, eloquent thing. There is in it the earthy aroma of a frankly peasant effluvium. It is filled with a rude and healthful vigor, renewing itself from its own sources. Above all, there is no self-consciousness, no sophisticated striving after simplicity. The artists are one with a people simple as nature is simple: that is to say, direct and savage, beautiful and terrible, full of harshness and love, divinely gentle, appallingly honest.

No folk art is ever wholly satisfactory to those who love smooth surfaces and artificial symmetry. They cannot approach a living thing that grows as a tree grows, thrusting up from its roots and saps, knots and fruits and tormented branches, without an uneasy feeling that it should be refined a little for art's sake.

Yet the fineness is there, not only in feeling, but in countless small delicate objects: in woven baskets fit to nest an ant, in lacquered gourds smooth as enamel, in necklaces of filigree gold. Countess Evelyn Martinengo Cesaresco, in her essays in "The Study of Folk Songs," understood this perfectly when she wrote: ". . . no touch is so light and sure as that of the artificer untaught in our own sense—the man or woman who produces the intricate filigree, the highly wrought silver, the wood carving, the embroidery, the lace, the knitted wool rivaling the spider's web, the shawl with whose weft and woof a human life is interwoven."

From this viewpoint, then, we must consider the Mexican arts and crafts as they are, having outworn or assimilated their foreign influences. If they seem a trifle endangered by modern contacts, however remote these may be, let us keep in mind that they have always been, not only a record of the racial unfoldment, but a personal diary, if you will, of the craftsman himself.

This accounts for the objective precision of that pictured account the Mexican left to us, of the first Spaniards: there they are, seen by implacably honest eyes, those helmeted conquerors on horseback, those wide skirted,

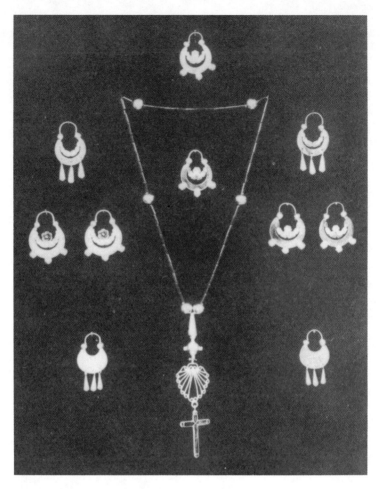

Silver Necklace and Ear Rings—Michoacán. *Outline of Mexican Popular Arts and Crafts*, p. 32.

stiff waisted ladies with monstrous coiffures, those imported dogs and incredible household furnishings. Painted chests and wooden trays of that period silently point to the ugliness of our kind of civilization as beheld by the civilized of another race and ethical code.

Today it is the same. I saw a classically formed pot from Tonalá, fresh from the potter's kiln, a masterpiece of design and glaze. One side was covered with figures done in the old style—ancient Mexican hunters drawing their bows against fantastic animals, all leaping through forests such as one is accustomed to see only in dreams.

Decorated Clay Pieces—Tonalá, Jalisco. *Outline of Mexican Popular Arts and Crafts*, p. 34.

The reverse side was even more interesting, for it bore the detailed drawing of an automobile, of outmoded fashion, brimming with men wearing foreign hats, hastening down the streets of an Oaxaca village—the potter's own village, no doubt, and this a first impression of the only automobile he had ever seen. Viewed through his amazed eyes, it is more mad and strange than all his warriors and animals and forests.

No doubt that most of us would think it in lamentable taste. It warns us, too, that if the artist were removed from his fructifying contact with his mother earth, condemned daily to touch instead the mechanics and artifices of modern progress, he might succumb, as do the aristocratic arts, each in turn, to the overwhelming forces of a world turned dizzyingly by a machine. But where the civilized arts, so-called, many root themselves in another imported and cultivated soil, where the individual artist may triumph by the strength of his unique genius, the peasant workman may have none of these resources. In his own earth—his native tradition, are his strength and his happiness.

The Mexican has a name for his home place. He calls it his "earth." (Mi Tierra.) He means literally the very spot where he was born, and where his mother nursed him, is his own. There he belongs, and there he will

Decorated Clay Plate—Tonalá, Jalisco. *Outline of Mexican Popular Arts and Crafts*, p. 35.

return inevitably, no matter how far he goes away, nor how long he must stay in foreign places. His life is bound to this beloved earth: gray-brown, fertile, spread unevenly as a tired man asleep, obscure and humble and filled with richness, compounded of all the stains and tints of fruits and flowers and iridescent stones.

In this village where he was born, the Mexican sits with his family and his neighbors, making household wares for himself, and for the nearby markets. Today, they make pottery and serapes in Guadalajara, in Oaxaca and in Texcoco; lacquered gourds and painted trays in Olinalá and Uruapan, chairs and tables in several parts of the states of Jalisco and Michoacán, saddles and charros and rebosos in Puebla and Guanajuato and Zacatecas.

Each community has its own particular craft, and not even the smallest painted box or clay figure but bears plainly the stamp of the place where it was made, by some unmistakable character of decoration or form, in color or material.

Grey Clay—Asompa, Oaxaca. *Outline of Mexican Popular Arts and Crafts*, p. 36.

Jars and Cups—Texcoco. *Outline of Mexican Popular Arts and Crafts*, p. 37.

We have seen that the early Mexican art was formed and ruled by the idea of religion. Later it overflowed into profane life as well, and became a personal, intensely human thing. But the forms had solidified, and during the later years of the Aztec dynasty, design assumed almost the rigidity of hieroglyphic writing, dogmatic and inelastic as the final stage of Egyptian art.

The inflood of foreign elements during four centuries, disastrous as it was in many ways, possessed one merit: it diffused and softened this dogmatic quality, and restored Mexican design to its early freedom and pliancy. Today, those ancient sacred and mystic shapes survive, but as decoration merely. They have lost their symbolism, and have become pure design. But they have not the haphazard, meaningless air of patterns invented merely for the sake of their cleverness; the dignity of their great origin saves them from superficial smartness. For example, the ritual cornflower is woven again and again into the reed fibre baskets and mats, in the traditional colors, blue and green; but the weaver cannot tell you why he does it in that certain way, or why, indeed, he uses the design at all.

Weaving and ceramics, wood carving and embroidery, these natural crafts of the peasant, are now the most perfectly developed and eloquent of the Mexican arts. There are many variations of method and style, depending on the climate, the characteristic woods or clays of the regions, the conditions of life of the workers; while the ultimate decisive factors are the special social customs and needs of each tribe.

Changing levels of merit divide the work of the individual artists, certainly, but it is not an overstatement to say that every village in the states of Jalisco, Oaxaca, and Puebla has its guild of craftsmen devoted to some special art, and within this circle there will be smaller guilds composed of entire families who have the secret of extraordinary skill in some chosen craft.

But all of them share ideas, intuitions and human habits; they understand each other. There is no groping for motives, no divided faith: they love their past with that uncritical, unquestioning devotion which is beyond logic and above reason.

Order and precision they know by heart. Instinctive obedience to the changeless laws of nature, straight fidelity to their own inner sense of fitness mark all they do. Without analysis they can perceive and design all the infinite harmony that is in a flower, a flying bird. Looms and wheels and edged tools are the same, their uses unchanged. By these means they have achieved innocently, without premeditation, the perfect speech of their hearts.

Of late, the Mexican students, writers, painters, the vivid group which makes up the National University life, has discovered anew the principles of design in this neglected native art. They have realized that in those undeciphered characters on temple walls is buried the history of the lost races of Mexico. With admirable humility they have set themselves, unreservedly, to the task of re-discovery, free of pre-conceived theories, not committed to faith in the obvious. The submerged period which preceded this revival, when no one remembered the native artist, did not bring about a decadence, or failure of creative energy as would occur to any art or industry depending for its life on a changeable public taste. The Indio labored as before, with the inspirations and materials that were his, rejecting and disposing and adding where he chose, completing his destined task in quiet certainty that it was good, whether the world remembered him, or forgot.

The state of Oaxaca is the very source of traditional folk art in Mexico. It is true that the pottery of Jalisco is more complex and mobile. But with this single exception, all things made by the Zapotec and Mixtec peoples have a deeper, more personal value. It may be because they, themselves, have retained their languages and laws more perfectly than the others.

The atmosphere of the tiny villages in this state is not old world in the ordinary sense. It blows mysteriously from the very ancient world, a time immeasurably removed from us. It is caught and held, however precariously, in the spirits of a race which preserves its past realities, surging with warm life, a quiver of living nerves, flowing and changing of itself within its own limitations.

This will all pass in time: even now is passing, maybe. But there is no sign of it yet, and it will disappear utterly only with the race itself. The tiny pueblos have a look of relaxed and unresisting permanence. The inhabitants have invested their surroundings with their own deep and slow moving rhythm of life. The rows of flat-topped houses lean together securely, the silent streets, cobbled or floored with earth, are clean and wide. Their open markets are centers not only of commerce, but of social exchange. Their manner would be good manner anywhere, they walk splendidly: they are those who rest on a sense of friendly and eternal kinship with each other, with their native earth, and with their destiny.

The serape they wear is the classic garment of the Mexican Indio, once used in many ways, woven of cotton, of rabbit fur, draped as a mantle,

Glazed Clay Ware—Tonalá, Jalisco. *Outline of Mexican Popular Arts and Crafts*, p. 41.

cloak alike of the nobility and of the poor. Now it is a simple square of woven wool, depending for beauty on design and color rather than material. Each Oaxaca village has a guild of weavers, under the authority of a master weaver. The best workman is their most important citizen, and his disciples, after learning their craft, unless they can surpass him, usually remain as simple weavers in the group. They work slowly, and every serape is individual in design, woven from wool they card and spin and dye themselves.

These garments are woven music: songs and legendary figures and the dreams of the weaver go into them. A sombre brown or black serape will be suddenly joyous with tight little nosegays of green and red and yellow flowers, precisely the shape and tints of the bouquets sold in the flower markets. A serape of scarlet and black will bear an angular, stylized horse's head, in hues unknown to that animal. Figures of Aztec warriors taken from the ancient codices, bringing to mind the later figures of Egypt, and the mythical cepactli, after all merely a tiger with bared teeth, are among the favorite designs used by the Oaxaca weaver with endless variations.

One man, master weaver of a certain small Zapotec pueblo, makes a smaller, simpler serape, woven lightly of fine spun wool, almost as pliable as velvet, and very delicate in design. On a foundation of white or gray or brown he weaves narrow bands of color in the ends, scatters small geometrical designs loosely over the surface, with a double line of the same

pattern in the center. The wearer slips his head through the straight opening where the seam is left unjoined, and this delicate wreath encircles his
shoulders.

It is not fantastic. It is simple and touching, it belongs to the wearer as
he belongs to the land about him. He seems not merely in sympathy with
the trees and hedges of cactus and the gray road, he literally is one with
these.

The women make their chemises of cotton, embroidered in colored
beads, or smocked at neck and sleeve ends in heavy blue or scarlet threads.
The beaded chemises, meant to be worn on days of fiesta, swing loosely,
weighted with the strips of glittering tinted glass grains, a classical
rounded band at the shoulder releasing the soft brown arms and necks in
a line of tender beauty.

Second to the pottery of Guadalajara, the earthenware most prized by
the Mexican is the thick yellow pottery made in the Tonalá village. It is of
common baked clay (loza vidriada), very gay in coloring and varied in
shapes. On a foundation of deep cream the stains are splashed on with an
effect of casualness, in orange, in vivid blue, and green with occasional
touches of brown. At first glance it appears to have been blurred, or "blot-
ted" on, as their phrase has it, but immediately the eye perceives the outlines of birds and butterflies and flowers, very fantastic and charming.

The glaze of this ware is thick and clear, but brittle. It flakes off easily,
carrying the pattern with it. But for all its evanescent character, it is most
appealing: the pots and bowls and platters spread in small booths in the
sunshine resemble a Mexican garden in full bloom.

There are other kinds of ware in the northern part of the state. Simple
vessels of white clay are molded without the wheel, and left unadorned.
The shapes are primitive, the jugs with tiny ears, the flat, round water jug
with a thin spout and a round handle at the top, and the cups tall as vases,
with straight edges. Black clay, engraved and glazed in the natural color, is
also made here, and is very attractive. One village specializes in small toys
of black clay, money banks for children, and whistles in the shapes of animals. The grotesque sense is perfect in these, the distorted little figures
possessing a sardonic quality of humor. But it is a grotesquerie still unin-
fluenced by the Oriental or the Western idea of comedy.

This portion of Oaxaca is peopled largely by the Zapotecas, and their
objective temper is expressed by the things they make: knives and swords
of a special kind of finely tempered steel come from here. The handles are
of wood or bone sharply carved, and engraved inscriptions, usually of a
sinister or slightly Rabelaisian humor, run thinly along the nervous, pli-

Clay Incense Burners—City of Puebla. *Outline of Mexican Popular Arts and Crafts*, p. 43.

able blades. "Do not unsheathe me without reason, nor fail to draw me through fear," says one. "I am the Peace," announces another. And still another identifies itself thus: "I am not the friend of cowards, nor the servant of the timid."

Here also we find a certain type of charro, the national riding costume of the ranchero, in which the Spanish love of magnificence is projected in terms of silver and gold embroidery, and hand tooled leather. The wide brimmed hats of heavy felt are weighted with borders of flowers and leaves, and great cords of metal thread knotted and hung with tassels depend from the inside of the crown. But the charro has its own place in the Mexican arts. Our present interest is with the pottery and weaving.

Guadalajara pottery has an older and more truly national history than the better known Puebla ware. But it has come into esteem only of late years, being rather overshadowed by the more obvious qualities of the imported Talavera style of ceramics. The Talavera has its own place, and a definite value, but it is considered even today as a modern importation by the makers of the older kinds of ware.

All the ancient city of Guadalajara is, in effect, a huge pottery. The state of Jalisco (of which Guadalajara is the capital) is indeed second only to Oaxaca in its devotion to the folk arts. Many smaller villages near the capital are given to this work, Tonalá being the leader. The most perfect pottery in Mexico is made by the guild in this tiny community. The inhabitants have been potters from the beginning of their history. When the Spaniards found them, Tonalá was the capital of a kingdom of the same name, and its potteries were famous. There are now only about five hundred people in the town, whose sole industry is the making of earthenware.

In idyllic peace and simplicity the villagers sit before their door steps or under the trees, or in their tiny clean houses with their open doors, decorating jars and jugs. They make, even more beautifully than the potters of Guadalajara, who invented the style, those splendid water jars and pots covered with fine tracery of design in white and delicate shades on a pearl gray ground.

They have created a type of ware even more interesting, though less subtle: a hard baked clay covered over with designs in white and brown. They superimpose a fine pattern of thick white paint on the dark copper red surface, and glaze it as hard as glass. It is extraordinary in effect, and they say, very difficult to make. Though it is the custom for the artist to sign his work, this type of pot is a veritable scroll of records. Infallibly it is not only signed, but dated, with the name of the village, and it is further dedicated to some individual, or christened with a name. It has, more than any other pottery of the Mexican, the faults, the imperfections, the unevenness of the handiwork of a human being who is "untaught in our own sense"—but it has this priceless value of the human sentiment, a loved thing created for its own sake. One comes to love better than any other thing in the native arts these brown humble bits of clay, done so exquisitely, so gently, so irregularly.

The potters of the city of Guadalajara have many ways of making beautiful things, but two types of their ware are of superior quality. They are fortunate in the quality of their clay: it is smooth, resilient and easy to stain. The old-fashioned potter puts a thin clear glaze over the design, which was very fragile. They cover the entire surface with nets of brush work too intricate to accept at a glance. The eye must follow patiently, unravelling that precise, unhurried mesh that never breaks nor interrupts itself. There are in them the full bodied gold of pumpkins, the glossy green of foliage, the tints of mangoes, of poppies, of bougainvillea blooms, woven together with slender markings of gray.

The newer style is more brusque, not so precious, the big flaring leaves are applied with broad stroke in one color, usually, on a ground of clay-red, ochre, sage green, or dull black with gray all unglazed, slightly rough to the touch. Yet this very slight, almost imperceptible, relief offers a fine depth of perspective.

The painter manages to convey, in this method, without shading or foreshortening, a foreground, a middle distance, a far distance. There are strange rhythms of loveliness in them: the darkness of forests, the curve of boughs laden with uncanny fruits, the sophistication of pointed fern fronds minutely accented as filagree; or brilliant with dyes and stains in color associations strange to us, full of gayety, balanced with shadow. They offer the paradox of gorgeousness balanced by restraint, an exuberant yet disciplined spirit, in which elements apparently unrelated are reduced to a simple and profound harmony.

After the Oaxaca and Guadalajara ware, the Puebla Talavera seems always a trifle naïve, rather lacking in imagination. But it has its perennial charm of blue-and-white, the Chinese inspiration—filtered through from Spain, absorbing the sturdiness and solidity of Holland blue-and-white on the way. We have seen that the Puebla Mexican did not long confine himself to the original colors. Today, all colors go into the tea pots and plates and flower vases of the thick, hard glazed ware. It is the most utilitarian of all the Mexican pottery, being near akin to a coarse and porous porcelain, or stone china.

Mexican artists have recently discovered that the Puebla ware lends itself to the use of their designs, and many of them have plates and jars for their collections made in the Puebla potteries, done in the old manner, and often in precise reproduction of the early examples. The tile work is very popular, and the individual with a taste for design may draw his own patterns for the tiles to be used in his house, in mantels, for fountains, or wall panels.

Many of the older tiled churches have fallen into decay, and are being restored with tiles that are such exact copies of the original, it is difficult to distinguish the old from the new. When the famous Casa de los Azulejos (House of Tiles, in Avenue Francisco I. Madero, Mexico City) was restored a few years since, it was necessary to add an entire new wall where the new street of Cinco de Mayo was cut through; the tiles were made in Puebla, in the same pottery and by the same methods as the original ones made in the seventeenth century, and the reproductions are so perfect only the connoisseur can detect the difference. Close examination shows that the old glaze was more clear and even, the blue is deeper, the clay is softer. The ware has deteriorated in quality by these shades of decline.

The two large tibores, great jars standing six feet or more in height, brought from Puebla for this present exhibition, are unusually splendid examples of the Talavera ware at its present best. One is developed in the blue and white, an ordered confusion of fleet winged birds and swift footed animals. The glaze is exceptionally fine. The other is in colors, a happy blending of yellow and green, of fruits and leaves. They are master-pieces of the Puebla method, prophetic of a renewed interest in making this ware the thing of beauty it once was.

There are many other kinds of earthenware in Mexico. Every region produces its special type of clay household vessels, made of the clay about the village doorways, and each has the merits of honesty and simplicity. It is not always artistic, judged even by the most liberal standard, but it has the profound appeal of ardent human expression.

In Cuernavaca, one of the most beautiful of the smaller cities, they make good use of their light red clay, almost a pale coral color, in molding bottles and jars without painted surfaces, but inlaid nicely with bits of half precious stones.

From Metepec near Mexico and Quiroga, a village of Michoacán, comes a very distinctive and curious sort of pottery. It is glazed in glossy black, decorated with vivid flowers, streaked with silver or gilt paint. It is gay and frivolous in effect, of no special importance except for its nonchalant prettiness. Set among a group of sedate Guadalajara bottles, or the sober plain gray and black pots from Teotihuacán or Texcoco, a Quiroga pitcher will decidedly convey the effect of a bright-skirted dancer in a company of Quaker ladies.

The "loza" from Texcoco is quite primitive, the very rudiments of earthenware, unpainted, often of a noble beauty of form. The specialty of the Texcocan is weaving, and he makes a serape that appeals to a discreet taste. Blue is his color, and on this ground he weaves his simple designs in black, white, or gray. The rugs are usually large and very heavy. The wool is more coarsely spun, which makes the Texcoco serape valuable for use as floor rugs. They are not so original or full of splendid associations as the serapes of Oaxaca, nor are they proof against rain and made for horsemen to wear in bitter weather, as are many of those woven in Guadalajara. But they have their soft enduring charm, a civilized restraint in tone, that makes them exceedingly livable.

After all, it is useless to attempt a rigid classification of the arts of Mexico, or to draw definitive boundaries beyond those here set down. For bits of loveliness spring up here and there, unexpectedly, like the sudden clumps of sweet blooming small flowers along a Mexican lane. For example, take those adorable little wax figures, dressed in the national costumes, made of real fabric stiffened with wax, that you see in the shops, or in the small booths called the "puestos" set along the borders of city parks at Easter and Christmas and other feast days . . . they are made in the suburbs of Mexico City, and so far as I was able to discover, they are not made anywhere else. Their variety is endless: patient little mothers carrying their babies on their backs, cradled in their rebosos: men bending under panniers of fruit: children dancing, men strumming guitars, girls and men mounted on splendid rearing horses, wearing the China Poblana, and the Charro. They are so delicately tinted, so fresh and lifelike, they seem veritable living people, seen through the reverse lens of a field glass.

The skirts of la China Poblana fly discreetly, as she curbs her mettlesome horse, glimpsing lace petticoats whose ruffles are fixed in billowing flight, real thread lace, waxed to maintain those spontaneous looking folds. Her knee curves easily over the horn of the saddle, her smiling face is always turned toward the caballero who rides beside her, gorgeous in his riding dress of tooled and embroidered buckskin.

From a village called Santa Cruz de los Monos (literally, Holy Cross of the Monkeys) in the state of Jalisco, comes another kind of small image, but made of clay and painted, of these types beloved in the popular imagination. There are mounted ladies and gentlemen, young country lads and girls dancing the Jarabe, a favorite folk dance seen at its best and most joyous in this part of the country. They also make fruits of painted clay, while the waxen fruits, perfect even to the bruised spots, the broken twig, are made only in Mexico City. Madame Calderon de la Barca, wife of the Spanish minister to Mexico in 1840, exclaimed with delight over the artfulness of these fruits, declaring herself completely deceived by their realism. They are deceptively luscious indeed.

This aspiration after a perfect realism, a complete statement of the thing they see, is the essence of their arts, the key to the racial temperament. I am reminded of a certain man, in the tiny pueblo of San Esteban Titzatlán, who carves walking sticks.

This man sits every day before his house, on the hard naked earth, behind his enclosure of organa cactus, and makes every sort of walking stick from the heavy cudgel of defense to the airy wand a man might add to his costume as pure decoration.

He works with a small sharpened knife on saplings of various native woods, dried and polished to the color of ivory. He carves designs in high relief on these wands, sometimes almost the entire length of them, after the fashion of the things he knows: lizards and beetles and cacti, eagles and dogs and leaves and men wearing charros. Each stick is a chapter in his life's experience, a record of what he has seen and felt. Sometimes he is more than a month in carving a single stick. When he finishes it, he sets it aside and begins another. Carving sticks, beautifully, painstakingly, endlessly, is his vocation and his pastime. He sells them occasionally, at prices which elevate them to the dignity of gifts. He works with a preoccupation entirely untainted by any knowledge of popular taste, and utterly refuses to teach any one else the technique of his carving. This is characteristic of the Mexican peasant artist. He guards jealously his working formulas.

Master potters have been known to create certain designs, to perfect an excellent glaze, and to teach them only to a carefully selected group of disciples, or more often, not to teach them at all. Several years ago a painter of boxes in Michoacán who had discovered a superb method of fixing his colors, died without revealing his secret, and left only a few examples of his work.

In Oaxaca there is a woman who makes a curious little incense burner, not particularly beautiful but intensely individual, rare in shape and violent in coloring. She instructs her daughters as they grow up in the method of making these burners, but the art remains strictly in her family, and no one else would even presume to inquire into her technique, nor to imitate her work.

The city of Aguascalientes contributes a wide assortment of crafts, the natives there being more versatile, if less classical in spirit, than in any other region.

Rather sophisticated tastes demand, in Aguascalientes, chairs made by hand, all painted in green and yellow and blue, or else lacquered in black and decorated with gilded flowers. The seats are made of woven rushes, or of maguey cords, woven stoutly in red, green, blue or white. Tiny chairs for children will be charmingly adorned with birds and animals, small flower wreaths, naïve and old fashioned as fairy book pictures.

Wall cupboards with shelves for books and pottery are also made in this style, quite often being painted in a sulphur yellow, the back panel carved at the top not infrequently with birds amiably touching beaks, a favorite device in wood carving with the Guanajuato cabinet maker.

A wool garment called the tilma is much worn here. It is a smaller and lighter weight serape, of wool of fine spun henequen fibre. They are cheerful in hue, fit for the bright soft weather of this region. On such a tilma was imprinted the miraculous image of the Virgin of Guadalupe, now the

Embroidered Waist Band—Tehuantepec. *Outline of Mexican Popular Arts and Crafts*, p. 49.

patroness of Mexico, which may be seen at her shrine at Villa de Guadalupe near Mexico City.

There is, in all, a progressive modern air about the arts of Aguascalientes, mingled with a native quaintness; their most dignified art is lace making. Needle lace, as it is called, and the drawn linen lace, were derived from

Italy in the seventeenth century. The women work marvels with their fine needles and linen thread on their smoothly woven linen, making table cloths and napkins, curtains and old-fashioned counterpanes, handkerchiefs, and lingerie for brides. The work has that remote and unworldly beauty of convent needle craft, and serves much the same uses. No Mexican bride, at least in the country, would forego a chest of this linen and lace for her new household.

Italy contributed also the small square shawl of embroidered silk in white or pale colors, adorned in the corners with thread lace. They are called chalinas, and are much worn by the young girls on haciendas. A few years ago they were worn also by the beautiful ladies of the cities, chiefly in Guadalajara, where the women are noted for their splendid hair. They wore these filmy mantles instead of hats, allowing them to slip lightly about the shoulders, thereby revealing the most carefully dressed heads in the Republic.

Aguascalientes has a rival guild of needle workers in the small town of Silao, near by. Here also they make those painted chairs and wall cupboards; and here they excel in the ancient art of mat and basket weaving from reeds and palms. The petate, the pliable mat used as a bed, or as curtains before doorways, even as wall partitions in the houses constructed of woven palm withes, is here at its glorified best. There are pure white ones, bleached like flax, with maybe only the national escutcheon, the eagle and cactus and serpent, in the center; or more thickly woven ones with diagonal stripes in many shades. Some of them rival a Quiroga pot in brilliancy, though this is more often found in the basketry. Whatever the shape, whether flat, made into halves that slip one over the other like a pocketbook, or round and handled like a flower jar, there is always in these baskets a shocking juxtaposition of color, raw and unrelieved. Often one sees in a single basket, red and rose and orange, with sulphur yellow and cobalt blue, without even the relief of a white line dividing them.

We have noted how this use of violent, unshaded pigment gives an effect of depth, of actual penetration, to the surfaces of pottery. In the painted boxes and chests from Michoacán, the lacquered gourds and bateas from Tehuantepec, whether encrusted or painted, this use is carried to the ultimate possibility. The result of this flat opaque unmixed color is to give an amazing clarity and sweetness of tone, where it is used with artistic discretion. On these chests and jicaras, also, the schemes of color are very ardent, but more ruled by the associations we are accustomed to accept: blue and clear red, orange and green, gray and black and rose, with bands of silver. They take on a delightful tone of mellowness with age. When new they are as irresponsibly brilliant as Russian embroideries.

In the Isthmus of Tehuantepec, these fragile seeming gourds are used daily for carrying fruit and vegetables, or water. The smaller ones serve as water dippers, and for chocolate. The chocolate will be beaten to a froth with a beautifully carved whip called a molinillo (little mill), sometimes inlaid with bits of jade or bone. The Tehuantepec woman wears, more often than not, a strange, flaring headdress of starched and pleated white lace, which rays out from her face like the coif of a sister of charity. But there is nothing nun-like about this enchanting dress of la Tehuana. She is given to all the vanities, from her perfectly arranged head to her embroidered short blouse with its short sleeves and low cut neck, to the rustling lace-trimmed and embroidered skirt, to her very feet, lightly bound in thin sandals or satin slippers with ribbon bow knots, embroidered on the straps.

Her jewelry is the airy gold and silver filagree, akin to that of China and Naples, but distinct from either, since it was an old art before either the Chinese or the Italians came to Mexico. The huge ear rings of the women, their necklaces, the splendid rosaries and crosses, the very auras of the saints are contrived of this delicate web-like gold. Their pins and combs, rings and bracelets are also of spun and filagree silver, set with jade and turquoise, or more rarely, with opals.

In Yucatán, the Mayas defeat their tropical heat with lightly spun fabrics, thin silks, pale colored, fine embroideries. Here, they import their cloths, and their embroidery is a comparatively recent imitation of the Chinese, which lessens the value of their contribution to Mexican arts. However, there is a certain charm to the curious satin shoes and thonged sandals of the women, with their sharply upcurved pointed toes and high heels. Their most unique and interesting work is done with henequen fibre weaving. They make hammocks, used instead of beds, of henequen (sisal) thread, in which they sleep suspended in air, cool as a spider in his web.

In the more temperate states, Jalisco, for example, we find serapes of moderate weight, furniture designed for comfortable living in a fairly equable climate, such as those cowhide easy-chairs, bound together with thongs of undressed cowhide or buckskin, known as "equipales." Stretched on stout wooden frames, the hide left in its natural color, they are much used in the country, and are meant to withstand hard usage.

The ceñidores, long narrow bands used as belts, woven in rigid figures in bright colors, are made in many districts, though they are used almost exclusively among the rural Indios. The reboso, that indispensable article of attire among Mexican women, is also made in every part of Mexico, though the finer ones come from two places only: Santa Maria, in the state of San Luis Potosí, and Tenancingo, state of Mexico.

The reboso is a long scarf, woven commonly in two colors, one the warp, the other the woof, so that it appears to be one shade except in the fringe, where the different colored threads will be woven alternately and knotted into an effect of square blocks of contrasting shade. For the poor, blue cotton is the favorite. The handsomest ones, made in Santa Maria, are of raw silk, in delicate tones of jade green, pale yellow, ashy violet, gray, and rose. The flat spun thread weaves into a very supple, sinuous length of silk, with a silvery shimmer, or overgleam, like the shine of a snake skin. Dr. Atl has touchingly described its use among the poor, in his monograph on "The Popular Arts of Mexico:" ". . . With the reboso the women of the village cover themselves. It does not only serve as a head covering, or when crossed over the breast, as a simple adornment, but it is also the provisional cradle of the poor children, the handkerchief with which the women dry their tears, the improvised basket in which the Indios carry their vegetables to the market, the cover of the infant who sleeps tranquilly beside the working mother. When it is twisted and placed on the feminine head it serves as a seat for the filled fruit basket which, skilfully balanced, is thus carried through the streets; or when extended, makes a shelter for the kettle of tamales in the angle of a street. . . ."

In its more luxurious aspect, it is used among the ladies of the haciendas, and is an important part of the riding costume, being folded about the hips, over the knees, adding its weight to the flying skirts of the rider. It was originally a Spanish garment, but its shape and uses have vastly changed. It is the familiar garment of many classes of women, even among the bourgeoisie, where it takes the form of softly fringed black silk or thin woolen nun's veiling.

El charro! He is the beau ideal of the romantic imagination in Mexico. He is the symbol of her old society, her truly Mexican old society, not the eternally foreign-souled Spanish grandee, but of the Spanish who were Mexican-born in their love of the country, who were genuinely native to the soil, to the struggles, to the dreams and aspirations of their country. Some of these had Indian blood, and in them the new patriotism burned with the ardor that quickens new nations, and is the clean animating force that welds a race indissolubly from the beginning.

The development of the charro, the national dress of Mexico today, is a little history of Spain in Mexico. The Spaniards brought horses, and with

Wax Figures—City of Mexico. *Outline of Mexican Popular Arts and Crafts*, p. 52.

them prodigious saddles, high pommelled, of leather and metal, with ponderous stirrups, leg guards of leather, and high chair-backs. This is the present shape of the Mexican saddle—La Silla, the chair of the horseman—often for the ranchero the only chair he knows day upon day, as he goes about his affairs on the cattle pastures and enormous cultivated areas of the haciendas.

From the Spaniard also he developed the dress itself, the short jacket, the tight trousers strapped under the boots, the wide sash fringed and knotted at the side. The great wide brimmed hats were designed for protection from the sun: it was the caballero's own manner of wearing them that made of them the most dashing and devil-may-care fashion of headgear ever devised by man.

Because of the necessity for country life in Mexico, the horse became the most important of all their domestic animals. Man must spend his life in the saddle in pursuit of either business or pleasure. The horse, the saddle, the accouterments of horsemanship became objects of care, of costly and expert attention. In this way it became a symbol of the national life and customs after the conquest. It is today worn with pride as the distinctive dress of the country, the mark of a special patriotic devotion. Members of old country families, and certain distinguished persons, make a point of appearing in the charro on all occasions of holiday and festal costume, notably in the paseo in the park of Chapultepec on Sunday morning, when the President, the members of the Cabinet, and Mexican society and officialdom in general drive slowly back and forth on the Grand Avenue, under the shadow of Chapultepec Castle.

In the country the charro is not a ceremonial dress, but the ordinary habit of the man on horseback. Here it appears in all its variations, from the humble suit of tough blue drill ornamented with black bone buttons, to the splendor of hand-dressed buckskin in chamois color embroidered in spun silver and scarlet.

The charro indeed is subject to all the caprices of taste of the individual in respect of material and color combinations: it is in the cut and the design and placing of decoration that do not change. They are made by Mexican leather workers and embroiderers in small towns, each one catering to the local taste. In Salamanca, state of Guanajuato, they band cream-colored buckskin with tooled leather flowers of golden brown; they make for this jacket a waistcoat of golden brown buckskin, with gold embroidery, and trousers to match the waistcoat. A hat of brown beaver or felt, very peaked in the crown, will be weighted with gold flowers and a long cord with gold thread tassels . . . gloves and boots, a whip of light tan leather, with gold or tooled leather head, a wide smooth leather belt with gold buckles, and a flowing gold-colored tie, will add the small final touches to a theatrically beautiful and impressive dress. In Salamanca also they have the habit of cutting strips of thin leather into complicated designs and stitching them on flat, to resemble braiding.

The town of Jerez, in the state of Zacatecas, has a famous guild of leather workers who make the finest possible quality of softly dressed buckskin; exquisite metal embroideries come from this place also. The finest hats come from Puebla or Guadalajara, being distinguished by their slightly tilted crown and deeply rolling brim. Aguascalientes contributes charros embroidered in thick brightly dyed thread, mingled with silver. In this region there is a taste for trousers and jacket of contrasting shades and materials. Charros of black cloth or leather, embroidered in silver or colors, are very much worn. Gauntlets have flaring wrists, fringed and stitched.

Like the manufacture of saddles and stirrups, this craft is somewhat modernized, since the demand is so wide and the buyers are drawn from every class and section of Mexico. But still the charro "shop" is apt to consist of one master workman and his apprentice, usually his son, and one or two employees.

Stirrups and saddles are made in several towns, but Amozoc, Puebla, Andeleon in Guanajuato is easily in the lead. Here they make great saddles

Clay Water Jar—Michoacán. *Outline of Mexican Popular Arts and Crafts*, p. 55.

of soft firm leather, delicately tooled as a lady's pocketbook. They embroider saddle flaps in shining threads of spun silver, and make saddle horns of carved wood or bone mounted in silver. There is no way of generalizing them in descriptive terms since every saddle is unique, with small details of decoration, the treatment of the leather, the pattern and method of tooling, the use of colors. They are finished with rings and stirrups of dark polished blue steel, encrusted with gold or silver flowers, gleaming like great jewels—a horseman's dream of stirrups!

The saddle flaps, the bridles, even splendid blankets of chamois colored buckskin or fine wool are bordered with banded designs of flowers in leather, are weighted with this lovely metal work and gay silk thread flowers.

Bridles of woven horse hair, hard as iron and pliable as wool, drip with prodigious tassels in red and blue and green. Less magnificent ones of maguey fibre are quite as durable and colorful. The designs are woven the full length of the reins, the head pieces are joined with buttons of bone, representing bulls' heads, or rosettes of metal or leather. To the final touch, it is all splendidly and perfectly made. Saddle cinches, lassoing gloves (strange mitten-like affairs, with fingers joined loosely to the body of the glove with light leather thongs for the sake of ease at the knuckles), lasso-ing ropes of maguey fibre, with tasselled noose ends: in everything there is a brilliant taste, a sense of beauty, a handsome abandon to their ideal of gallant living, that is deeply characteristic of the Mexican people.

One is loath to leave a subject on which there is so much left unsaid . . . but it was not my intention, indeed, it was not within my province, to write a complete analysis and history of so complex a subject as the Mexican Popular Arts.

My aim is to present to you, in its human aspects, this profound and touching expression of a very old race, surviving and persisting in its de-votion to ancient laws with a steadfastness that is anachronism in this fluc-tuating age. These pages will perhaps help to explain many things to those who will see, for the first time, examples of this art extending over a period of at least fifteen centuries. In doing this, the aim of this short study will have been fulfilled.

Finis

Two Ancient Mexican Pyramids— the Core of a City Unknown until a Few Years Ago

Christian Science Monitor (September 19, 1922): 7

Having toured the Christian temples of San Juan and neighboring villages of Teotihuacán for her 1921 "Notes," Porter returns a year later to the temples of a mysterious ancient civilization, the chief of which are the impressive pyramids of the Sun and the Moon. In contrast to the "Notes," this essay is depersonalized, giving a straightforward overview of the archaeological region and the many theories about its ancient inhabitants. Throughout the article, Porter is once more indebted to Manuel Gamio, whose work is described therein. The theory of the Chinese origin of the civilization was advanced by amateur archaeologist William Niven, whose own digs at Azcapotzalco Porter frequented; Niven served as the model for Givens in "María Concepción."

Two Ancient Mexican Pyramids—the Core of a City Unknown until a Few Years Ago

In Mexican mythology there is a lively account of how the gods met in council and decided that their newly-made world was perfect except for the lack of light, and therefore they must create a Sun and a Moon.

Two of them voluntarily offered themselves to the ritual by fire, and emerged immediately, first one, and then the other, as Sun and Moon, lighting the universe. Indeed, there was much more light than the gods had counted on. The new planets, stubbornly fixed in the heavens, blazed away together insupportably. So the remaining gods allowed themselves to be swept away by the Wind, in order that the planets might be moved, and persuaded to roll across the firmament at regular times, and allow the earth periods of rest in darkness.

This episode occurred, they say, at Teotihuacán, in the valley of Anahuac, now the valley of Mexico; and certainly there stand today, in this very spot, the two splendid temples built in honor of those two valorous deities who transformed themselves in order to give light to their creatures.

Compared with the other ruins of old Mexico, these are virtually unknown. The Maya temples were crumbling when the Spaniards found them, but they were never covered over with earth. The mystical city of Tula had fallen into the twilight of legend even before the Aztecs came to found the city of Tenochtitlan. Of late there is even tentative speculation that this Teotihuacán is identical with that lost city, said to have been built by the Toltecs.

But the word Toltec means literally "builder," and is the description of an art epoch, not the name of a race. . . . So the question remains archaeologically almost where it was before the discovery of this city of Teotihuacán, which is a Nahoa word signifying "The Place of the Gods." These Nahoas, it is now believed by many scholars, were the tribe that brought ancient Mexican civilization to the higher flower of its culture, thereafter to be gradually absorbed by the more aggressive and war-like Aztec.

Let it be understood that I cannot, after so short a period of study, advance the ideas of any certain group, or present theories of my own on this amazingly complicated and difficult subject. I wish merely to give a simple outline of later results of research, for the most part being carried on by Mexican historians and archaeologists. The younger scholars have brought about a renewed interest in the archaeology of their country, being animated by a spirit intensely nationalistic, which seeks to discover in the racial sources the answer to some of their latter day social and ethical problems.

The temples now uncovered and in process of restoration in San Juan Teotihuacán, commonly called the "Pyramides," are the most fascinating of all the Mexican ruins, not only in themselves but because they are the core of a city literally unknown until a few years ago, and totally unaccounted for in all Mexican legend and history. It stands now, partially uncovered and darkly splendid, dominating a wide deep fruitful valley, gracious as of old, wrapped within itself, keeping a curious secret to which we have not yet found the key.

It is a very short time since the task of excavating, restoring and preserving the records of this place has been undertaken seriously. Désiré Charnay, a visiting Frenchman in the year 1880, touched the city of San Juan Teotihuacán and discovered the temple now called "Subterráneos," a mere surface of paved floors and low walls, with another larger temple buried immediately beneath it.

No further attempt was made to bring this city to light until about 1905, when D. Manuel Gamio, a native Mexican of Spanish descent, began his study of the vanished civilization of Mexico. Teotihuacán was his special field of interest. Mr. Gamio was educated in France and America, and was a disciple of Franz Boas of Columbia University. For the last four years he has been Director of Anthropology in connection with the National Museum of Mexico. The work of restoring the "pyramides" and the city of Teotihuacán has been intrusted solely to Mr. Gamio, and by agreement with the Mexican Government, the work is being carried on through the Department of Agriculture and Improvement.

The results have far outrun the hopes of even the enthusiastic workers themselves. Here within less than 30 miles from the present capital, they have unearthed the throne city of the ancient Nahoas, and presently we have there before us, a silent strange capital of the past, inexplicable and impressively beautiful.

Who were those people? We call them Nahoas. But when did they flourish? Where did they come from, and why did they vanish so mysteriously? Some of the historians believe, and Mr. Gamio shares this theory, that in remote times the region of San Juan Teotihuacán was inhabited by peoples of the Otomí race, whose cultural type we now term archaic. The oldest traces of this race were found in San Angel Pedregal, about two miles from Mexico City. The structures of adobe and of clay found here are without doubt the remains of a very early race. Later on numerous human groups of different racial and cultural aspects arrived—from whence is a matter full of discussion—of whom the highest type was the Nahoa. They brought different habits, customs and industries, and effected radical changes in the architectural and sculptural forms. Gradually out of this fusion came an advanced group whose civilization created two ages of culture as they have been discovered in this region.

That there were two epochs is clear enough. The excavations have disclosed the remains of two cities, plainly divided, one built over the other. They follow a natural pattern of development; the first city was massive, simple, with a powerful art of sculpture. The second had more color, but was less painstaking, less sincere, not so sharply defined.

Both cities were beautiful. There was freedom enough for all the graces of wide streets and spacious gardens and houses. The valley is like an enormous bowl rimmed with mountains. On the north the now extinct volcano, the Cerro Gordo, shut off the winter winds. The lava that formed and cooled on the sides of this mountain was used by the people in building the entire city. A wide quarry at the foot of the mountain furnished the huge blocks of gray and reddish stone for the pyramids. The black, flint-like volcanic glass, called obsidian, was used almost exclusively for the making of knives, razors, arrowheads, and tools for sculpture.

Both cities came to an end by agencies unknown, in spite of many venturesome theories. But here they are, buried at two levels. Of the two cities, the first one must mark the period now known as Toltecan. Traces of other influences exist also—chiefly the Totonaca, the Zapoteca, and the Maya, the civilization of Yucatan. These vanished builders knew the secret of harmony, of symmetry, not only in planning a city, but in building it up as a natural spontaneous part of the landscape. Their architecture was in perfect accord with the line of mountains, with the very forms of trees and cacti. The Pyramid of the Sun dominates the whole, a solitary brooding thing, rising splendidly at the foot of the volcano. It is, as a matter of detail and comparison for those who know Egypt, larger at the base than the great Cheops, and slants away swiftly to an altar elevated more than two hundred feet—220, to be exact. It rises more steeply at first than the pyramids of Egypt, but is broken in six levels, each diminishing sharply in diameter. A diagonal stairway of stone is set at either side of a square platform at the foot of the pyramid. An immense soaring flight of steps begins here and ascends to the high altar, pausing at each terrace, but breath taking in their effect of ascending at one sheer sweep. These steps are very high and narrow, and the priests performed the feat of descending them backward, in order not to turn their faces from the altar.

From the top of this pyramid the city plan becomes clear. The lines are often mere raised veins in the earth, marking the streets and the walls of houses. A few feet under the earth is the pavement, bared here and there, disclosing a perfectly smooth surface of large squares of artificial stone, or cement. This belonged to the second city.

The far-flung valley is dotted with small villages, and many glimmering white spires of churches; the first Spanish church in Mexico still stands in Acolman. Under a mountain shadow, one sees this little village drowsing, scene also of the Aztec legend of the creation of man.

Near the Pyramid of the Sun is the Pyramid of the Moon, newly un-covered, of smaller size and importance because the second of the two gods, it is said, hesitated at the ritual of fire in his work of helping to light the earth. Therefore his planet is second to the first, and his temple also. We see near by the beginnings of the work on the temple of Tlaloc, god of water, and a whole cityful of mounds hardly touched as yet, each one concealing a smaller shrine.

Across the wide irrigation canal, standing alone in a glory second only to the Pyramid of the Sun, the square terraces of Quetzalcoatl's second temple appear in the limpid air like two huge solid blocks of stone. Back of it, almost overwhelming it, is a ponderous, shapeless mound. Within lie, only half explored, the most mysterious of all the discoveries of Teoti-huacán, the most difficult to decipher. This structure is sometimes called the temple of the god of the winds, but Quetzalcoatl has many names and many legends. The mound is set in a wide square, surrounded by a guard of smaller shrines, similar to those we have mentioned, each now hidden entirely. There are 15 of these special votary mounds, arranged probably in symbolic order, four on three sides, three on one side. These will be opened in time. At present interest is centered on the larger mound.

In this place many wells were opened, discovering treasures of carved stones, clay faces, ornaments and jewelry, ear plates of polished jade, ritual vases and arrow heads. The temple is of incalculable age. The walls are built of blocks of carved stone, cut and fitted together with geometrical precision. The figures are deeply carved, and were painted in brilliant col-ors, traces of which survive.

It is the stronghold of the great Mexican deity, Quetzalcoatl. Through the narrow deep passageways winds the endless body of the plumed ser-pent, the writhing line broken now by an upreared head, fanged and flat-tened, or an altar stone in the form of an owl's head. The significance of this owl, the exact meaning of this serpent are unknown. Attempts have been made to explain them after the same principals of symbolism of the Greeks, of the Romans, of the Egyptians, and of the Chinese. But the scholars at work here say, "We are not sure of anything where this temple is concerned." Which is probably the beginning of knowledge.

Another head is found here, neither serpent nor bird nor human, said to represent the mythical animal, the Cepactli. This is also the name of the first day of the Aztec month. What the meaning of it is has not been discovered. The image recurs with sufficient frequency to give it interest. It rather resembles a tiger with bared teeth.

Many other symbols occur that have been found in other ruins in many parts of the world, especially in the Orient. One or two archaeologists in Mexico have accepted the theory of the Asiatic origin of the Mexican and they attempt to decipher the characters on the walls by the Chinese characters. This idea is energetically opposed by other schools of archaeology, who claim no kinship with China, but rather with Egypt . . . and still others are working on the premise that the races of Mexico were here from the dawn of humanity: if they sprang from Asia, it was at such an early time it does not weigh in considering their civilization, which is proved by its very findings to be a culture distinct from all other ancient worlds.

The controversy makes for ever-freshening interest in the subject, and stimulates thought and study. No man's word has yet attained to complete authority. There is really only one legend completely authenticated, and it has endless variations. It is the story of Quetzalcoatl. It is the most involved and imaginative of all the Mexican myths. He was once a human being, a good and wise man who taught many arts and devised many crafts for his people, as well as bequeathing them an ethical system. He disappeared, and promised to come again as a god. His relation to the planet Venus is not clear, but appears in at least one version. Also he went away by sea in a magic skiff of snakeskins, and the sculptured shells that follow his path along the lower walls of the temple reiterate his affinity, in Mexican thought, with the sea. His plumed and glittering body winds irregularly, and bore in their imagination, probably, a resemblance to starlight on glowing water.

The first temple, now restored, was built in a less religious and artistic age. It is an arrangement of flat, square terraces, built of lava, stone and adobe, cemented over and painted red. The reconstruction was comparatively simple. The classical method of excavation used in Europe and Asia was followed by Mr. Gamio. The walls were built up of the original stones, and protected against the weather. The older carved walls are simply uncovered and fortified, with no attempt at restoration.

You spend many days in wonder, baffled in attempts to study because there is no beginning to take hold of. And there you leave the ancient city, her secret untold, sitting mightily in her silence, dreaming in a cloud of ghostly remembrances . . . the very Sphinx of cities, Teotihuacán. But beauty was there, and a magnificent concept of life. Incalculable faith in mysteries set those stones one above another, and carved those images. A superb race flourished there, and a wise one. Their religion was by evidence their reason for being. The whole valley is a place of temples.

Corridos

Survey Graphic 5 (May 1924): 157–159

Porter returned to Mexico for a third time in 1923 as art editor of *Survey Graphic*'s Mexican issue, whose contributors—Robert Haberman and Felipe Carrillo Puerto among them—read like a who's who of her acquaintances in Mexico. This charming essay has the personal stamp of her earlier sketches and would have found a proper place in her once-contemplated book on Mexico. She had read Dr. Atl's chapter on corridos in his *Artes Populares* and a book of corridos borrowed from Bertram Wolfe, but most of all she delighted in the songs she heard sung on street corners and marketplaces, the very setting of the singing adding to the appeal of the song. Since the corridos' "stories are always concerned with immediate fundamental things: death, love, acts of vengeance, and appalling malignities of Fate," of all the Mexican folk arts, it came closest to her own art. Her sketches and stories are filled with song titles and snatches of songs. "Noon Wine" and "Pale Horse, Pale Rider" allude to songs in their titles. Commenting on the spiritual appearing in the latter story, Miranda states that "Death always leaves one singer to mourn," that singer being the artist. Porter first sounded that motif in "Corridos": "No man can be so utterly brought down but there will always be left one devoted, steadfast woman to come, weeping, bringing what consolation her love can devise."

Corridos

In Mexico, most of the birds, and all of the people, sing.

They sing out freely and cheerfully, to the extent of the voice Heaven has endowed them with, in all places, and at all hours. The lover warbles serenades under the balcony of his lady, the children sing on their way to school, the truck drivers and pedlars whistle and sing, the beggars fiddle and murmur doleful songs about love and death. High pitched, untrained voices of girls murmur sentimental songs softly to the set waltz accompaniment of pianos, from *patio* after *patio* the music floats out as one passes along the bright streets. In a cafe across from my hotel, a set of lively youngsters used to gather almost every night in the week and sing at the top of their voices until the very sunrise. On birthdays and feast days, the guests begin singing at the windows of the celebrant a little after midnight, and sing until breakfast time. These charming songs are known as *las Mañanitas*, (morning songs) modern sister to the old Provençal madrigal. There are marching songs, dancing, wedding and funeral songs: no possible occasion for singing has been overlooked, and the gayest, freshest, most spirited popular music in the world can be heard in Mexico.

There is still another type of song, altogether distinct from these popular airs; these are ruder, lustier, they have a unique flavor. They are meant to be listened to; one could not dance to them, the measure is too erratic, and besides, one would miss the story. This type of song is called the *corrido*, and it is the primitive, indigenous song of the Mexican people.

The *corrido* is, in effect, a ballad. Mexico is one of the few countries where a genuine folk poetry still exists, a word of mouth tradition which renews itself daily in the heroic, sensational or comic episodes of the moment, an instant record of events, a moment caught in the quick of life. They are informal, copious, filled with irrelevant matter. The story wanders on by itself, filled with minute details, often with meaningless words tacked on at the end of a phrase in order to make the rhyme. But the form is quite definitive, four lines to the verse, eight syllables to the line, and a refrain. If the perfection of this ideal is not always achieved in the stanza, the music takes care of that by deftly crowding the two or three extra syllables into a note meant for one. The effect is hilarious in the extreme, and is usually deliberate.

These *corridos* are composed and sung by the people all over Mexico. The Indians, the country people and the very humble folk of the town, all know these stories. In them are contained their legends and folk lore. Most of them are handed on by word of mouth, and only a comparatively small number have been written down. But for the past twenty-five years the publication of *corridos* has increased. They are printed on spongy, luridly dyed strips of paper and sold, two for a *centavo*, in the markets.

The composers are usually anonymous, so far as the printed sheet is concerned. Theirs is the more subtle fame of the enlightened word spoken among the elect. Popular singers vend the wares during early mornings when the citizens crowd to the narrow cobbled streets of the markets. Among the open booths hung with streamers of bright muslins and thin silks, mounds of pottery and colored glass, the heaped melting fragrance of figs, apricots, mangoes and peaches, birds in wicker cages (those sweet-throated doomed creatures whose modest colors have been disguised with brilliant lead paints, which will shortly bring them to death), withies and mats of palm fiber, fowls whose legs have been broken to keep them from wandering, intricate foods simmering over charcoal *braziers*, soft-eyed, self-possessed Indian girls with small stands of brass and silver jewelry, a huddle of beggars and dogs: there, in some accessible corner, the singers squat, strum their guitars, and sing.

They are uniformly hoarse of voice, but no matter. A certain sweated, rugged earnestness in the telling merely emphasizes the innate quality of the narrative. The *corrido* should be shouted. Shouted it is, and the presence of three or four rival vendors, each with the fixed intention of shouting down his competitor, makes a fine, exciting racket. The crowd collects, it takes sides, offers odds on its favorites. Sometimes an entire family, father, mother, and children even down to the five-year-old, sing turn and turn about, until all are hoarse as corn-crakes—and why not? But the bright colored strips of song sell instantly, everybody wishes the newest one, they go away memorising the story, humming the tune.

The homely, earthy soul of a people is in them: Gay, tragic, superstitious, devout, cruel, in love with life and a little desperate. The stories are always concerned with immediate fundamental things; death, love, acts of vengeance, the appalling malignities of Fate. They celebrate heroes. A hero is usually one who kills huge numbers of his enemies and dies bravely. He must be a bold, high stepping and regardless person, whether he gives his energies to saving his country or to robbing trains. Motives do not matter. They love deeds, concrete and measurable. They wield a truly murderous bludgeon of sarcasm, they have the gift of the grand manner in relating a love tragedy. An amazing air of realism is achieved through their habit of giving names, dates and places. The tune is composed or improvised on the spot, maybe, by the singer. Or they squeeze the lines of a new story into the measures of an old, familiar melody. Either way, they will be remembered, and sung.

A collection of these *corridos* which I have seen,* dating from about 1890, has a curious sub-historical value. Revolution after revolution has risen, broken and passed over the heads of these singers, and there is not a single revolutionary *corrido*. With the true temperament of the minor poet, the folk singer concerns himself with personalities, with intimate emotions, with deeds of heroism and crime. If many of their favorite subjects were revolutionists, it is because the men themselves possessed the admired qualities of nonchalance, bravado and quickness in action. Carranza was not loved by the *corrido* singer: Madero was loved as a saint and a hero. The difference was not one of revolutionary spirit, but of personality. Victoriano Huerta was rightly dubbed "butcher" in several *corridos—and* a poltroon. He let other men do his fighting. That is the root of the *corrido* singers' contempt for him.

Emiliano Zapata, the bandit general who made of Morelos the first genuinely socialist state of Mexico, was a popular subject of *corridos*. At the time of his assassination, hundreds of rhymed narratives appeared, reflecting every shade of provincial opinion. He was martyr, hero, bandit, a man who betrayed his friends, the savior of his state, a scoundrel who destroyed churches, all depending on the section of the country and the personal bias of the composer . . . but not one of them mentions that he revolutionized the agrarian system of Morelos, or was one of the first Mexicans to apprehend the principles of soviet government. . . . Such things are ephemerae to the maker of ballads. He is concerned with eternal verities.

The records of accident and murder are set down with a taste for explicit horror; after thirty stanzas the singer will break off by saying he cannot finish the sad tale for weeping. It is their habit to begin by asking the attention of those present, in the manner of the Irish "come-all-ye" and to finish by asking prayers for the soul of the singer, or less often, by mentioning the composer's name, adding that he is one of the most talented *corrido* makers of his time.

*Loaned me by Bertram D. Wolfe, of Mexico City.

Within two days after the death of Pancho Villa last year, the street singers were shouting long histories of the event, with melancholy insistence on particulars. "He was dishonorably killed, his entrails were out," sang one, gayly, a literal fact proved by the photograph of the body printed at the top of the sheet. Villa was the hero of hundred *corridos*, and his exploits took on, even while he lived, that legendary character which is the very heart of romance. When going on raids he flew in aeroplanes at a speed of fifty kilometers a minute. He vanquished one hundred fifty thousand Gringos who came to capture Villa, looked about for him, did not see him, ate a great quantity of corn and beans, and so went home again . . . the subject was meat for their intensely personal kind of humor. One says that the poor Texans were so tired when they reached Mexico, the ones on horseback could not sit, and those on foot could not stand. So they all drank freely of *tequila* and lay down.

These ballads are saturated with faith in the supernatural. A very recent one tells of a man born with the head of a pig, who grew up into an extremely disturbing demon in his community. Devils are gravely accused of aiding a man in Guanajuato to murder a helpless female. Divine Providence in the shape of a white angel with wings intervened when two bandits attempted to rob a priest. The apparition of the Virgin of Guadalupe takes place somewhere in Mexico, and endless *corridos* piously give the facts of the event. Illustrations sometimes accompany them, rude cuts used many times over, of strange devils, horned and tailed and saber-toothed, blood kin to those of Albrecht Dürer. They urge weak mortals into crime, usually murder or sacrilege.

Laments for the dead are often joined with the story of how the mourner has seen and talked with the ghost. Beautiful young ladies who died unwed are notably restless. They are always rising and frightening their families by appearing at the midnight hour, wan, covered with grave mold, bitterly complaining of their too-early fate.

The laments have passionate, grieved choruses: "Oh, Death, why didst thou turn thine eyes toward my little flower, the white rose of my heart?" sings one. "Oh, Death, thou monster, why didst thou take my child, and leave my step-daughter?" inquires another. And one sturdy souled singer counsels a ghostly wife to return to her tomb, and leave her husband, now happily re-wed, in peace.

The loneliness of the men facing death far away from home and friends is the recurring motif of many *corridos*. They turn their eyes toward the sky, they invoke birds as messengers. A young soldier of fortune, finding himself back to wall and the levelled rifles at his heart, calls on a swallow to fly swiftly and tell his mother how they are going to kill him. The swallow takes the message, and the mother comes weeping to kiss her child goodbye. Ah, the weeping women of the *corridos*. No man can be so utterly brought down but there will always be left one devoted, steadfast woman to come, weeping, bringing what consolation her love can devise. "Pray for her who prayed for me," sings a dying man after battle, "She who bound up my wounds and brought me water, she who will remember my grave when all others have forgotten!"

Corridos celebrating the executions of men taken bearing arms against the government are curious mixtures of admiration for valor come to a hard death, and cautious warning to all who revolt against the government.

This adding of a postscript, slightly moralistic in tone, is merely a gesture of good manners, a courtesy nod to convention. The story is the thing, and a deliciously terrifying ghost story will end with a warning against faith in apparitions and false miracles. The story of some glittering escapade in outlawry will conclude with a word of caution against hateful anarchy. This is done with perfect gravity, tongue in cheek, eyes beaming with charming, natural malice, all a trifle "edgy" a little impious, perfect complaisant mirror of the popular mind.

A *corrido* still popular, with the wicked mother-in-law motif, has many marks of extreme antiquity. It is called "Marbella and the Newly-born," and resembles the old English carol of Mary and the Cherry Tree, in which the unborn child speaks in defense of his mother.

Marbella, the *corrido* begins, was in the hard pains of birth that brought her to her knees. Her lord the Count was absent, and the deceitful mother-in-law advises her to return to her home, where she will be in more skillful hands. Marbella utters a moving plaint of homesick longing: "Oh, if I were once more in Castle Valledal at the side of my father the King, he would give me help and comfort. . . . But when my lord comes home, who will give him his supper?" she asks the mother-in-law.

"I will give him bread and wine. There is barley for his horse and meat for the sparrow hawk," answers the wicked woman.

After Marbella has gone her husband comes home and asks for his mirror. The mother asks whether he wants his mirror of fine silver, or the one of crystal, or of ivory? He answers that he wants none of these, but Marbella, his wife, his royal mirror.

The mother tells him that Marbella has betrayed him with a Jew, and has now returned to her father's castle to hide her guilt, and to leave her child there.

The husband, with the fatal credulity of all lovers in tragic love stories, sets off to Castle Valledal and finds Marbella there, surrounded by her maids, her newly born child at her breast. He commands her to rise and come with him. He places the mother at the pillion and the child at his breast straps. They ride for seven leagues without a word, so fast the horse's hooves strike fire from the stones. Marbella implores him, "Do not kill me in this mountain where the eagles may devour me. Leave me in the open road where some merciful soul may find me. Or take me to the hermitage yonder where I may confess, for I am at my last breath." At the hermitage she is taken down, dying, unable to speak. But by the never ending grace of God, the newly born child finds language: "I tell you truly, my mother is going at once to Paradise without a stain on her soul. And now I must go to limbo unless I am baptised, for I shall follow my mother into death. But my wicked grandmother shall suffer eternally for this work."

Over their bodies, the Count swore by the bread and wine that he would not touch food again until he had slain his wicked mother. He placed her in a barrel lined with iron skewers and cast her over a mountain side; because, the song hints, he could invent nothing worse.

A race of singing people . . . used to sorrowful beginnings and tragic endings, in love with life, fiercely independent, a little desperate, but afraid of nothing. They see life as a flash of flame against a wall of darkness. Conscious players of vivid roles, they live and die well, and as they live and die, they sing.

To a Portrait of the Poet

Survey Graphic 5 (May 1924): 182

Porter's translation of this sonnet of Sor Juana Inés de la Cruz and brief introduction to her life also appeared in the Mexico number of *Survey Graphic*. Her third contribution to the issue was "The Guild Spirit in Mexican Art" by Diego Rivera, "as told to Katherine Anne Porter." (In 1928, she began an essay on Sor Juana and Gabriela Mistral, whom she met in Mexico in 1922.) The subject of the poem complements Porter's comments that stress Sor Juana as a beauty and a legend.

Porter paid tribute to other legendary heroines, including Joan of Arc, over the years. Upon discovering the mummy of Thaïs in the Paris museum in the 1930s, she wrote, "All my life I had loved Thais. She was to me a symbol of all loveliness hastening to decay. . . . call it by a name—whatever name is your symbol for eternal beauty. And Thais was my symbol. . . . Here was my dream, here was my gathered and stored beauty."

Sor Juana's sonnet insists on the body's mortality, but its living voice has not perished. And so her "pure and candid legend persists and grows." Porter may have had Sor Juana in mind when she began "Old Mortality" with a description of Miranda's legendary Aunt Amy, "forever in the pose of being photographed." In the tombstone poem composed by her husband, "she forgets/The griefs of old mortality."

Portrait by Miguel Cabrera of Sor Juana Inés de la Cruz (1750), Museo Nacional de Historia, Castillo de Chapultepec, Mexico D.F. This portrait was reproduced with Porter's translation of a sonnet by Sor Juana in the May 1924 issue of *Survey Graphic*. Reproduced here by permission of INAH. Photograph: Archivo Fotográfico, Instituto de Investigaciones Estéticas, Universidad Nacional Autónoma de México.

To a Portrait of the Poet

By Sor Juana Inés de la Cruz
Translated by Katherine Anne Porter

This which you see is merely a painted shadow
Wrought by the boastful pride of art,
With falsely reasoned arguments of colours,
A wary, sweet deception of the senses.

This picture, where flattery has endeavored
To mitigate the terrors of the years,
To defeat the rigorous assaults of Time,
And triumph over oblivion and decay —

Is only a subtle careful artifice,
A fragile flower of the wind,
A useless shield against my destiny.

It is an anxious diligence to preserve
A perishable thing: and clearly seen
It is a corpse, a whirl of dust, a shadow,—
      nothing.

Juana De Asbaje, in religion Sor Juana Inés de la Cruz, was, like most great spirits, at once the glory and the victim of her age. She was born in Mexico in 1651, of aristocratic Spanish parentage, and won the respect of the most advanced scholars of her time by her achievements in mathematics, astronomy, languages, and poetry. Her austere, impassioned and mystical mind led her to the cloister, where she ended by renouncing her studies, and writing out her confession of faith in her own blood.

She was, in her beauty, her learning and her Catholicism, the perfect flowering of seventeenth century European civilization in the New World, a civilization imperfectly transplanted, imposed artificially, due to be swept away by the rising flood of revolution. But her own pure and candid legend persists and grows, a thing beloved for its unique beauty. She died in her forty-fifth year of a plague which swept Mexico City. This sonnet is almost literally translated.

The Lovely Legend

(unfinished story, 1923, 1925, 1929)

In the draft of a 1923 letter to Freda Kirchwey of the *Nation* Porter offered for publication "The Enchanting Legend of Rosita," whose outline she gave, promising that it would not exceed 2,500 words: "It is one of a group of stories told around one central figure, Rubén, the Mexican painter. . . . The first one ["The Martyr"], which is really in proper order the last, will appear in the July *Century*." Apparently Porter worked on this story throughout the 1920s. Part of the manuscript is dated "1925," and there are references to it in several of her letters to Matthew Josephson in 1929. Among her papers is a first page of what looks to be the final version of a story reentitled "The Lovely Legend," which deals with the painter Rubén. The rest of the manuscript consists of earlier drafts, with some overlapping passages, of a main character called Rafael, but the story itself conforms to the outline Porter gave Kirchwey. In our reconstruction of the story we have retained the name of Rubén.

Both "The Martyr" and "The Lovely Legend" take as their subject matter Diego Rivera's stormy relation with Lupe Marín, whom he married in Guadalajara in 1922. If Porter meant us to take the two stories in relation to each other, then Isabel of "The Martyr" is a reincarnation of Rosita in "The Lovely Legend," for both pointedly resemble Marín physically and temperamentally. Porter astutely recognized that Marín represented ideal beauty to Rivera, but she assumed that as an artist he amorally exploited her beauty. For that reason she has the reincarnated Rosita, in the form of Isabel, revenge herself on Rubén for the callous way he treated her earlier incarnation.

If Rubén is a moral monster who sacrifices all human relations for his art, he is fully aware of the price he has to pay. Not so Amado, the point-of-view character in "The Lovely Legend." Unlike Rubén, he is an inferior artist and sentimentalist who deceives himself about art and human relations. Only when Porter has others humiliate him over his insincere ballad on the death of Rosita, who he mistakenly thinks was killed, does he have some inkling of the way he convinced himself that his love for Rosita depended on her being dead, that "he had been tricked by his own invented emotions." He finally sees her as Rubén does: "a noble arrangement," a subject for art. Porter clearly portrays the exploitation of women in this story and avenges their victimization in her unflattering portraits of Rubén and Amado.

The Lovely Legend

<(I dedicate this story to the characters in it, and I freely acknowledge my debt to one of them for some of the more intimate details here related.) *The Author.*

The face of Rubén loomed full of disordered curves, behind his rubbish heap of emptied coffee cups and tequila goblets. The monkeys painted on the walls were experimenting with cinematograph effects, the tittering suggestiveness of their usual attitudes broke up in a series of frantic poses, not to be accounted for, Amado decided, even on the score of tequila with a dash of vermouth. It occurred to him that Rubén would be entirely contemptuous if the phenomenon were mentioned; he would not even be amused. There was a fatal, indestructible sanity in Rubén—he did the same things drunk that he did sober, only with more reasonableness.

Amado leaned nearer Rubén, and began one of his endless tales of erotic personal experience in the sub-cellar stratum of romance; he was annoyingly conscious that he must have passed his twentieth drink.

Whether he was in Paris or London, in Madrid or Port Said, in Pekin or Mexico City, the tales were monotonously uniform. The woman herself varied but in the matter of shades; from shell-rose to amber, to gold, to bronze, to ebony itself—pigmentation was a fascinating subject to Amado.>

<Amado said, [. . . .] "I once slept a whole night in a wine cellar with a girl, black, this was in a village in Porto Rico. She was a servant there in an inn, she smuggled me into the place after dinner and at midnight she

came down and took off her dress by the light of a candle in a cone of white paper, and she was black every inch of her except the palms of her hands."

"You were surprised?"

"But you cannot imagine unless you have seen it . . . a minute figure hewn in obsidian, polished to smoothness, with coral palms: her breasts were like sharpened stones, and when I touched her, she was soft, the flesh laid on like warm oil over the truly female muscles, curved and short and woven in fat. And rank as a wild cat, a different smell for every part of her. We rolled among the wine barrels until she was covered with the wine-saturated mold. I have not forgotten her delicious fat that had the look of stone, nor how sweetly she balanced a basket of clothes on her head when she went to the river the next morning. I said, 'Goodbye, God bless the womb that bore you!' And she said, 'What's my mother to you, you who were born an orphan?' I have not forgotten her. She spat on the stones at my feet and walked on swinging her hands. Hi-Hi!"

"You remember them all," said [Rubén], "with their color schemes, their smells, their sayings always so ungracious. After complacency but never before. Was there not one of them who clouted you over the head and stole your money? You see, these stories are in me now, like some indigestible substance, I shall disgorge them. Some day you will not recognise them! . . . the colors: shell-rose and amber, gold bronze, lemon citron, almond white, fig purple, baby-pink—"

"These colors are important," said Amado. "They are mixed with my memories of cities; I have seen them on walls and on fruits. The women I have known and shall not see again share these tints alike with indestructible or recurring things; it is a second, a third, a thousandth re-incarnation for them in my memory when they, the least fortunate of living creatures, are vanished out of youth. . . ."

[Rubén] swore and pounded his fist on the table. A heap of coffee cups slid off the edge and committed suicide on the stone flags.

"I am sick of buttocks round as billiard balls and breasts which stare like owl's eyes," he shouted, and relapsed quietly into bitterness. "Was it for this you were born? To nibble the gilded finger nails of the whores of Port Said, to sniff around the perfumed monstrosities with hair bleached to dried straw who sit so noisily dead in the High Life Cafe at Santiago, to jumble the partridge-shaped girls of Cracow? Had they no faces, these creatures?"

"They did not need them. Faces are over praised. A fictitious value attaches to that set of organs, for the most part ill-arranged and devoted to a number of our most revolting functions, which by practical necessity man has habituated himself to expose without shame. . . . I do not remember their faces, nor the tones of their voices. I remember them in the tips of my fingers, in my nostrils; I have smelt death on them. I have feared the loss of my soul in them."

"Do you want me to puke?" asked [Rubén].

"No," replied Amado with noble simplicity.

The waiter said uneasily, "In that case, this way, sir," and pointed to a large sign. GENTLEMEN, TO THE RIGHT.

"In Amecameca," said Amado, "on Good Friday, I saw an innocent little thing, thirteen years old, ascending the Via Dolorosa on her knees. At this sight the prodigal bright day was spoiled for me. I knelt beside her, grass grew between the stones of this cruel stairway in a natural hill shaded with heavy trees, and I whispered, 'Do as I do. Set those darling knees on the soft grass. God would weep to see you bruised.' She was fresh as a pat of butter just lifted from the spring, and she could have taught tricks to a Viennese. . . ."

[Rubén] said, "What color was this phenomenon?"

"She was like a softly modelled clay jar, the reddish sort with the thin glaze from Tonalá. Her arms were curved in handle shape, she lifted them to hold her jar on the braids of her hair, wrapped to make a little crown, or a platform on which to balance burdens. When she squatted on her round haunches she was a jug. An admirable vessel of clay saturated in vital essences, warm as sunshine, soft as grass. . . .">

"Enough," said Rubén. "I know that one by heart also. The worst of the lot. Give it up, Amado, your invention is failing you. This love of soft women and decorated surfaces, how debased it is. This amateur taste for purple eyelids! Do you want me to puke? <I need a model for the Maya fresco.> A lean tall woman who does not simper or paint her finger nails; who has long hard hands and feet, and a nose with a hooked bridge, that is the one kind of beauty I can endure in a woman: and her hair must be black. Blonde hair smells like decayed tuberoses."

<"The odor of decayed tuberoses also haunts convents," said Amado. He began to weep and the tears rolled down over his nose, over his mouth. He licked them away, but one continued and ran into his collar. "She did, she did," he sobbed. "She danced for me on broken glass with her white feet bleeding. I knelt and kissed the wounds through the cold iron grill of the gate. I wiped away her blood with my handkerchief."

"It could be true," said [Rubén], wishing to console him. "I have seen some very odd things."

"She was the daughter of a curio vender in Sixteenth of September

Street, and once in her father's shop, before she went to be a nun, she tried to entice me behind the tall glass cases full of clay heads and painted gourds and beadwork: I ran because I feared I should have to buy and I had no money. On the day she became a nun I said farewell to her at the little barred window, and she whispered that she would see me at the gate that very night. It was not the fate I expected for her. . . . Now, do you see, there was one woman who was not beautiful, except for this one night in a white veil under the white moon, who had failed to enchant me once and yet who did enchant me finally, and there was nothing soft in her. I stood in the shadow of the wall, and she danced lifting her long skirts, and I saw the glass shining like naked sword's points under her feet. She came with her sharp teeth bared laughing, and offered me her feet to kiss through the bars. Then she said, 'It is nothing, you must not pity me, it has made me happy, it is not for you I did it,' and she ran away!">

<"Ah my memories! Some day they will cease to rise coolly in me a perpetual fountain. I shall be as dry as the basin of the Lost Child. . . .">

<He leaned his head on his hand. "You are right, it is intolerable that I should have exchanged my youth for these things. And what an exchange! For the thing bargained for has vanished with the gold I gave for it, and as for my poems, who reads them?">

[Rubén returned to the subject of his model.] "If I could find such a woman, I wouldn't be wasting my time here with you. The sketches for the Maya fresco are not even begun, and I have searched Mexico for the woman. Where is she?"

"I have seen such a brute as you describe. Her ears stand out like shells, and she is dying of tuberculosis. I wouldn't touch her with tongs, she has been the dubious ornament of a pleasant dive in Calle de la Palma for five years past. She is part Indian and part any other animal you choose, and if you care to look at her, come with me. It will cure you of your infatuation."

"She must have a chest, not a breast," added [Rubén]. "I insist on shoulders, also, and eyes that bore sharply into distances: if she were a deaf-mute, it would be supernatural good fortune."

"I wish I could make it clear to you that if you should find such a creature, it would not be a woman."

"If she is not, so much the better. I wish not to be distracted. Let her remain as the armature for my idea. Stop telling me your wet dreams, Amado," [Rubén] said, after a long walk. "Go sleep with a live woman once, and come back and I will listen to you, though I know already what you will say— Is this the place?"

"Not these cribs. At this gate." Under the red lantern he knocked gently. Even from the cobblestones there rose a vapor blended of onions, wine, fermenting orange peel, stale perfumed arm pits. Amado sniffed with pleasure. "All over the world it is the same," he said. "The odor of venery. . . . These little streets all smell alike. I love them tenderly. As for your insults, say what you please. I am sorry for you, I at least shall not be disappointed here."

An old woman smothered head and mouth in her reboso dragged open the grille. As they passed, she squatted asleep again upon the stones.

The square patio was clothed with orange trees, growing in painted barrels; a small fountain wept incessantly to itself, many little starveling tables stood about washed clean for the night, chairs were interlocked upon each other. A respectable place, where the guests retired early, or caroused discreetly behind the barred windows. The cloister-like verandah was black except for slivers of light under the blinds: silent except for the voices of servants in the kitchen quarters. Three men sat at a table near the fountain, heads together over their goblets, talking. A girl sat with them, either listening or asleep, present as their own shadows were present, no more. They had forgotten why they had asked for her.

"We wish to sit here a little while," Amado explained to the duena. "We are in a fit of nostalgia for lost simplicities."

The duena was past boredom with imbeciles. "Sit here, if you please, gentlemen," she said seriously. "This is your house. You do not wish entertainment, then?"

"No . . . or rather, yes. Send Rosita."

The wind cut the soiled white wool bedroom robe sharply about her fleshless thighs. She came with an air of dim, indifferent boldness, and sat down without a word. She drew her garnet-colored knitted shawl about her sunken neck and shivered. They gave her wine and she drank. The harsh caverns under her fixed brows were fierce and blind looking. She was tall as a ghost.

"The awareness of her ferocity," whispered [Rubén] to Amado in delight. "There is a menace on her very clutch on the wine glass. She could cut one's throat with the rim."

"She is merely dead, I tell you, and you are mad. . . ."

[Rubén] stood up and ran the flat of his palm delicately over her shoulder blades and spine. Her nostrils pinched together and relaxed again. "A truly noble arrangement," he commented. "Balanced and true and simple as a triangle. . . . Chica, I think you are very sick and this is a ridiculous life for you. Why don't you come with me? You have beautiful bones, just what I am looking for. You have only to keep still when I tell you, and I shall draw pictures of you. You won't find it a bad bargain in the least. Come along, eh? Get your cloak. Do you owe anything here?"

She flattened her hands on the table and raised herself to her feet. "You are drunk and making fun of me. You may go to hell."

"I am maybe a little drunk, but I mean what I say."

"Wait a minute, then. There is some one I must say goodbye to."

They took her to [Rubén]'s house. Her breathing rattled with the jolting of the cab. Amado felt a fearful desolation all through him, as if there had been poison in his tequila. [Rubén] was happy, he whistled and sang a little.

Amado waited outside while [Rubén] helped her undress, and put her to bed. [Rubén] came out after a while, shut the door and whispered, "Come now and see her." The woman lay asleep, an effigy of herself, stretched out stiffly, long arms at her side, the sheet drawn up to her chin and sunken into the hollows of her body like a thin fall of snow. [Rubén] gazed, shaking his head a little. Tears stood in his eyes.

"Poor child, what beauty! I never hoped to find it . . . those flanks, that gaunt shallow torso—a young Christ on a Byzantine crucifix! That exquisitely laced corselet of ribs—how did they happen to be so right? I thank you for this, Amado."

"I suggest that you wash her, and burn her clothes, and be careful of your hands," said Amado, his stomach rising.

"Go away, my friend," said [Rubén] gently. And he closed the door after him.

Amado went away thinking that a door can be opened to you rightly only by the one who closed it upon you, and he waited for word from [Rubén]. But nothing happened, he knew well that nothing would be different this time from all previous times. Having grown tired of that empty place in him that was filled by [Rubén], he would go back. As always, he forgave [Rubén] in secret for the wounds given so unconsciously, this cleansed him of the need for pride, and restored a balance between him and his friend. Holding this balance carefully within him then, he went back once more.

[Rubén] said, "Hello, keep your feet out of that pile of drawings," and went on with some story he was telling Ramón, a caricaturist who daily distilled synthetic venom in a daily newspaper. It was his duty to be malicious, and so he found it easy to take a harmless rabbit-faced politician, and give him the features of a pig or a tiger, and make the reader say: "How mistaken I was in this man! See how Ramón has uncovered his true character!"

Rosita had changed much during her month with [Rubén]. She seemed merely hungry, not famine stricken, her hair was braided Indian fashion, her eyes were cleared with sound sleep. But she was implacably silent, and she did not even glance at Amado. She stood holding up a hand the color of dried corn, the fingers admonished silence. [Rubén] drew the hand on a magnified scale, she looked away from the drawing.

"Let me tell you about that woman," said Ramón. "She is a virago, I would as soon keep a leopardess for a house-cat. There is no end to her anger. [Rubén] is wrong in being so mild with her. He will end by beating her every day."

He walked on with Amado, accompanying him to the Cafe de los Monotes.

"I insist on her less dramatic aspects," said Amado. "Without [Rubén] she has nothing to hope for but death in Calle de la Palma. She is a raw, sulking beast, but she knows who feeds her. Already she appears to have gained ten pounds. Soon her bones will be of no mortal use to [Rubén]."

"I think she has a certain beauty."

"She is more hideous than any nightmare."

"Nonsense, you don't know what you are saying. She is architecturally impressive, I'd rather look at her than at the Tepozotlan cathedral any day."

"Women, cathedrals! Cathedrals, women! You don't know how this confusion of perception bores me!"

"Since when? Only I remember that you prefer to confuse your images of women with lengths of silk fabric and over-ripe fruits. Where is the difference?"

Amado grew uneasy; he made a rite of seeing Rosita every day. He distrusted his own taste for the first time, and timidly sought for signs of beauty in her. Her sullen silences, the ugly twist of her bitter mouth, these things lost their importance for him little by little, and he began to look at her through [Rubén]'s eyes, to judge her by the heroic sketches which were filling the walls of the ruined church that [Rubén] used as a working place. His enchantment grew, and his horror. He continued to scoff, but he was won to a passionate secret cult of a stern, relentless and emphatic beauty. He shuddered when he remembered his fancy for moon curves. Certain perfumes he had loved now revolted him. He tore up a dozen sonnets he had been working on as trivial and unworthy of his new mood.

Rosita despised him calmly, and he feared her with a mortal fear. She lay on a pile of sacking in the corner and ate figs and bread crusts, pulling out the center of the loaf for [Rubén] to clean his drawings with. When Amado talked, watching her raised knees, she pushed out her under lip and stared at the ceiling. This disheartened him, his thoughts seemed like filaments of cobweb hanging between him and her violent colored reality of feeling. She never spoke to him, or seemed aware of him, except as a slight disturbance in the air about her.

He knew that when he was gone, Rosita and [Rubén] would continue with their existence together, that had all the force of a secret alliance, expending itself in scandalous scenes and noisy quarrels that drew passersby to their windows in the romantic hope of witnessing a love murder. He resented this, for they never quarrelled in his presence. Even Ramón had witnessed their battles, and their tranquility in Amado's presence had the quality of a confidence withheld. He wished to provoke them, even to share in an intimate scene, to be the object of dissension between them. But he could think of nothing, and he began to feel a stranger to them, though he could not keep away from their house.

One afternoon he was passing the door of the church, determined not to go in; but from the choir loft he heard such sounds of screams and noise of breaking pottery, without knowing what he did he ran in. Rosita leaned over the choir railing and threw bottles and painted pots at [Rubén], who ran about, laughing, holding up a chair before him. His shirt was in tatters, his hair full of clay dust. A small cut on his chin bled in streaks down his throat. With the face of a fury, Rosita aimed again. Amado felt without surprise a brittle shower over his head. Trembling with shock and tenderness, he ran into the street, hearing [Rubén] call after him, "Don't go away! We are about finished!"

Amado, wiping his hair with his handkerchief, waited until [Rubén] put his head out. "Come in, come in, the volcano is asleep!"

[Rubén]'s calmness was a part of him. "My life is a long uncertainty," he explained, "but I share with God and a few inspired architects a passion for structural perfection. I need that woman, I cannot do without her just yet; I am damned glad she chooses Guadalajara pots to throw, it is a soft clay. She likes that type of jug because it has a neck."

"Where is she?" asked Amado, still trembling, and feeling as if his blood had turned to acid.

[Rubén] waved toward the choir loft. "I always leave her to sleep there after these little exercises."

"To sleep?"

"When I have had enough, I give her a little love tap under the chin—careful not to mark her, you understand—and she rests quietly for half an hour or more. When she wakes, she is docile, and remains in that state for three days or more. During that time I paint."

"Ridiculous—obscene! How can you live with a woman on such terms?"

"Can you not distill the essence of experience from the mere episode?" inquired [Rubén], patiently brushing bits of debris from his hair.

"I cannot."

"No, you cannot. It is your supreme limitation. This violent empty creature, useless as a human being, has for me the value of a work of art. If I make love to her, it is a mere matter of etiquette. I permit her to satisfy her grosser impulses by smashing water jugs on my head. These things have no relation to my Maya fresco."

"They are closely related to Rosita."

"Ha, Rosita! a simple accident of nature . . . an upheaval of misdirected forces. It is baldest chance that she has not the temperament of a milking cow. She will pass, and be no more remembered than last night's thunder shower."

"But she will have occurred—how can you deny it?"

[Rubén] was pulling off his shirt. He turned now and looked at Amado suddenly, clearly, his brown eyes male and ruthless. "To you, my poor romantic, I understand she will have occurred. . . . Well, that too is unimportant."

Amado glanced toward the choir loft. He felt Rosita lying there, hidden behind the railing. About the walls he saw her, recreated in splendor, her likeness raised to the stature of a goddess, set forth with mighty attributes. For the first time he wished to leave [Rubén]. "I must go now."

"Stay a little while. You may see her later."

"NO." And this time he went away as far as Nicaragua, and to the little town where his mother lived. He stayed there three months, re-writing all his poems, sending no letters and receiving none. At last it seemed pointless, there was nothing in the present for him, and he spent his time remembering Rosita as he had last seen her magnified portraits on the walls.

The evening of his return, he walked up three streets away from [Rubén]'s studio, and over seven streets and down three again, and retraced seven more streets, and so found himself at the church portal asking for Rosita.

[Rubén] was alone, and about the walls the completed drawings for the fresco were arranged in order, the red chalk seemed almost black in the candle light. [Rubén] embraced him, beating him affectionately on the back. "You must forget about Rosita," he said. "I have sad news, and I want to tell you now before you hear it from my enemies. You will accuse me of cruelty, but not more than I accuse myself. No denying, Rosita as she flourished regained all those qualities for which she was renowned in the beginning of her career. Her violence became that of seven gorillas, I swear! It was no longer safe to allow her free play for her little fancies. The jars grew heavier, her aim more certain, the impact more deadly. My health began to suffer. At last, she would not even pose except when she pleased. . . . By some mysterious process of reasoning, she regarded those gorgeous bones as her own property. Imagine! So I said to her one day, a last kiss, my tender little Rosita, and we part. It was so. I went away. I did not see her alive again."

A pause. "Well, Amado, she was really a child, I was no fit guardian for her. You remember that she went to say goodbye to some one the night we brought her here? That person was a woman infatuated with Rosita, and no sooner was I gone than this woman, moved by a monstrous jealousy, took Rosita by surprise and stabbed her to death. Yes, that is what happened to her, all through my impatience, my haste to go. Within an hour I was called back to her, and I saw her with three narrow wounds in her poor heart, her lips the color of wet clay. My God, I still cannot believe it. But it is surely ended."

Amado waited a moment, but [Rubén] said nothing more. Amado could not read the look on his face, where one emotion lay always on the surface and another flickered like a smothered light beneath. Amado felt it would be better to say, "I loved her," and he lingered trying to form the words. He did not speak, for [Rubén] would laugh, without amusement. It was bitter to discover that his friend must be treated as an enemy: that terrible enemy who tempts the confidence and despises the suffering heart that reveals itself.

In his own house, Amado sat for a long time with his head in his hands, grieving formlessly. Afterward he began to think of her, lying very still as he had seen her that first night in [Rubén]'s house: but now she breathed no longer, being eased and rested—poor Rosita, poor thing! He began to cry, and felt as if he had been crying, so, for a long time somewhere inside him, and the tears were just now finding a way out. This sudden refreshment of tears and the thought of death broke down for him his fear of Rosita's resistance to his humanity. Now it seemed merely stupid of him not to have spoken to her when he first wanted to: he might have gone to her so simply at any moment and said, "Rosita, it is like this with me, don't trouble to despise me any longer, but let me love you." Now the words sounded right, he wept again because he had not said them at the perfect time. She would certainly have answered, and it seemed now it would not have mattered much what answer she gave, only he would not have been left wondering, as he must wonder all his life, what might have happened if he had spoken.

No, for the first time he could not bear the past. Remembrance was altogether a waste. He went to his table, arranging his thoughts as he dried his eyes and selected a pen. He wrote steadily for a number of hours. The rest of the night he spent pacing the room, reading aloud to himself in a frenzy, now and then stopping to correct slightly, a poem covering several large pages.

The following evening, very early, he went to the Cafe de los Monotes, looking for [Rubén]. He found him, already a little drunk, sitting with Ramón, Pancho Guerra, an Indian sculptor with a face like a sacred tiger in greenish stone, and Cristina, a little dancer who talked only when she had a new dirty joke to tell. This was not the audience he would have chosen, but he read his poem just the same.

It was a fine swinging ballad in a hurrying medieval style, relating the sorrowful life, the tragic death, and the triumphal entry into a waiting heaven of Rosita. [Rubén]'s superhuman charity to her, and her angelic gratitude, were the two balancing themes. At the climax, she was passed safely through the awful gates of Paradise by Saint Peter, who made her a low bow. The angels welcomed her, and the Blessed Virgin kissed her, and the Lord Christ married her. . . .

They had listened with smiles pressed tight into the corners of their mouths. At this, Cristina tittered, then her throat cracked with tiny explosions. Amado saw their mouths open, their eyes close, and the shocking sound of laughter poured about him from these distorted faces. The veins rose in [Rubén]'s forehead, he beat the table with his fists. Amado rose peering at them as if he saw uncaged wild beasts, and knocking over his chair, he ran for his life.

Thud, thud, came [Rubén]'s great feet after him, [Rubén]'s huge voice calling, "Wait, wait, don't be a fool—" On the sidewalk he seized Amado. . . . "Listen, this has gone too far—let me explain—stop, now, I WILL tell you—"

He chuckled, his chin shaking, but his eyes were drunkenly serious. "It was a tale, I tell you—a tale invented for your amusement! Rosita? My Jesus Christ who could have dreamed—Rosita? She is back in Calle de la Palma, sound, alive—wait, you fool! Amado, dear friend, stop while I tell you—that not a word of the tale is true! I sent her away because the work was finished! She threw everything in the place at me and left—How could I know you would feel her death so seriously?"

"You mistake—it is not her death I feel. It is this outrage to my feelings, this insult to her very existence that you offer as a joke! My ballad! Leave me, leave me—the whole thing is a filthy farce, there is no place for my ballad but the fire!"

Amado stammered and strangled, and when [Rubén] put an arm about his shoulders he broke free. "What you have said about me so often is true, Amado: I am hardhearted. Aside from your sufferings, this seems to me an episode comic in the extreme, a comedy most fruitful for us both. You have your poem, I have my fresco: they are the ends, what else is in the least important? Rosita? pah, dead or alive, how does she figure in this now?"

"I don't know," answered Amado out of his confusion. "I only know she is in it. I loved her," he said after a pause. "It is too bitter."

"I tell you, you loved some fancy you had of her, nothing more. She is not a woman to love, she is a bitch and ugly to her core; any beauty she possesses you added to her yourself. I clothed my idea with her outlines, and I love that: but I never confused the two things."

"Go back to your hyenas in the cafe, I shall go to see Rosita."

"If you must, you must, and afterward, come back and let us be as we were—friends."

They parted.

The duena nodded and inquired, "Shall I send little Sancha? She is a rose for freshness this evening." Her pride was to remember the individual tastes of her patrons.

"I wish to sit alone."

He waited drinking his cognac, now and then glancing slantwise at the girls who entered down the shallow stairway from the patio balcony in the manner of popular actresses, with fixed greasy red smiles and soot-smudged eyelids. At last she appeared at the stair head, and his stomach began to thump like a drum. The garnet colored shawl was twisted around her neck, her ruined face was stiff with rouge. She was more hideous than he remembered her the night [Rubén] came to take her away.

Her eyes were pale blanks in their oval black smears, her glance trailed over Amado and beyond. She moved over to a small table nearby and sat with her back to him.

Amado, his heart contracted now to a hot needle point, sat and watched her for a while, blinking his eyes a little and whirling the liquor round and round in his glass. It was no more possible to speak to her than it had been, and besides, there was nothing to say. Death had dropped between them easingly for a moment, making everything whole and clear, but for him only. She had shared none of that bath of tears, no honorable burial, no tremendous resurrection in Eternity. It had all been his own, made up out of fragments of an idle cruel tale. As for her, she had been cheated of her death when the labor of dying was half done, and now she must begin all over again her interrupted business. All the beautiful thoughts he had had about her sickened him now: he did not love her, he had not loved her, again he had been tricked by his own invented emotions. He was ashamed of his ballad, she would have laughed with the rest, and she would have been right. . . . Yet his feeling toward her persisted with terrible gentleness, as if she were really dead.

Her fingers had not once tightened around the stem of her glass as her hand lay on the table. Limp, full of angles, the wrist protruded from the white sleeve that muffled up the noble arrangement of shoulders and neckbones.

Amado began to hope she had not seen him: but if she had, what possible difference could it make now?

After a little while, he got up and went away.

The Evening

(unfinished story, 1924?)

This story seems to be related to both "Trinidad" and "The Lovely Legend" by virtue of its depiction of cafe scenes and the appearance of some of the same characters. It is also related, in its depiction of the character Gordito, to Porter's 1921 plans for a "Mexican book." The historical reference to the De la Huerta rebellion dates the chronological time of the story to late 1923 or early 1924, although the allusions to General Sidronio Méndez connect it to Porter's 1920–1921 visit to Mexico. The story may have grown out of Porter's 1923 visit to Mexico on assignment for *Survey Graphic*. We believe it was part of the material she planned to publish in a novel to be entitled *Thieves' Market*; in early 1930, Porter signed a contract with Harcourt, Brace which specified publication of this novel in the autumn of 1931.

The story also bears a resemblance to another story on which Porter was working in 1924, "Holiday." Porter's recurring theme of estrangement appears in both. In "The Evening," a "gringa" very much like Porter listens to but does not wholly understand the Spanish chatter of artist friends in a cafe. The language barrier in Mexico deepened her sense of alienation, triggering her memory of an earlier experience in Texas depicted in "Holiday." In both, an alienated female character is at the center of a group who do not speak her native tongue.

The story is also important for its interesting delineation of this central female character, the American dancer Alma. An earlier draft of the story outlines her "insatiable thirst" for excitement, "her eagerness to be beautiful in their eyes," her desire "to inspire love, not to love," "her malice, her sensuality, her instinctive worldliness, her waywardness," and her essential "modernness." These traits suggest a self-portrait of Porter in 1924, who like Alma had "fine eyes," "slender ankles," and a "too thin" mouth. Alma also resembles Laura of "Flowering Judas," whose notorious inaccessibility is meant to frustrate the predatory male who rightly suspects her frigidity, a condition from which Porter apparently suffered.

The other characters who frequent the cafe are members of Mexico City's artistic and revolutionary circle, the fictional counterpart of the milieu from which Porter's own Mexican circle was drawn. The central male figure, the fat, romantic poet and revolutionary called by his friends Gordito, is an early version of Braggioni, whose primary prototype was Samuel Yúdico. Yúdico was one of the four revolutionaries Porter had planned in 1921 to portray in her "Mexican book." The only obviously recognizable portrait is that of Roberto, who is clearly modeled on Adolfo Best-Maugard; little Lino is probably based on Miguel Covarrubias; and Gatita de Oro, on María Conesa (Gatita Blanca), a famous headliner of Mexican popular theater in the 1920s.

The Evening

Gordito stood before the mirror in the coatroom while the girl drew the topcoat from his shoulders. He examined his face carefully for signs of agitation. No, the eyes of a man well established on his center of gravity. He shook his head to rid himself of the buzzing in his ears, and stood on tiptoe to glimpse his waistline in the new riding trousers. Much, much better. Four kilos lost in eleven days. It was really a record. He glanced through the half open door of the cafe with a look of homecoming, and sniffed a good smell of food and wine. He needed both.

Yes, there they were, loafers all. They were grouped exactly as when he had last seen them, three nights before, one might believe they slept in the place; he despised them warmly and affectionately, wishing to embrace them for being there when he had come hoping to find them: Ciro, Vicente, Roberto, little Lino, and with them a girl whose face was turned away, but whose long shoulder line and lank thigh identified [her] as the American dancer.

Lino saw him first. "Zzzzzt!" he whistled through his crooked front teeth, "Gordito!" The others turned and took up the call. Their faces were mirrors of welcome, but the detested nickname hurt his ears. They made a great space for his chair, and Ciro poured him a glass of wine, with his air of deliberate elegance, watching the thin clear stream as if it were a work of art. Gordito responded with a dignity he had not intended when he came in, slid into place purposely making himself as small as he could, and managed to create about himself an atmosphere of gloom.

He had just risked his life—not that it mattered, but still, there you were!—in a cause that intimately concerned them all. Besides, he was not so fat as he had been: why could they not see it? All of them gathered here, drinking their heads off, getting the orchestra to play their favorite tunes, discussing Ouspensky no doubt, since Roberto was present, and all the time he had been riding for his life—for their lives too! He measured them resentfully with an eye that reduced them to worms; it's no joke to dodge twenty bullets that come from nowhere in a darkness blacker than a pocket. He had not been so close to death since the time Casa-Mero had emptied his revolver down the center of Fabacher's cafe by way of a little Sixteenth of September prank. And always that gringa with them. Gordito distrusted her. She was not really beautiful, in spite of her fine eyes and slender ankles. Her mouth was too thin, she was not by any means young enough. Twenty-four at least. A cold woman with an experienced glance. He knew them well, these visiting gringas frias. They let you make love to them as if they thought you meant to pick their pockets. So cold it made a man chatter to touch them. He remembered his unhappy year in a military school in Virginia, and all those self-possessed virgins who went about without a chaperone, leaving so much to be inferred, defending their virtue single-handed after they themselves had raised a question of it. Brrrr!

"Are you chilled?" asked the gringa fria, amiably, smiling at him with smooth white teeth. "You are fairly chattering."

"I had a thought of death," Gordito answered, giving her all his attention suddenly. "A death I lately witnessed." He told her about it carefully, trying to match her childish Spanish with his own. A dear companion riding with him on an errand of some military importance had been shot from ambush. He carried in his coat a communication from General Rioseco to General Mendez, a document of incalculable moral weight. In a few words, while the others were silenced for a moment, he made them see that the whole current of the present revolution might be altered by this death, a death which in fact had not occurred, because the man named had never been born. As for the communication, it was infallibly delivered—he omitted to say by whom, it was so easy to guess—only a little late, true, but maybe too late.

It was a perfect story, and in it he glorified somewhat the history of that soiled packet of papers he had just placed in the hands of General Mendez, they being merely a half dozen intercepted letters from minor trouble makers in the opposite camp, and a manifesto to which several leading generals had foolishly set their names: an act they might be much troubled to explain later, in case their cause failed. The campaign, explained Gordito, might now go forward, but never never by any chance so well, now that his devoted friend, Angel del Castillo was dead. The group listened, their faces darkened and grew tragic. Ciro, who had been dipping lumps of sugar in brandy and burning them for the sake of the exquisitely coloured flame, had tears in his eyes. Or what looked like tears. Gordito leaned toward him.

"You remember poor Angel, then?"

"Perfectly, perfectly," muttered Ciro, thinking that surely no such name could exist outside of a fancy novel, "an ardent and heroic soul." His look met Gordito's, vanished under his lids, he burned another sugar lump.

"Yes, yes, yes," murmured the others, a vapour of elegy breathed above their heads. The gringa watched, listened, sighed, shuddered, took a deep swallow of wine. Her eyes deepened, her lips warmed and softened. Now she might be called beautiful, but it was the beauty of mood only. An uncapturable thing: he must look at her now while she was lovely. Tomorrow in the streets she might be drawn and hideous as he remembered her once before, dressed in American flannels, with imitation man's shoes. For a flash some bubble in his mind held a pre-vision of her face, relaxed and pale in sleep on a tumbled white pillow after a night of love. Brrr! She would look like a dead woman. She was too thin: she was eating jellied broth, my God, imagine! He shuddered again, the flesh prickled on his bones. Truth was, the entire day had got on his nerves. He was sick of his own thoughts, and decided to dismiss them as unworthy of him and of his recent experience.

Ciro and Vicente were in a mood of indulgence for Gordito. He had done well with his story, silly as it was, but he usually blundered, poor fellow. As for the ambush, it might have happened to any one of them, and was not much more exciting than a dash of good brandy. Little Lino was unimpressed by Gordito's adventure, but it had set him off on his own prospects. He had reached that stage in his evening's development where he was again vowing to take horse no later than tomorrow and ride south to General Gomez, and help scatter the de la Huertistas to the four cardinal points, to say nothing of the earth and sky. His youth's face, shallow as a mask, tightened up a bit and he looked around, but no one took him seriously. "If you should go, your little brother would have no one to quarrel with," said Roberto.

The girl sat among them, her big hat shading her eyes, hoping she looked like a Mexican. She had that pleasant sense of social anonymity which in certain moods invites to the expansion of the personality. She felt deliciously lost to her familiar background, restored to her proper self. But she knew the fat one was indifferent to her, the one who was called a good poet and a bad joke by the others, and she despised him because he was fat, and because the others ridiculed him a trifle uneasily, and because he was indifferent to her. She dimly felt that he rejected her on some intimate prompting of personal taste, and she was affronted. They all recognised her essential qualities . . . did he, also, and were they unattractive to him? She herself did not know precisely what these qualities were, and they did not tell her, but they cast delightful hints. . . . Among themselves they were quite frank. By a myriad subtle signs they read her: her malice, her sensuality, her instinctive worldliness, her waywardness; and that indefinable thing they called "modernness." At this altar they would all consent to worship for a moment. Even her imperfections were not defects, because they were appealing. Thus Vicente assured her, studying her features with intimate candour, exclaiming against the appalling perfections of the Classic Greeks, praising the sensitive distortions and irregularities of modern beauty, that delicate enchantment, fluid as the poses of a dancer, which could never be measured, analysed: The adorable beauty-in-ugliness which baffled the mind and from which the heart could never free itself: a thing never to be lost, because never wholly captured. . . .

He convinced himself. He suffered in his heart for love of that ideal. He convinced all the others save Gordito.

"The romantic attitude merely," he began conscious that he was being heavily academic. He cringed innerly expecting the foul word to smite him before he could get on with his argument. He felt it settling upon their minds as they listened, closing the channels of their interest. "Also the preoccupation of an inadequate esthetic which dares not aspire to the awful grandeur of perfection." He made his attack personal in order to get their attention. "You are in point of fact a snob, dear Vicente . . . and you have a fashionable mind. It is fashionable to love the ugly, the second-rate, the half-alive. . . ."

"Half-alive!" shouted Ciro, who had been amusing himself looking at his own reflection in the bowl of a silver spoon. "But that is the point! The perfect thing is already dead. It dies of its own consent. . . . To be perfect is to commit suicide. The living thing is that which struggles, the beauty must labour to be born out of the ugliness in which it is enclosed. Oh, the beauty of that distortion! The line of a woman's cheek a little wrong, the pose of her head almost in complete harmony with her neck as it slides down to the exquisite line of her too-thin shoulder. . . ." He did not glance at the girl, but the others did. Her vanity trembled under the regard, receded a little, swayed back reassured. . . . "*But not quite!* You feel the breath of beauty, you shudder with its nearness, it does not quite touch you . . . but from that moment you are a pilgrim in search of that harmony you have missed, oh, by a breath only, you die seeking it! Away with your classicists! . . ."

Vicente burst in, a little annoyed that Ciro had taken up his idea and expanded it as if it were his own. And he was bitterly offended at Gordito.

"It is true there is no longer a canon of beauty. We are not governed by an esthetic hierarchy . . . but it is also true, lamentably, lamentably! that a preference for one's own bad taste is no warrant of authority for making new laws. . . . I distrust empiricists, I reject that amateurish emotionalism which considers all things beautiful that move the enthusiasms. . . . There is a definitive ugliness, there is an ideal Beauty . . . a profound, unalterable Law exists. . . ."

"Where? Who makes the law? Who will enforce it?" They all talked at once. "Is art governed by the caprices of a military occupation?"

Roberto, raising his voice, began explaining that Beauty was the manifestation of the divine Energy, the Creative Principle which could not be less than perfect. "This Energy was in everything, yes, in absolutely everything, our failure to perceive beauty was a perversity of vision in ourselves. . . ." He looked about him for something sufficiently hideous to point his example. "No created thing, down to the very atom, was without beauty. . . ." His wandering eye lighted on an amazingly decorated cuspidor, a monstrosity in gilt and scarlet bulbous roses. The impact on his eye nerves seemed to tie knots in his stomach. He blinked, looked away again. But the others were too quick for him. "The cuspidor!" they chanted in chorus. "Even the cuspidor—even that—is beautiful, no?" Roberto was wounded in his love of his idea. But continuing, he affirmed nobly that the impulse back of the dreadful object—he did not glance at it again— was to create an image of beauty. "The impulse, then, came from the soul of man, and was therefore beautiful . . . sublime, even. Unutterably moving to the heart, that terrific will to make out of one's own material an expression of harmony, of obedience to the majestic law of Energy. If it had failed, it was only because of our blindness. It was right, it had its place in eternity. It was no more ugly than a cripple could be ugly: A blind and limbless beggar carried in him the God-head, his share of divinity. The Spark, the impulse, was divine, was immaculate. . . ."

The girl, sitting quietly, knew they had not forgotten her presence. But as their voices rose, they talked so rapidly the language became a blur. They dropped into the elaborate invented argot of their group, confusing her further. . . . She could no longer understand the words, so she leaned back and closed her eyes, and the sounds translated themselves to her in terms of emotion. No great problem was being settled, or even discussed, really. It was a personal contest, they were trying to silence one another, they were all a little bored. And boredom was a confession of inner resourcelessness. . . . They must not be bored. . . . They had lost sight of the subject, and now the subject itself suddenly vanished. It was time for her to come back. She opened her eyes and sat up as Vicente said to Ciro, in a changed, dry voice—"I mean to go to San Luis Potosi tomorrow or the next day." They leaned together, and the argot crept back into their speech. But Gordito said clearly, "My plans are what they were. I go to Baja California. . . ."

The girl saw them for a moment as phantoms, dissolving before her eyes, floating away in whispers. That they all were entangled in some way in the coming revolution was plain, they all had plans, but what they were, and the reasons for them, she could not grasp. And she could not greatly care. She wished them to talk to her again, and about her.

After midnight a half dozen more friends dropped in, the men with their air of living in cafes, the women with theirs of being on exhibition. The women were all dancers or actresses from the Esperanza Iris or the Teatro Lirico, they all stared at the American dancer whose show had been a complete failure, but who had stayed on in Mexico. She felt herself again a foreigner, and the men at her table were strangers. The famous Gatita de Oro was present now formally rouged and dyed and laced, but with Parisian discretion and resource. She would say, "Being the pet of the Mexican public is a martyrdom!" But still she danced, and if her fortunes failed, she went to Yucatán for a half a season. Her appearances were more than mere performances, they were nightly battles with a lover. She purred and fawned and sang her famous songs, challenging even to the cynical imagination of a Mexican audience. Her voice shamed the peacock, and she danced with ferocious energy in the old style. The people applauded her with endearing phrases, with flung coins, the men would cast their hats upon the stage. But there were nights when she did not please them. Something went a little wrong, and the audience would rise, hissing and shouting curious epithets at her, until she would stand defeated, shaking her fist at them, and the curtain would plump down between them like a barricade between two skirmishing parties.

This redoubtable woman gave the foreign girl a look which disposed of her as a presence, and sat down by Vicente, who flung his arm across the back of her chair. They were old friends, he had been her lover, every man present had been her lover. She glowed, present like a ruby-lamp upon the scene.

Gordito sat and ate cold chicken with slices of bread and cheese and quince jelly. Nothing could be worse for him than sweets. In a world so utterly dull, what could be more stupid than going to Baja California and getting full of fleas in the desert, in the hope of killing a few de la Huertistas? But his friend Gomez was there, now a general; Gomez had a great quarrel with the de la Huerta general in that part of the country. . . . Loyalty to other people's causes was one form of imbecility. Still, he would go. . . .

Ciro watched the girl, whose name was Alma, and wondered where he should take her, since his friend Vicente had borrowed his lionera for the night, meaning to go there with Cristina, a plump gay girl with breasts like tight pink toy balloons. Cristina even now was showing her legs to Lino under the table. When he got up to dance with Alma, Ciro made up his mind. They would go early, Vicente would find the door barred, he would have to take his Cristina somewhere else . . . surely a friend must be expected to comprehend and pardon an emergency. Alma's body when she danced was like a long velvet scarf, warmed and electric. For a moment he had a complete illusion of love.

Gordito watched them go, his eyes like lusterless brown agates. Lino forgot Cristina's legs, and Vicente remembered them. Roberto, head on hand, felt the nerves in the corner of his mouth twitching.

"The business ended well, then?" He asked Gordito at length, without interest, for he had lived in Paris from his childhood until the age at which his mind no longer accepted the possibility of affection for his own country, and Mexico troubled him like an inherited weakness.

"Well enough," answered Gordito, "I left the Villa Guadalupe at dusk. Really, nothing happened. On the edge of Churubusco, I was fired upon. I came on, precautions mean less and less. . . . This carrying of pointless messages between Generals who will do nothing until the plans of the enemy are published in the papers must go on without me. . . ." He looked about the cafe where Americans with blunt, suety faces were experimenting with guacamole and broiled gusanos. The women were applauding the orchestra after drinking too many strawberry pink cocktail novias; under the fixed constellation of green white electric bulbs above their heads, they looked dazed and melancholy; the men usually quarrelled with the waiters . . . an imperfectly domesticated, semi-barbarous race, who still looked upon cafes as feeding places merely. Places where one might get more drunk than was permissible at home . . . a race of tourists. . . . The capital was insupportable: he breathed in harsh nasal noises with the smell of mixed liquors. He thought of the desert where he would soon be with longing, as an incorruptible thing. "I shall join Gomez, there is no need to delay any longer." As he spoke, his own plans depressed him. He had meant to spend the summer at Lake Chapala in the village where time forgets to move, and it is always a clear summer, and the girls came down at early morning to bathe in the rosy-lighted lake, splashing and calling to each other without disturbing the white herons at the water's rim. Now, nothing. Vicente and Cristina were gone, little Lino was yawning, having grown bored with his own obscene caricatures of the nose of the man at a near table. Roberto said nothing. The evening was dead. It had been slain at last, it sprawled there clammily on the table between them.

The Princess

(unfinished story, 1927–1928?)

Like the three children's stories Porter interpreted from legend for *Everyland* in 1920, "The Princess" centers on a woman who gets her own way and becomes the subject of legend. The main character is a royal princess, as are those of "The Faithful Princess" and "The Magic Ear Ring." Like Nayagta in "The Shattered Star," her lack of conformity to the norms of her culture brings her suffering and ostracism. There also seem to be intimations of this fictional princess in Porter's poem "Requiescat—" in *Measure* 38 (April 1924), reprinted as "Little Requiem" in her *Collected Essays* ("the state of a king's daughter"; "a scaled silver armour for a breast cover"). The story rehearses a common theme in Porter's work, that of a woman who is forced to make the choice between the traditional roles of women and her desire to be an artist. Clearly this is a decision fraught with pain, as suggested in "Old Mortality," in which Porter's alter ego Miranda rejects husband and family.

In its exploration of this subject, "The Princess" exhibits a strong resemblance to an essay on which Porter was working in 1928; it exists in two drafts among her papers titled "Notes on Two Spanish-American Poets" and "Sor Juana Inés de la Cruz, Gabriela Mistral." Porter's interest in Sor Juana dates at the very least to her translation published in 1924. The never-published and incomplete essay contrasts and compares Sor Juana and the twentieth-century Chilean poet, centering on the conflict they suffered because they were women artists and thus caught between the physical ("ardor for human love, for maternity, for the earth," "the world of the senses") and the intellectual ("the world of ideas"). Each was, unlike the princess, "the willing victim of her times" because she accepted the "limitations of sex" and "played a classic feminine role, though somewhat on the grand scale": "poverty, chastity, obedience, and perpetual enclosure." The princess has chosen to suffer for her art and to reject nature, both its biological and aesthetic dictates. Her decision results in her death, but also in her immortality. The young acolyte who becomes her betrothed immortalizes them both: his fine poetry records both her history and his love. The story suggests what Porter averred in 1940, that the arts "represent the substance of faith and the only reality" (introduction to Modern Library edition of *Flowering Judas and Other Stories* [1940]; reprinted in *Collected Essays* [1970]). We have dated the story 1927–1928 because of its affinities with the Sor Juana–Gabriela Mistral piece and because of the similarity in physical appearance of the typescript of the most polished part of the manuscript with typewritten letters of Porter from this period.

The Princess

When the Princess arrived at her thirteenth year she refused steadfastly to remove her white linen shift and walk naked among the other marriageable virgins of her father's kingdom.

This caused a scandal among the people, especially among the elderly women of the tribe, who, as a sign that they had buried their youth, had returned to shifts of grey sack-cloth. The young girls made round eyes and mouths at her, and the lads looked with their eyelids askew. The Chief of the Royal Council called a secret conference, and the High Priestess retired within the inner temple for the space of nine days. She emerged with the word of divine revelation on her lips.

"Let the Princess come alone to the altar and cast her shift upon the fire in a special ceremony, and the taint of heresy may even yet be lifted from her." And the youths and maidens who had taken part in the spring feasts gathered about and implored her to listen to the commands of the gods.

"I will not disrobe," said the Princess, sitting among her maids, all naked as asparagus stalks and as thin. She crossed her arms wax-tight over her bosom so that no one could remove the garment without disturbing the royal person.

"She is a little mad, no doubt," said the High Priestess, whose only garment was a hieratic nose ring of polished iron.

The Queen was royally upset at this. "She read the magic runes on her father's sword at the age of five and that without instruction! No other child has done this."

"A certain sign of holy madness," amended the High Priestess firmly. "That is too great wisdom for a natural infant."

"We cannot afford any holy madness in the family at this moment," cried the distracted Queen. "The succession of our dynasty depends on this girl!"

"That is worldly talk, and the gods are not deaf," answered the High Priestess, who never hesitated to rebuke the Queen her brother's wife when the dignity of the Sacred Office required it.

"The people will think the Princess has a crooked back, or a twisted knee, and for this she will not show herself," ventured the old nurse, who had both of these afflictions, and so could think of nothing else.

"They know she is straight and full of sap as a young tree flowering for the first time!" answered the Queen. "They have seen her thin legs running under her shift!"

"I will not disrobe!" said the Princess, smoothing out the folds of her white garment, and drawing them closer over her bosom.

The Queen, innocent of raiment save her ravelled hair, covered her eyes to shut out the sight of her shameless daughter.

"Then we will speak to your father, the King!" cried the High Priestess, quite beside herself.

"Speak to him. And when I am Queen, for every word you utter now, I promise you a year in prison when you are old!" answered the good natured Princess, shaking her long red hair like a flag at the High Priestess.

"But it is strange, it is incomprehensible, it is monstrous and now what shall we do with you?" complained the High Priestess, bitterly.

"I do not know. But if you annoy me further, I shall put [on] two shifts," said the Princess. And very much annoyed as she was, she instantly put on another shift over the first, and sat where the whole court could see her.

The High Priestess went into retirement for another nine days, and the Chief of the Royal Council called a second conference, and the Queen lay on her cushions and wept. The King, who left all affairs of government to the Chief of the Royal Council and all affairs of religion to the High Priestess, and all affairs of the palace to the Queen, now took a firm hand in the matter. He issued a manifesto to the people, assuring them that in this, as in all other things touching the happiness and welfare of his beloved people, he, their King, would remain in full command of the situation, and would bring this slight disturbance shortly to a just and peaceful conclusion.

Thus pacified, the people waited, for they loved the Princess. And strange things happened. Among a people so dedicated to the love and worship of nature that food must be eaten without the pollution of fire, where no woman bound up her hair nor man hindered his beard, the Princess sat in her father's palace, and directed her maids to weave lengths of cloth for new garments. The simple looms which served to weave the scant garments of the little girls, and of the women past the time of bearing were not enough, and she devised new ones. Soon three maidens were employed in the sole task of pressing out the juices from berries and leaves wherewith to dye these robes, and the Princess walked abroad wearing them, vari-coloured and to the number of five, one over the other, and when she stirred her knees she rustled like a tree in full leaf.

There was at this time in the temple a young acolyte, a youth of eighteen years, who with others of his kind served his turn at assisting in the rites of the spring sowing, when the betrothed maidens of the kingdom went in a procession to the inner temple to bid farewell to their virginity.

This was called also the feast of marriage with the god, and even maidens not betrothed were eager to offer themselves, for to continue a virgin beyond the fifteenth year was cause for shame. But the Princess continued to clothe herself strangely, and to attend the feast of marriage by the side of her mother, and for two years she refused to offer herself. When the people talked among themselves, the High Priestess spoke sternly to them, as if they blasphemed, and the Queen would say in the court: "This is the curious whim of a child, and will pass."

The Princess came to the third feast with the Queen, and all her maids in attendance. She wore three robes of scarlet and blue and purple woven of the threads made from a strange worm she had discovered in the mulberry grove, and now she caused the trees where these worms fed to be cared for by men who did nothing else, and her garments glistened and crackled like flame as she walked. The young acolyte saw her there, with her red hair braided, her grey eyes wide and cold; he felt a strangeness about her, and a terrible fated loneliness, and afterward he could not forget her.

When the brides came out of the inner temple carrying their lighted torches and singing above the sound of the drums, the Princess did not join the others in the dancing, but walked among her maids with her head bowed, looking about her not at all, and if she heard the murmurs of distrust and unbelief from her future subjects, she seemed not to hear them.

Day by day she went about devising new ways of covering herself. Her robes grew heavier and more ample, and the cloth was of bright shining substance, as if she had learned to spin gold and silver into airy threads.

When she went into the streets of the city even her maidens blushed for shame of her strangeness. The women twisted their mouths and said, "Because she is not beautiful, she does this in order to snare a lover in a new way!" But the men searched the folds of her robes with cautious stares, wishing their eyes were hands; and turned away, saying each one to himself, "Not even the gods know what manner of woman is concealed in that robe!" Many a youth tossed and sweated at night with the thought of her, and groaned in his sleep as if his bed were full of stones: but they dared nothing, for fear of her answer.

When the Princess came to her eighteenth year, it was common scandal that no man had ever asked for her in marriage, nor had she been known even so much as to glance at the acolytes of the temple, who were the most beautiful youths in the kingdom. She sat on a dais all day in the King's palace, directing her maids in the art of beating heated metal into divers shapes, and fashioning splendid ornaments of brightly coloured stones. And when these were done, the girls would look about them to make certain no one saw, and then would try them on their wrists, and about their bodies for a moment, blushing at their own reflections in the oval pool of green water; this always pleased the Princess, who would say, "Some day you will wear these things without blushing. And at last you will wear them with pride." But they would take them off again in silence, and the Princess would wear them.

One day the youth who had been acolyte in the thirteenth year of the Princess came to the palace, and presented himself before the King and Queen. For he could no longer bear the trouble that was in his heart, and he prayed that the Princess might be given in marriage to him.

The King said privately to the Queen: "I had hoped it might be the son of the Chief of the Royal Council. But whoever wants this mad girl may have her and welcome, and the gods grant he may work a change in her.

If she rules alone, this kingdom will be corrupted and go the way of the Blaisians, who covered even their fighting men with cloth and steel, so that the nation perished of a plague; or of the Ruzanites who put their food in the fire before eating it, so that their stomachs rotted while they yet lived. . . . I am resolved that this people shall not be destroyed in such ways, even though our dynasty disappear with this girl."

The Queen answered, "Never let it be hinted that this dynasty shall end. A husband will cure her of all these fancies, and we shall have twenty grandchildren and a happy succession to the throne even yet."

So the royal pair welcomed the youth, and asked him fewer than three questions before they gave their consent to his marriage with the Princess, which might be arranged to take place within the very month.

The news of the betrothal of the Princess was called every where in the city by messengers from the Royal household, who ran through every street beating upon drums and shouting, and a great feast was given to the populace. The King and the Queen appeared and the Chief of the Royal Council in a great voice announced that the Princess even that moment was preparing to lead a procession to the temple, where she would lay aside her adornments, and partake of the ceremonies natural to her state.

To the sounds of singing and laughter, and the light of bonfire that turned even the clouds red as a sunset, the Princess came before the people. Two of her maids held up her hands, and she walked slowly under the weight of her robes, for she wore now a flexible breast plate of silver and blue stones, and a wrought girdle of blue stones and silver tassels, and her arms were weighted with like jewels. Her hair was woven with golden threads, and she kept her eyes hidden. A dark silence fell about her as she came, and her sandals of gold clashed musically as bells upon the stones, and her bracelets jingled a sweet tune. And such was the silence that came upon all the people as she passed, no sound was heard except this music as the procession came into the temple.

The Princess went up to the altar, where the High Priestess sat with folded legs and crossed hands. "Bring the youth to me," said the Princess in a clear voice. And when he approached, she looked at him a long time in silence.

"Disrobe and cast upon the fire your heretical garments," commanded the High Priestess.

"I will not disrobe," said the Princess. "Nor will I suffer one fold of my robe to be touched by any living creature." She turned to the youth. "This is the beauty I have created out of a dream and a vision, and I shall wear it until my death. But if you will, let us be betrothed, in a way I shall devise, and not by ceremonies full of blood and the smell of scorched grain. . . . And in time, when I am Queen, you shall be King. But by no means shall we touch even the tips of our hands together until our dream shall be made perfect."

And the youth said, "I accept all, for the sake of our dream."

At this the High Priestess rose, and lifted her arms saying, "There can be no betrothal rightly celebrated which omits even a nod of the head from the canonical ritual! Let this blasphemy cease!"

"We have no further concern with this place," said the Princess to her lover. And they moved a little toward one another, and walked at the head of the procession smiling, and so went out from the temple . . . and the High Priestess in a rage went into retirement for nine days, and emerged with tight locked lips and a frowning brow. And what the gods had whispered to her she refused to tell even to the King her brother. But she warned him most gravely: "Look well to this, O King, my brother, that the sacred earth and the venerated fruits thereof be not violated and the hands of your people be not wasted in the service of the idol-maker. Remember that the holy river shall wash away all that is dust."

The King could make nothing of these words, and repeated them to the Queen, who found them so puzzling that she repeated them to the Chief of the Royal Council, who promised to ponder them long, and if possible discover their meaning, and so make it known to the King and Queen. And that night he started from a sound sleep remembering that in the old days it was the custom to drown heretics in the holy river that flowed past the east wall of the city. Being Chief of the Royal Council and therefore discreet, he slept again, and said nothing of his recollection to the King and Queen.

Now the lover of the Princess took his place in the palace, and on feast days he faced the people beside the Princess. But the people did not understand, and they complained, "What manner of betrothal is this between a heretic Princess and a man who is afraid, and consents to her heresy?"

But these murmurings were in whispers among themselves, and they waited. For they had once loved the Princess. And the lover of the Princess sat at her feet and said, "Let me kiss your hands, O delight of the World." And she promised him, "Tomorrow."

And when tomorrow came he held out her hand, but it was covered with a glove of woven silver, and set with thorny jewels, so that his lips bled at the touch. And he said then, "Not your cruel hand, O Princess, but your soft woven hair—Let me kiss your hair!" And the Princess promised, "Tomorrow!"

And when tomorrow came, the Princess sat on her dais, wearing upon her head a tall crown of white jewels which flowed with pale coloured [light] as if fire burned in the hearts of icicles, and the braids of her hair were woven with these same stones, all sharpened like little daggers. And the lover could not touch them without cutting his hands cruelly. So he said, "Our dream is one of sorrow, my adored and my beloved, yet I would kiss your eyelids. Let me kiss your eyelids, and I shall love you forever."

And the Princess promised, "Tomorrow."

All night the Princess sat among her maids who worked with molten metals, and they said not a word, but worked as if they kept a secret under their fingertips. And when the morning came, the lover saw not the Princess, but an image in stiff woven robes of gold, with corselet and girdle of jewels, and a tall crown of pointed crystals, and the face of the image was a golden mask, with eyes of amethyst. Yet the voice of the Princess spoke from within the mask.

"Am I beautiful in your eyes, my beloved and my betrothed?"

"I see an image with the voice of a woman," said the lover, "but for the sake of a dream I had I will remember you forever."

The maidens danced and sang, shaking out their long hair, and splashing in the pool, they kicked up their rosy heels. The lover watched them, and said, "They are like the petals of many-shaded pale flowers after rain."

"They are like little statues of amethyst," said the Princess.

"I see only a group of young girls in a state of holy nature," said an older dame of the palace lately returned to a shift.

"Nature is abhorrent, a vulgarity perpetually to be denied by the soul of man," answered the Princess.

"Soul?" pondered the dame. "And what part of man is that, pray, my Princess?"

"It is the only part of man which he creates himself," answered the Princess. Then she turned away the golden mask, and the dame dared not question her further. But she repeated the strange word here and there, and it came to the High Priestess that the Princess declared man to have some quality or element other than that held in common by all sentient things, and that she had given a strange name to it. The High Priestess talked long and earnestly with the King, who promised that the Princess would be cautioned with great severity against her habit of making riddles in public.

"The whim of a wild, but good hearted girl, my dear," urged the King. "All this nonsense of dressing up in unheard ways—the high spirits of youth. Let her be a little while longer."

"It is time something were done about it," said the High Priestess. "The gods will not have patience forever. Nor will your subjects continue to be uncorrupted by the sight of a heretic in the palace of their King."

The King was troubled. "You cannot suggest a remedy stopping short of harshness to my child?"

"Let her strip herself of these baubles, and celebrate her marriage with the youth you have given her, and that will be the end," said the High Priestess.

But the Princess said, "The day of my marriage is far off. There is one thing more I wait for, and our dream shall be made perfect."

The lover pondered what the thing might be, but he could not guess. The King said, "You may have a carpet of woven silver to walk upon, if only you will put off these strange things, and be Queen over these people after the old way, when I am dead."

The Queen said, "May I live to dandle my grandchildren upon my knee." And the Chief of the Royal Council said, "Why do you suffer the torments of these robes and the dark mask and the sharpened jewels of your gloves?"

"I will make beauty after my own secret thought," said the Princess, "and I will also devise my own cruelties, rejecting utterly the banal sufferings imposed by nature."

This saying, a little distorted, came in time to the ears of the High Priestess, at that very moment in throes of a sacrificial potion, compounded of bitter herbs which she drank at the full of the moon as vicarious easement of women in childbirth. Her contortions were dreadful to endure and behold, and this frequent necessary ritual of her exalted station was gradually souring her temper. <She was therefore enraged against the willful princess. "Tell the Princess," she said, between throes, "that if she scorns and rejects the natural office of motherhood it is written that she will never rule over this kingdom. For the fruitless woman may not inherit the throne, no, not even if she is the sole child of her father."

When the Queen heard that the High Priestess had, to all practical intents, delivered the canonical curse against her daughter, she hastened to the temple and remonstrated urgently with that Sacred functionary, who was now recovered, and in better humour. "But still we cannot permit it," she reminded the Queen. "A ruler must be a mirror wherein the most simple of his subjects gazes, seeing reflected there all his own virtues and traits, but magnified and made royal: So that a poor woman may say with pride, 'I bore my child on the same day when the Queen was delivered, and she sent me a shift for the child, cut from the same cloth with that of her own infant.' Or a wood cutter may say, 'True, I suffer with the cramp when the wind is in the south east but so does the King, and the great Zehdrah give us both strength to endure it!' It is with these invisible threads that we weave a mighty bond between ruler and subject, and if the Princess persists in her madness, there will not be one loyal subject left to her when she is ready to take up the scepter."

"Beside, it is immoral," said the dear good Queen.

"Oh, that! . . ." answered the High Priestess, and immediately added, "Your most gracious majesty is such a refulgent example of all that royalty should be, I wonder at your daughter's blindness in her course. . . ."

The Queen bowed, the High Priestess bowed, though a shade more profoundly. This was because she could afford a gesture of humility before the Queen, who must cajole her subjects, while she, the High Priestess, commanded them.

The Queen knew well enough why the High Priestess bowed lower than she, and resolved not be outdone in pride. She therefore bowed again, exceeding the depth of the bow of the High Priestess by several inches. Whereat the High Priestess bowed until her forehead almost touched the floor, and the Queen, who was the elder of the two and not agile, bent over as far as her spine would permit, but could by no means equal the obeisance of the High Priestess. Whereat she gave up, and the two great ladies kissed each other amiably on the cheeks and parted, without another word about the Princess.

But the Queen complained to the King afterward that the High Priestess was getting more and more high and mighty every day and that the Queen was quite sick of the sight of the High Priestess giving herself airs. The King understood the Queen very well, and loved her dearly. . . . He thought that he understood the High Priestess also, and therefore admired her exceedingly. So he said, "Never mind darling, it is hard on the High Priestess to suffer the pangs of labour every month, and yet to be a childless virgin, while you a Queen are married, and have suffered them only once, and have such a fine daughter to show for it. . . ." The Queen saw at once that this was the perfect reason for the conduct of the High Priestess. . . . "If you look at it in that way, for certain she is merely a cross old maid," she agreed cheerfully and was cheerful for the balance of the day.

As for the High Priestess, she was a busy woman, and could not trouble even to laugh at the Queen once she was out of her presence. But she had by no means forgotten the conduct of the Princess, nor did she loose her from the bonds of the canonical curse. . . .>

*   *   *

So the lover became a poet and wrote songs about the Prin[cess.] If he heard running water, he thought of her voice, and any flower that was sweet to smell was her breath, and the glitter of sunlight on water made him nostalgic for the flash and blaze of her jewelled robe; and he grew to loathe the sight of the moon because he could not see the sickle shaped emerald that the Princess saw through her jewelled eyes. In short, there was no beauty but that which came to him through his dream of the Princess, and he came to see all things through her. What was hateful to her, he loathed utterly; and the things [she] loved he worshipped. In short, he became a poet, and wrote songs to the Princess.

The lover looked about him as one who takes his leave without regrets.

She became even as she lived among them, a legend. There were many who professed that they could not remember her face. . . . Some of them remembered that she was oval faced, with a skin the colour of a buttercup: others said she was hideous, and that her eyes were set awry in her head. It was even said an evil fiend in the shape of a bat had torn her face and wounded and spoiled her beauty, and this mask was her way of concealment. Every one remembered her in a different guise, so that at last there were so many legends, no one knew which was the truth.

The women said, "She does this in order to ensnare a lover," and the men said, "Not even the gods know what manner of woman is concealed in that robe."

"This is the beauty I have dreamed and made, and that is the only beauty. . . . If you should strip me, you will find nothing but that beauty I have made . . . and if you kill me, you cannot destroy my dream. . . . If I am heavy with it, it is because the love of beauty is a heavy sorrow, and the making of beauty a task too great for the soul to endure for long."

When she had finished speaking, no one answered for a time. Then an old lawgiver spoke and said, "The woman is mad."

"And a heretic besides," added another. "Since when has she become a god, to create with her hands?"

*   *   *

"We accuse Her Royal Highness with the following offenses against the dignity of the throne, the peace and welfare of the sovereign realm, and the Temples of the most High Zehdrah and of the Woman God."

"Ha, Ha, Ha," laughed the Princess, clearly and suddenly. A terrible silence followed. The judges stared at one another. Had they really heard this sound? The Mask gleamed smooth and golden, the emerald eyes were blank.

"Of unholy practises."

"Ha, ha, ha," laughed the Princess.

This time it was a certainty. . . . The enchantress, the stone image, the heretic, was laughing at her sacred tribunal.

They proceeded solemnly: "Of corrupting the youths and maidens of her court."

"Ha, ha, ha," laughed the Princess.

"Of conspiring against the power of the High Priest and especially of the High Priestess."

"Ha, ha, ha," laughed the Princess.

"Of wantonness with her favourite courtier, who was of low birth."

"Ha, ha, ha," laughed the Princess.

"And for these and other crimes here not to be named, but written in the state secret parchments, and preserved sealed in the archives of state, we do now pronounce sentence of death upon the [Princess], and we purpose therefore, to escort the [Princess] down to the river's edge at sunrise of tomorrow and with due and appropriate ceremonies to drown her as a heretic."

"Ha, ha, ha, ha, ha," laughed the Princess, so gayly and lightly that some of the people forgot themselves and argued with her [when] suddenly [they] remembered things that hurt, and wept.

And those who stood near the Princess saw with amazement how tears suddenly streamed from the emerald eyes of the mask, as if it wept for the Princess while she laughed.

The executioners took her away to the tower to wait for the sunrise. She sat gleaming in the moonlight at the window, and it was whispered about in terror that the Mask wept until the hour of midnight without ceasing. And at this time the watchers slept. So that the Poet came silently, and saw the Princess sitting upright, and the tears rolling down the Mask to her jewelled hands, so that the moonlight glittered and flowed among the coloured stones like water.

"Come with me," said the Poet. "You shall not die. I will take you across the lake, and tomorrow we shall hide in the deep forest beyond, and at night we shall travel, and by this means we shall come to another country, and you shall live forever!"

"I will go with you," said the Princess who always kept her word, "to the lake." And the Mask wept no more. A step at a time the Princess descended the stone steps like a moving statue, and the points of her jewels and the sharp edges of her gloves cut into the hands of the Poet as he supported her. They went through the dreaming street under a sky festooned with white stars and a great scared faced moon, and came to the lake that was clear as a tourmaline to the depths.

Here the Poet knelt and prayed the Princess to be rid of her robes and jewels and so make flight easy and safety certain.

She would not. Then he prayed, "Oh Princess, I have not seen your face since that day we were betrothed, and I am sick with longing to look upon your face! Take off the mask!" But she would not. . . .

"Oh, Princess, let me kiss your bared hand once more, and not this cruel glove of sharp silver and cutting jewels!" But she would not take off the glove.

"Oh Princess, what a cruel thing that your tender breast, the little shy breasts of a young maid, should be crushed under such a corselet. . . . Take off your shield of woven silver and let me heal your bruised breasts with kisses!" But she would not. And the Poet despaired and said, "It was you I loved, oh, Princess, I loved your eyelashes and your nostrils and your thin rosy fingernails, and your naked heels . . . and now these things are hidden, are gone, and I cannot see them any more—and what good is it to me to love a stone, an image wearing a mask?"

"But you will make songs about me until your last day," said the Princess. And with that, she leaned straight over the brink of the lake, and slipped into the water like a falling stone. The water parted for she trailed like a falling star to the bed of waterfern, and lay there glimmering under the moon [and] the little shining silver bubbles frolicked joyously up and danced a moment on the surface.

The Poet lay and watched her until the dawn, and before his eyes there transpired a marvelous and joyous thing.

The Princess lay still in her deep cradle of transparent water, and the waves lipped back and forth over her heavy robes and the cold inert jewels . . . until softly, oh, softly, they were loosened from about her throat and hands and ankles. . . . The crown slipped away and released the long red hair that streamed out like a soft flame, the mask slipped and fell aside.

*   *   *

She lay like a tall thin statue, naked and glistening, her half opened eyes regarded the peering faces above her with drowsy sweet malice. . . .

"Ah, do you see!" cried one of the women, in a voice cold with spite. "She was not so mysterious! She was like the rest of us, simply a woman, after all!"

The lover of the Princess sighed. "She was the most beautiful woman in the world!"

"She is dead!"

"She is still the loveliest thing on earth!"

"She is a half-fathom under water!"

"She is the most beloved thing under the sun!"

∗   ∗   ∗

So sitting there waiting for his death, he made his last song about the Princess. In it he told of his faithful love, and her unrelenting cruelty, and how now at last she had brought him to the dark grave. Indeed, the song was not at all about the Princess, but about himself. . . . And it was from this song of his that I learned about the Princess, about how cruel she really was; and of how the Poet loved her, and of what a faithful lover he was, and how fine a poet.

Return

(unfinished story, 1928)

This is another of the pieces that anticipates "Flowering Judas"; it must have been intended for *Thieves' Market*, as the setting is Mexico City's El Mercado del Volador, known as the Thieves' Market. The beginning of Porter's typescript of the text appears under the heading "History of Slavery in New England/George Moore./John Cottons Body of Judicialls." This heading is crossed out; "Return" and "1928" have been added in Porter's hand. The date and the evidence of the crossed-out heading would suggest that Porter was working on it in 1928, when she was researching her proposed biography of Cotton Mather.

The central figure, Anna, is clearly based on Porter herself, who loved to buy Mexican treasures and admired the carved crystal rabbit, still housed today in Mexico City's Museum of Anthropology. The allusions to a plaster bust and to an attempt to get José out of jail refer to incidents of Porter's life in the summer of 1921. The dead Felipe may be Felipe Carrillo Puerto, who was assassinated on January 3, 1924. The Students' Riot probably refers to the June 25, 1924, mutilation of murals painted by José Clemente Orozco and David Alfaro Siqueiros at the Escuela Nacional Preparatoria.

The piece is unusual in its use of a male character as the central point of view observing the central character, who is a female.

Return

He saw her one morning haunting the puestos in the Thieves' Market, in her no-coloured clothes and her irrelevant hat. Her face was pale as ever, she picked up objects, examined them near sightedly, and dropped them again. He wished to disappear without speaking; he felt that it would wound her if she knew, and this idea drew him toward her.

"Hello, Anna," he said. She did not seem surprised or pleased or annoyed, or indeed, anything else.

"I am on my way to the Museo," she said, dropping his hand after a moment. "But you know? it's funny. To this day I can't remember whether you turn down [this] street, or go straight on by [that] street."

"I thought you would probably be lost," he said.

"No more than usual. Tell me, are these things any good? I'd hate to spend the money if they aren't, and I hate to let them slip if they are."

"Well, do you really want them? They are nice, you mustn't expect to find real treasures, except very very tiny ones. Mexico is picked clean, the good things are in the museo or in the great private collections. It's pretentious to hope for anything more than amusement here. . . ." His voice trailed, the sun was warm on the top of his head, he wished to put on his hat and be gone. She peered at him a little vaguely, felt his vagueness, and resented it vaguely. She desired a little to pick a quarrel with him; when she was angry she found her speech and a point of view, people remembered her if once she really quarrelled with them. But there was nothing now, really nothing to quarrel about. She would have to begin it, it was not worth the trouble.

"Well, thank you, I don't want them badly enough: there's always too much luggage anyhow. Tell me again how to get to the Museo? and good bye. Have you seen anybody I know lately? Tell them hello if they remember me. . . ."

"How long has it been? Four years, Anna! Well, I saw your house the other day, I was passing by accident, there was a great plaster bust sitting in the front window, it looked very strange . . . and I couldn't believe my eyes. It was that great bust Cardenas made of you the summer you were trying to get José out of jail. My God, I said to myself, that's Anna! How she would laugh!"

"I left it in the corner of the bedroom," said Anna. "It was too heavy to carry around. . . ."

"It was good, I thought. . . ."

"Did you? I'm sorry I couldn't keep it. . . . Well, good bye."

"Oh say, I'll walk over with you. . . . Do you know, I always feel I should do something about you, Anna. Something."

"Well, what? But you can't think of anything, can you?"

"No, I can't. Sometime I will explain how I feel."

"I can't, either. Nobody else can. Oh, don't bother, there mayn't be any sometime: and I can find my way. I always do, really."

"What are you going for? Did you find something interesting?"

"Well, yes. . . . I mean, I want to see my crystal rabbit again."

"Crystal rabbit?"

"It's about the size of a lemon, a pure transparent little young rabbit, with fat ears. . . . I always go to see it when I'm here."

"In the Museo?"

"Certainly. Who was living in my house?"

"Oh, just one of our copious Mexican families. Very cheerful, but they don't have red checkered curtains, so it can't look the [same."]

"I was happy there . . ." said Anna, after a short silence. "It was a perfect rook's nest, wasn't it?" She blinked up at the sun, tossed a small scrap of bronze into the air and caught it absent-mindedly. . . . "Some odd-looking dogs lived on the roof. . . . Well, good bye."

"Good bye, then. How long do you expect to be here this time?"

"Oh, I haven't an idea. It depends on whether the money holds out, and whether I can get to Tehuantepec before the rainy season, and some friends were coming down to Vera Cruz in a boat—you know, if I can make it I might go back with them . . . but that's in July, and I thought of Tehuantepec for much later—I can't tell, you see. I thought if I found Felipe I might stay here. He was doing a book or something. You know, he can't write. It's too bad. He spoke of getting me to look it over for him. I don't know. I can't write either, so it seems sort of silly . . ."

"But Felipe is dead, Anna." There was no use in sparing her: he had spent too much time selecting his words, making careful phrases meant to soften facts to her ears. She cut through impatiently, she didn't hear phrases. Her mind stripped off words, reached in and scored out the quick of a communication. She took it as he knew she would: her eyes blazed with pure shock: without grief or regret, without comprehension. He felt again the impossibility of sharing her emotions, no matter how she convinced him. Her emotions affected him as a work of art: with its separate reality, its permanent effect on the imagination. But he could not console a work of art. And he could not say to Anna, "It's all too bad, and I'm sorry." His sympathy half aroused, wore thin. There was nothing to say further.

She spoke, but there was nothing personal in her voice or manner. "I never hear of things until so long afterward," she said without complaint. "I meant to write to him. . . . When did it happen?"

"Well . . . in December I think. He died very simply of pneumonia. Suddenly. In Oaxaca. He merely disappeared, Anna. It is always unexpected."

"Yes. In all my life in the United States, even from my childhood, I have lost only three friends by death. But here in Mexico, whenever I come back, even if it has been only a year, I find two or three gone . . . for all sorts of causes."

"Maybe you have more friends here." She looked up at him, and he saw again that her beauty was so much a matter of identity: Cardenas had said she had the most superb cheek bones in the world. It was true. True and entirely unimportant. There was no release in her company. She weighed on him, beneath her reserves she always managed to make intimate confidences. It was terrible to listen to confidences about things so hidden there could be no bond of sympathy between the teller and the listener. He would go away knowing that Anna had lost one more essential element from her life, but how did it concern him? Still he stayed, and wondered a bit about her. What had passed between her and Felipe that he always thought of them in the one thought? Yet he had never seen them together more than twice. They had sat miles apart over a table, and talked of most improbable things. . . . There had been a bond, but nothing had come of it. Felipe being dead did not really interrupt anything. The sun was growing hotter, he desired to be away. The thought of Felipe oppressed him. Or was it Anna's face, now greenish pale with the reflection from the washed stones of the market floor. He remembered her when she was alive, slowly the life had been sapped from her, she was not related to anything that he knew or cared for any longer. He wished to say, "I was almost in love with you myself once, Anna, and now it is too late." He said nothing, they looked in opposite directions.

And shortly she drifted a step or two away, fingered a strip of dyed plaited leather hanging outside a stall, called back: "I may go to Morelia. If there's fighting, it would start there."

"Not this time. . . . The trouble will come from the North. What do you want with more revolution?"

"I like to see the thing move. But I want to sit in an Indian house and play with parrots. Good bye."

This time she was in earnest. She walked away rapidly, her black skirts bundling a little between her knees. The last petticoated North American woman. So, she had wanted to be rid of him also. He should have gone when he first thought of it.

Maybe this was the last time he would see her. When she disappeared around the corner, she would again cease to exist. Already her image grew dim. There was nothing in the line of her back to correspond with her face and voice. In him she lived simply as a remembered emotion, she was something formless and a little painful in him.

"I should have known her very well, or not at all," he thought to himself. And after buying a handful of ebony and silver rings for Alma, he strolled over to the Preparatoria to see the end of the Students' Riot.

Harcourt, Brace News

South Dakota Club Woman 12 (September 1930): 7

✺ Part of the publicity which Harcourt, Brace disseminated prior to the early September publication of *Flowering Judas*, this piece is of interest in documenting Porter's activities and attitudes during her last major stay in Mexico. The excerpt from her letter, written after July 4, 1930, indicates that she attended events of the American colony in Mexico. Though she had apparently retained some of her sympathy for the Mexican Indian, her view of Mexico and of the activities she observed there in 1930–1931 was jaundiced rather than enthusiastic.

There is ironic complexity in Porter's use of the word "savage." She mocks the holiday-making Americans, who disparage the Indians as savages, while praising the restraint and good manners of those noble savages.

Harcourt, Brace News

Katherine Anne Porter, whose first work of fiction, "Flowering Judas," will be published this fall by Harcourt, Brace and Company in a limited edition only, is living in Mexico City. In a recent letter she writes, "Today is very heavenly blue and sunny; the American colony, which is still in the raffle-and-potato-race stage of social development, will have fine weather for its peculiar celebration of July 4th. It might surprise you to know how amused they are at the quaint savage feast-day customs of the Indians. The Indian has a gorgeous comic sense in him, but still he does not smile at the quaint savage customs of the American colony. He just stands around looking slightly appalled. Appalled and polite. A savage, some student of human customs once assured me, is always polite. It is, he declared, almost a mark of savagery, or barbarism at least, to have really good manners."

Segment edited
from "Leaving the Petate"

New Republic 65 (February 4, 1931): 318–320

In a letter to Porter of November 30, 1930, Malcolm Cowley wrote that "'Leaving the Petate' came, was read, was universally liked and universally adjudged to be longer than we could possibly use. I was assigned to, condemned to, perform the amputation—and out came all the nice pages about your little Indian boy friend. I'm enclosing them, thinking that they might be used by you some other way." An examination of the manuscript of this segment in relation to the text of the piece as published suggests that this part of the text originally appeared after the end of the second paragraph of the essay. As published in *New Republic*, "Leaving the Petate" deals with changes "so gradual" it is impossible to say when they began. Porter uses the petate, the Indian's sleeping mat of woven straw, as her central symbol.

Porter's thesis is that the Indian, at first chance, "leaves his petate and takes as naturally as any other human being to the delights of kinder living." She describes how this homely object had been appropriated by those who waged the Mexican revolution to demonstrate their identification with Indian blood, points of view, and revolutionary aims. The Indians of this piece form quite a contrast to those of "The Fiesta of Guadalupe," "In a Mexican Patio," and "Xochimilco/The Children of Xochitl," who seem to be in harmony with nature or at least inured to the sufferings of the difficult lives they lead. Although the three native women depicted practice traditional medicine and continue to hold outmoded superstitions, these are thoroughly modern women: combative, acquisitive, secretive, bold, full of tricks and intrigue, mischievous, and carriers of gossip.

Porter implies the corruption of the Indian through the particularly negative picture of one of the three women, her maid Eufemia. The voice of another indigenous woman undercuts the romantic notions of foreigners about Mexican revolutionaries who "keep up the work of saving the Indians." The implication is that, like those who have institutionalized the revolution, the motive of individual contemporary Indians is simply personal self-interest.

The part of the essay that Cowley excised takes up some Indians who have not forsaken the petate and live simply and harmoniously. The contrast of these Indians, who incidentally reside in Xochimilco (scene of Porter's idyll of 1921), with the Mexico City servants couldn't be wider. The Xochimilco natives are also contrasted with a branch of their family that has almost totally escaped into the "immense petty respectability" of middle-class urban life. Even the least Europeanized of these relatives, "the charming little boy of twelve," who accompanies the narrator, presumably Porter, on the visit to Xochimilco, fears going back to the petate, "even for one night." The Indian branch of the family lives in harmony with nature, profiting from nature's bounty. The patriarch of this family, of wholly indigenous blood, is a "main citizen," a dignified property-owner and farmer, with a "serious grown son," a generous, hospitable wife, and respectful, polite grandchildren. However, Porter implies that the corruption of modern urban life is spreading even here: one of the granddaughters of the dignified old Indian "was trying to persuade her father to allow her to go to the city as a servant." This is Porter's skillful way of leading into her depiction of the three Indian servants, who are seduced by contemporary life in Mexico City.

The recovery of the excised portion of the text slightly alters one's understanding of Porter's view of Mexico in 1930–1931. Its effect is to soften the smart and cynical attitude expressed in the essay as it was published in 1931. But the underlying disillusionment and suspicion expressed here surfaced again in the two other Mexican pieces that follow.

Segment edited from "Leaving the Petate"

I know a charming little boy of twelve who brings notes from a friend of mine who lives in his aunt's house. He is an orphan, but he hardly knows it, for his aunt is one of the kindest women alive, and takes good care of him. She is the daughter of an Indian woman who married a middle-class mestizo. She and her two sisters are little round pretty dark women who were brought up in immense petty respectability in Mexico City. She married a German, is childless, and is periodically deserted by her husband as well. She rents rooms, and makes ends meet by working daily miracles of thrift and energy. She has foreigners in her house who are also poor, and when they cannot pay she feeds them anyhow, when they are sick she nurses them, and when one of them can afford to pay, she promptly offers to lend ten pesos to another who is hard up. She has not had much luck in her life, but she has a steadfast spirit, youth and in-grained good looks. Her sisters did better for themselves. One married a Norwegian of wealth, president of a public utility company in a provincial city. She lives in real luxury, with many servants and cars, and a handsome house. Once a year she goes to Europe with her husband and son, who are both very tall, aquiline featured, gray-eyed. The other married a Mexi-can-born Spaniard, a manufacturer. He is at least thirty years her senior, she is childless and a little neurotic, but securely placed for life in a class she considers above her own. The fourth sister disgraced herself in their eyes by marrying back into the Indian blood. She died, leaving this little boy who brings me notes, makes me a perfect bow, and sits with the most complete smiling dignity while waiting for an answer. He has a very dark skin and the slanting eyes of an Otomí.

The old mother's side of the family lives in Xochimilco. Her brother is a main citizen of the place, owning many houses, many plots of ground and a series of islands in the canals where he raises vegetables for the mar-ket. A friend of mine rented a house from him for the summer, and I went there to visit over a week-end. The house was a squarish room of adobe with a thatched roof, a door on the one side opening on the garden, a window on the other overlooking the canals and blooming green islands of flowers and vegetables. A low wall with an arched gateway enclosed all the front, and the hard baked surface of the garden seemed merely a con-tinuation of the house, being swept like a floor, and furnished with chairs and mats. The owner passed through this garden now and then on his way to the vegetable islands. He wore always the same wide peaked hat, white cotton clothing with a blue cotton sash, and thonged sandals on his feet. He carried a hoe and a garden fork, he had the stern unbending counte-nance of an old-time patriarch, and he was utterly indifferent to the occu-pants of the house. His niece in Mexico City had warned us against the Indians. "They will kill you for five pesos," she said. "You should not go there. It is really very dangerous. But if you must, do not let them see your money, and be careful to lock your doors at night. They are very evil people." There seemed nothing unusual in this dignified man, nor his serious grown son, nor in the old woman of the family who sent us a dish of turkey prepared with a savory red sauce. We simply did not believe they would bother about our five pesos. There was a wild disorderly crowd which drank and howled songs in the bar-rooms of the village, but these were blocks distant and we never saw any of its members astray. "Maybe we should take her word for it, I suppose she knows her people better than we can ever hope to do," I said. But there, in the place, we could not feel other than at home, and one does not feel danger in the place where one lives. Moreover, we decided we were veterans of the wars, since we had lived in Brooklyn and Chicago. We left our windows open at night, and slept with our pesos under our heads. The little grand-children of the family came to call. The elder girl brought in the younger ones ceremonially, and they curtsied and kissed our hands, as they kissed the hands of their parents and grand-parents morning and evening. They then sat with pretty solemnity in the rush-bottomed chairs, long skirts hiding their rosy-brown bare feet, listening to the victrola so long as the records held out. The little boy who brings me notes came with us, played a little, but distantly, with his cousins. He did not like the hut with its slatted beds and thin mattresses, the charcoal brasero under a tree where we cooked, nor the oil lamps—though there are electric lights in most of those houses—nor indeed, anything he saw. He longed with all his heart to get away, and fell into such martyred gloom we had to send him home next morning. He had stretched himself out on the smaller bed for the night, after crossing himself furtively. In the morning he was lying on his side, knees drawn up under his chin, and his blanket was wound snugly about him. When he opened his eyes and sat up, a fleeting glance of distress went over his face as he remembered where he was. So after breakfast he started for the village beaming with his car-fare in his handkerchief. He was not far enough away from the petate not to fear going back to it, even for one night. His wealthy aunts employ as servants Indians of almost the same class as their well-to-do relatives in Xochimilco. One of the daughters of this family was trying to persuade her father to allow her to go to the city as a servant. And the aunts never go to Xochimilco.

Parvenu . . . Review of
Mexico: A Study of Two Americas
by Stuart Chase

Rejected by *New Republic*, September 1931

In a letter of July 15, 1931, Malcolm Cowley asked Porter to un-
dertake this review for the *New Republic*. Porter apparently completed it
and sent it off to Cowley before she left Mexico for Europe in August 1931.
Cowley's letter of September 14, 1931, explaining to Porter why the *New
Republic* could not publish such a negative review of the book, prompted
a rather lengthy reply from her in a letter dated October 3. The review,
one of the last records of her attitude toward Mexico in 1931, forms a rather
neat symmetry with her first review in 1920; Chase had committed Blasco
Ibáñez's error of gathering information on Mexico "to stuff it all down in
a hurry and rush back with a book while the racket is still good." Where
Porter had faulted Blasco Ibáñez for writing an unfair evaluation of Mexico's revolution to appeal to U. S. prejudices, she excoriated Chase for his
"cautious bread-and-butter letter to a friendly host." She criticized him for
attempting "to be historian, explorer, critic and apologist of a way of life
strange to him," but betrayed her own mood in her chilling first sentence:
"Mexico is not really a place to visit any more, or to live in." It is this bitter
mood, rather than her accurate assessment of October 3 that the book was
"not only highly unnecessary, but pretty fairly jerry-built," that dominates
the review. Porter indicts Chase as another of the "parvenu" cousins who
had swarmed to Mexico, changing, commercializing, and falsifying. Her
letter to Cowley mentions some of them by name—Frances (Paca) Toor,

William Spratling, Fred Davis, Frank Tannenbaum—and further admits that the review was "an outburst" expressing "an ingrained point of view, a way of feeling I have." That chilling first sentence of the review neatly captures the tone of "Hacienda," clearly neither a bread-and-butter note to a friendly host nor "a machine-made hymn of praise to life without machines."

Parvenu . . .　Review of *Mexico: A Study of Two Americas* by Stuart Chase

Mexico is not really a place to visit any more, or to live in. The land has fallen prey to its friends, organized and unorganized; its arts and customs are in the dreadful convulsions of being saved, preserved, advertised and exploited by a horde of appreciators, amateur or professional. They swarm over the place and eat the heart out of it like a plague of locusts. Tourist busses go roaring over the beautiful mountain roads, loaded with persons carrying note books and cameras, and you may be certain that one in five of them is writing a study, or an interpretation, or a survey; hardly one of them will admit he is a simple traveller taking the air and viewing the scenery and buying harmless little knickknacks by way of proving to himself he is really travelling.

In a published letter Kay Boyle has written that Americans are the best travellers. In Spain they become entirely Carmen swinging her behind, they are each in turn Christ on the cross in Jerusalem. In Mexico, I find, they are all prophets and experts, flustered and uneasy, nosing about in a crowd of other self-appointed prophets, trying to squeeze themselves into the esoteric skin of the Indian; their ears buzz with the altitude and the cross-currents of misinformation, and besides, often they are under contract to stuff it all down in a hurry and rush back with a book while the racket is still good.

Most of these travellers fall with deadly monotony into the arms of the resident authorities on Mexico, who have placed the whole subject on production basis. They publish slipshod little magazines full of glib pieces about those native dances; they peddle Mexican painting, act as scouts for art shops, instruct the Indian craftsman how to make his stuff more acceptable to the tourist taste, and in every way help on the destruction of

Mexican art and life as much as they can. Next the visitor is introduced to a picked half-dozen of "representative" Mexicans, who speak English, and who are invariably courteous, hospitable and charming. He then goes, or is taken, on a sightseeing tour: to Xochimilco (floating gardens!), Teotihuacan (the pyramids!), the frescoes of Diego Rivera (the greatest painter in the world!), to a show school in the country (Actopan or Oaxtepec), Cuernavaca (Mr. Morrow's town), Taxco, with the only foreign art colony in Mexico, and Acapulco, once a great port. Back to the capital, and off again for a glimpse of the deep hidden Mexico: through Puebla to certain parts of Oaxaca and Michoacan, and if he is a do or die visitor, bent on making his study complete, on to Yucatan to see those oft-discovered Maya ruins. . . .

Mr. Chase did it all, and in record time. His *Mexico: A Study* is a got-up, trivial affair, concocted out of two short trips and two other books which had covered very thoroughly all the ground he goes over: *Tepoztlan* by Robert Redfield, and *Middletown* by Helen and Robert Lynd. The knack of re-writing other people's books, using other people's researches as one's own, is a trick on which many a journalistic career is based. One expects better of Mr. Chase, who has a field of his own and credit for original findings. Brilliant as his idea may have been of making a comparison between Middletown and Tepoztlan, he is the victim of his own mind, and has turned out a machine-made hymn of praise to life without machines. . . . Or is it a cautious bread-and-butter letter to a friendly host? For of all bad books written recently on Mexico, this is the most peculiarly irritating mixture of glossing over, of tactful omission, of superficial observation, of, above all, surprising errors in simple fact. It dashes in all directions at once, with a hasty flick at everything in sight, full of the confusions apt to occur when a trained economist attempts in one short volume to be historian, explorer, critic and apologist of a way of life strange to him. With a little patience and work he might have learned something. But he repeats at second, third, fourth hand all the old familiar jargon about the Indians (they are unchangeable, they have no nerves or inhibitions, they don't want anything, they are insulted if you offer them money for their work, and so on to eternity), takes a passing whack at grafting politicians but is careful not really to tell anything, praises all the things the professional propagandists have been paid for praising all these years; in short, there is not one shred of evidence that Mr. Chase ever set foot in this country, except for some rather sketchy glances at the scenery. Everything else, he could, and did, I believe, read from books, and most of them very silly books recently published on Mexico. His bibliography itself is a curiosity.

Mr. Chase winds up by some extraordinary advice to the Mexicans from a parvenu cousin. I know better than to give advice to Mexicans, after living here for four years over a period of ten. But I should like to seize this opportunity for a little advice to my fellow authors who come here. You would do well to visit Mexico quite as you visit other countries, without meddling, without presuming that you are a natural candidate for official favor, and without that condescending kindness which is so infuriating to intelligent Mexicans. If you really love the way of life you find here, keep your hands off it. All this uproar of publicity helps to change, commercialize, falsify it. Do not apologize for Mexican political corruption, any more than you would for your own rotten politicians. Mexicans are quick to resent this. The Indian arts are very beautiful, but so are the folk arts of other countries, and there is no special occult value to them. Their fiestas have about the same degree of meaning as popular fiestas in other countries. The nature of the Indian is as complicated and mysterious as human nature is, and if one of you would take the time and trouble to be well acquainted with even one of them, I think you might be ashamed to talk of him always as a problem, a spectacle, a kind of picturesque social monstrosity to be approached always in this arty-scientific-sociological manner. Americans, travelling, seem to believe there is nothing so integral, so good of its kind, but can be improved by their pawing and fumbling it over a little. It is better, when you visit here, to leave your superiorities at home, and if possible to shed your ignorances here, before you write a book interpreting Mexico.

With these farewell words, I sit back and wait for the next flood of books written by this year's crop of seminarists, folk lorists, prophets, students, friends of Mexico, propagandists, art enthusiasts, and the common carriers of good will. But I shall not read them.

Hacienda

Virginia Quarterly Review 8 (October 1932): 556–569

Porter characterized this first version of "Hacienda" as "only an article"; it had been intended, like "Leaving the Petate," as an American outsider's observation of Mexican life, an attempt to assess the changes since 1920, when the revolution had triumphed. Porter proposed it in a July 22, 1931, letter to Malcolm Cowley. ("Maybe I might do you a piece on Tetlapayac, but with names and such disguised. It would be necessary.") By November 5, 1931, Porter had sent the manuscript of this version of "Hacienda" to *Scribner's*. When it was rejected there, Porter sent it on to the *Virginia Quarterly Review*. It is based on an actual trip Porter made to the Hacienda Tetlapayac, northeast of Mexico City on the plains of Apam in the Mexican state of Hidalgo. The Russian film director Sergei Eisenstein had journeyed with his crew and his Mexican government entourage to this *pulque* hacienda in early May 1931 in order to film the second of four major stories of an ambitious work, tentatively entitled *¡Qué Viva Mexico!*, which was being financed by Upton Sinclair and other wealthy investors.

Eisenstein had initially come to Mexico in early December 1930 and had aroused such curiosity and apprehension in certain Mexican officials that he, his party (assistant director Grigori Alexandrov, cameraman Eduard Tisse, and business manager Hunter Kimbrough, who was Sinclair's brother-in-law), and several Mexican artists were arrested on December 21, 1930, although they were soon released. Porter's old friends Adolfo Best-Maugard

Diego Rivera, Frida Kahlo, an unidentified woman, and Sergei Eisenstein sometime between December 1930 and February 1932 when Eisenstein was in Mexico filming his ultimately abortive project *¡Qué Viva Mexico!* Sergei Eisenstein Collection, Lilly Library, Indiana University.

and Roberto Montenegro were among the Mexican government's advisers to Eisenstein during the period, from late December 1930 through late April 1931, when parts of *¡Qué Viva Mexico!* were filmed in Puebla, Acapulco, Oaxaca, Tehuantepec, and Yucatán. Eisenstein returned briefly to Mexico City between each of these location sessions, and, during one of these visits, he and his party met Porter, who was invited to visit the filming at Hacienda Tetlapayac in mid-July 1931. If Porter did, indeed, visit the hacienda on the day on which an Indian actor accidentally killed his sister, she must have spent Wednesday, Thursday, and Friday, July 15–17, 1931, at Tetlapayac. If one accepts as evidence this version of "Hacienda," she must have travelled to the hacienda by train in the company of Alexandrov and Kimbrough, met the Indian male lead of the movie on the train, and encountered Eisenstein, Tisse, Best-Maugard, Don Julio Saldivar (the heir to the owner of the hacienda), Don Julio's "wife," and "some sort of assistant to the art adviser" at the hacienda after her arrival. The "adviser" to Best-Maugard may have been Gabriel Fernández Ledesma, a Mexican artist who served in such a capacity on this film.

"Hacienda" has obvious connections to "The Mexican Trinity" of 1921. K——, Don J——, and the art adviser represent the trinity Porter feared would survive the Mexican revolution: the foreigners, the *hacendados*, and the Church. The hacienda had survived from the period of Spanish viceroyalty, as had the *hacendado*, represented by Don J——, whose immense ego reduces Justino's tragedy to the matter of property rights. He is, like the Spanish conquerors of the sixteenth century, an exploiter of the brown-skinned natives. K——, the contemptuous American who is fearful of everything Mexican, represents the "splendid horde of invaders" of Mexico with economic exploitation on their minds. He is as egotistic and inhuman as Don J——. The art adviser suggests the third part of the Mexican trinity: the Catholic Church. His "pontifical" gesture while offering the "easy words" of conventional consolation for the death of Justino's sister suggests his identification with the Church's tradition of privilege and power, which Porter made more pointed in the revised version of the story, first published as a monograph in 1934. This identification links the art adviser with corrupt cynical Mexican churchmen such as the archbishop depicted in "The Dove of Chapacalco." In fact, Porter's anticlericalism is quite overt in this version; she asserts that both the intoxicating pulque and Roman Catholic religion, as symbolized by the statue of María Santísima, are anodynes.

This version of "Hacienda" can also be directly linked with "The Children of Xochitl," the former a despairing negative view developed out of the positive hope expressed in the latter. The goddess Xochitl, who was a giver of life and fertility in "The Children of Xochitl," here becomes a goddess of death, reigning with María Santísima in the fetid vat rooms of Mexican pulque haciendas. Xochitl represents the enslavement of the Indians to the pulque, which induces a deathlike sleep. Pulque itself represents hopelessness, suffering, and corruption, because it is at the heart of the oppressive social system of the hacienda. Producing and drinking the liquor, the peons are doubly victimized by the greed of the *hacendados* and the corrupt "revolutionary" government.

Although the point of both versions of this story is that the Mexican revolution has changed nothing, the revised version is both more despairing and more personal. It clearly articulates Porter's disillusionment and her fascination with death.

Hacienda

We hung our heads out of the window every time the train stopped, raising false hopes in the hearts of the Indian women, who ran along beside us even after the train was moving away. "Fresh pulque!" they urged mournfully, holding up jars of thick grey-white liquor, and "Fresh maguey worms!" they called after us, waving lumpy viscous leaf bags.

K——, the business manager, shuddered. "Isn't it horrible, the things they eat and drink? I have just come back," he said, "from God's country," which we are to understand is California. He ripped open an orange trademarked in purple ink. "What a relief to eat fruit that isn't full of germs. I brought them all the way back with me" (I could fairly see him, legging across the desert with a knapsack full of oranges). "Have one, it's clean."

K—— is very clean too; washed, shaven, clipped, pressed, polished, brisk and firm looking in his new tweeds. But his nerves are bundles of dried twigs, they crackle at every touch, they jab his insides and keep his blank blue eyes fixed in a white stare. The muscles of his jaw jerk in continual helpless rage. Eight months spent piloting a group of Russian moving picture men through Mexico have about finished him off, he told me. "My heart skips every other beat. The altitude!" he said. But that wasn't all. These Mexicans would drive you crazy in no time. In Tehuantepec it was frightful. Those people don't know the meaning of time. It would take him a week to tell the whole story, but just for example, they had to bribe every step of the way. Bribe, bribe it was, from morning until night, from fifty pesos to the Wise Boys to a bag of candy for a provincial Mayor, before they were allowed to set up their cameras. Then they lost ten thousand dollars flat by obeying the laws of the country—something no one else does!—and passing their film of the earthquake before the board of censorship. Meanwhile some unscrupulous scoundrels who knew the ropes had beaten them to it and sent a newsreel to New York. "It doesn't pay to

Sergei Eisenstein, unidentified woman, Adolfo Best-Maugard, and Grigori Alexandrov. The three men are the originals of "the famous director," "the art adviser," and A—— of the 1932 version of Porter's "Hacienda." Sergei Eisenstein Collection, Lilly Library, Indiana University.

have a conscience, but if you have one, what can you do about it?" He had written and protested to the censors, charging them with letting the Mexican film company get away with murder, accusing them of favoritism and deliberate malice in holding up the Russian film—everything, in a five-page letter. They hadn't even answered it. Now what can you do with people like that? Bribe, graft, bribe, graft—well, he had been learning too. "Whatever they ask for, I give 'em half the amount, straight across the board," he said.

Crickle, crackle go the twigs at every slightest jog of memory, every footfall of the present, every cold wind from the future. He is afraid of his brother-in-law, a violent prohibitionist who would be furious if he ever hears that K—— is even now drinking beer, on the train. Beer is the only thing he can trust; fruit, air, and water are alike poisoned. But suppose his brother-in-law should hear? He is afraid the picture may not succeed, may not be finished on time. "What time?" asked A——, the assistant camera man. "When it is done it is done." "Yes, but it isn't enough merely to finish a job," said K——, going on to explain that making good involves all sorts of mysterious interlocking schedules; it must be done by a certain date, it must be art, of course, that's taken for granted, and it must be a hit. There are thousands of things to be thought of, and if they miss one point, bang goes everything. I thought of K——'s life in Mexico, of K——'s life any-where: lying awake nights fuming, rising in the mornings, grey-faced, stu-pefied, pushing himself under cold showers and filling himself up on hot coffee and slamming himself again into the fight. Everything is against him, but he will win! His loud voice and commanding stride must adver-tise to the world that here walks a man nothing can stop. As he sat there, eating American chocolate bars and drinking his third bottle of beer, sleep took him suddenly, upright as he was, talking as ever. Assertion failed, sleep took him mercifully. His body cradled itself in the tweed, the collar rose about his neck, his closed eyes and limp mouth looked ready to cry.

The famous director is making a part of his picture at an old hacienda in the pulque country, and all the peons belonging to the estate are work-ing in it. So much entertainment and excitement have not touched their lives since the last Agrarian raid. . . .

A——, the assistant camera man, went on showing me pictures from the scenes they have made on the hacienda. Here are innate outlines and postures of tragedy, the human body a thin shell stiffened in the shapes of pain; servitude has stamped these faces, so that the arrogant features are a mockery of the servants who live within. By now suffering is a habit of the spirit; the dark faces carry a common memory, as the eyes of cruelly treated animals look all alike: they know that they suffer, they do not know why, and they cannot imagine a remedy. So the figures move with the ritual solemnity of their burial processions with no symbol of grief omit-ted. These pictures are alternated with interludes of life in the master's house, where all the characters are dressed in the fashions of 1898. They seem to bring to life again a world long since dead, and always a portrait of Diaz looms in the background. Why is this? Only to show, I am told, that these conditions existed in the time of Diaz, but have been swept away by the Revolution; it is one of the requirements of their agreement here. This without cracking a smile or meeting my eye.

At the last station before we reach the hacienda, the Indian boy who plays the leading rôle in the picture came looking for us. He was already a hero in his village, being a pugilist. Fame added to fame has given him a brilliant air of self-confidence. He shines in new blue overalls, a red neck-erchief, a wide new straw hat. Ordinarily, his face has the histrionic fe-rocity of the professional boxer, but it is broken now by simple excite-ment, live, gleaming, dark, almost gay. He has news worth hearing and will be the first to tell us. What a to-do at the hacienda this morning;

Justino killed his sister, shot her, and ran for the mountains. Vicente chased him on horseback, yes, and brought him back, and now he is in jail in the village. He had been working all morning on the set. . . .

Neither A—— nor K—— speaks Spanish, the boy's words were a jargon from which I snatched key words to translate quickly. K—— leaped up, white-eyed. "On the set? My God, we're ruined!" But why ruined? "His family will have a damage suit against us!" The boy wanted to know what this meant. "They can collect money from us for the loss of their daughter! It can be blamed on us!" The boy was fairly baffled by this. "He says he doesn't understand," I told K——. "He says nobody ever heard of such a thing. He says Justino was in his own house when it happened, and nobody, not even Justino, is to blame."

"Oh," said K——. "Oh, I see. Well, let's hear the rest of it. If he wasn't on the set it doesn't matter."

All the way we asked questions and the boy repeated his story. Justino had gone to his hut for the noon meal. His sister was grinding corn for the tortillas, while he stood by, waiting, throwing the pistol into the air and catching it. The pistol fired, shot her through—touching his ribs level with his heart—, she fell forward on her face over the grinding stone, dead. Seeing what he had done, Justino ran leaping like a crazy man, throwing away his pistol as he went, and struck through the maguey fields toward the mountains. . . . His friend Vicente went after him on horseback, waving a gun and yelling, "Stop, or I'll shoot!" and Justino yelled back, "Shoot, I don't care!" But of course Vicente did not. He just galloped up and bashed Justino over the head with the gun butt, set him across the saddle, and brought him back. Now he is in jail, but Don J—— is already in the village getting him out. Justino did not do it on purpose.

We are jogging away in the little mule car, facing each other three in a row, with the bags under our feet and the straw falling off the seats. The driver, craning around toward the mule now and then, flicking the reins, adds comments. An unlucky family—this is the second child to be killed by a brother. The mother is half dead with grief, and Justino, a good boy, is in jail. The big man sitting by him, in striped riding trousers, his hat bound under his chin with red cords, adds that Justino is in for it now, God help him. But where did he get the pistol? He borrowed it from the firearms being used in the picture. It is true he was not supposed to touch the pistols, and there was his first mistake. He meant to put it back at once, but you know how a boy of sixteen loves to play with a pistol. No-

Hunter Kimbrough, K—— of "Hacienda," in Mexico during the period when *¡Qué Viva Mexico!* was being filmed. Sergei Eisenstein Collection, Lilly Library, Indiana University.

body blames him. The girl was nineteen years old. Her body has been sent to the village to be buried. Don J—— went according to custom to cross her hands, close her eyes, and light a candle beside her. Everything was done in order, they said, piously, their eyes dancing with rich, enjoyable feelings. It is always regrettable and exciting when somebody you know gets into such dramatic trouble. Ah, we are alive under this dark sky, in this thin air fresher than flowers, jingling away through the yellow fields of blooming mustard, with the pattern of spiked maguey shuttling as we pass from straight lines to angles to diamond shape and back again. A——sings: "Ay, Sandunga, Sandunga, Mamá, por Dios!" and the Indians shout with joy and delight at the new thing his Russian tongue makes of the words. A—— laughs too, this laughter is an invitation to their confidence: with a burst of song in Russian the young pugilist throws himself in turn on the laughter of A——. Everybody laughs loudly, even K——, eyes meet eyes through the guard of crinkled lids, and the little mule goes into a stiff-legged gallop. A jack rabbit leaps across the track, chased by lean hungry dogs. He is cracking the strings of his heart in flight, his eyes start from his head like crystal bubbles. Run, fellow, run!

The hacienda lies before us, a monastery, a fortress, walled, towered in terra cotta and coral, sheltered against the mountains. The heavy door in the wall opens, we slide into the main corral. The upper windows in the near end are all alight. The first camera man stands on one balcony, the art adviser on the next, for a moment the famous director appears with waving arms at a third. They call to us even before they recognize us, glad to see anyone coming from town to ripple the long monotony of the day. Horses are standing under saddle in the patio. Big polite dogs of expensive breed come out to meet us and walk with dignity beside us up the broad steps.

The Russians are concerned with aftermaths. It is not only a great pity about the poor girl, but both she and her brother were working in the picture; the boy's rôle was important, and now everything must halt until he comes back, or if he does not, everything must be done again. The art adviser is Mexican, full of Spanish elegance and detachment. "I am sorry for everything," he says, lifting a narrow pontifical hand, waving away vulgar human pity which threatens and buzzes like a fly about the edges of his mind. "But when you consider"—he makes a small bow in the general direction of the social point of view represented by the three Russians—"what her life would have been in this place, it is much better that she is dead."

With his easy words, she is dead indeed, anonymously entombed. A—— turns off the mechanical attachment of the player-piano, sits and sings his favorite songs. The Porfirian Gothic doorways soar toward the roof in a cloud of gilded, stamped wall paper, from an undergrowth of purple and red and yellow plush armchairs. Such spots as this, fitted up for casual visits, interrupt the cold darkness of the apartments marching along the cloisters, now and then casting themselves around patios, gardens, pens for animals. The week-end crowds are gone, the grandfather of Don J—— is absent, and our party scarcely occupies one end of the long dining table. The famous director sits in striped overalls; the camera man in flannel slacks and polo shirt; the art director in riding trousers and puttees; A——'s no-colored wool shirt is elbow to elbow with the brash tweeds of K——; all provide contrast for the young wife of Don J—— at the head of the table, a figure from a Hollywood comedy, in black satin pajamas adorned with rainbow-colored bands of silk, black hair sleeked to her round skull, eyes painted, apparently, in the waxed semblance of her face.

Don J—— joins her, and he is in a fury. This fury is part of his rôle. He is a blue-eyed Spaniard, formed and hardened by inherited authority, smoothed over and speeded up by life in Europe and the capital; a rich young hacendado having his fling before settling down to lord it over serfs

Isabel Villaseñor and Martín Hernández in the maguey fields of Hacienda Tetlapayac (the setting for Porter's "Hacienda") during the filming of ¡Qué Viva Mexico! This part of Eisenstein's film premiered in May 1933 as *Thunder Over Mexico*. The publicity caption for the photograph reads "Sebastian and Maria, the Mexican-Indians who play the leading roles in Sergei M. Eisenstein's 'Thunder Over Mexico.' If the great Russian director intended there be romance in the 'Maguey episode' of his picture, then these two characters must be considered, as they say in Hollywood, 'the lovers.'" In "Hacienda," Porter describes Hernández as "the Indian boy who plays the leading rôle in the picture." Sergei Eisenstein Collection, Lilly Library, Indiana University.

on the family estates. He has old-fashioned tastes for drink, for gambling, for ladies of the theater; he rides always at a tearing run, hurling himself at the saddle and careering out of the patio with his mounted man pounding at his heels. He drives his car at desperate speed, taking the road by right. He is thinking about an airplane to cut distances; nothing can move too fast for him, whether a woman, a horse, or something with machinery in it. If you opened his skull you would find there, neatly ticketed and labelled, a set of ideas unchanged in essentials since 1650. Life stales on him suddenly and unaccountably at intervals, and he lashes about him until the foam rises again. He is pleased and entertained to have the famous director making a picture on his hacienda, puts all at his disposal, and watches the mimic wars of his own peons against Oppression, symbolized by himself, if he bothered to think about it: but he does not think, his springs of action are automatic and ready, and he knows how to manage Indians.

He sits beside his wife and brings his fist thumping down on the table as he talks. That imbecile judge refuses to let him have Justino. It seems there is some crazy law about criminal negligence. "The law does not recognize accidents in the vulgar sense," said the judge. "That has nothing to do with it," Don J—— told him; "Justino is my peon, his family have lived for generations on my hacienda, it is my business. I know what happened and all about it, and you know nothing, and it is necessary for me to have Justino back again at once." It was no use. The judge wanted two thousand pesos to let Justino go. "Two thousand pesos!" shouts Don J——, thumping the table. "How ridiculous," says his wife, smiling brilliantly.

He glares at her impersonally for a split-second, as if he did not recognize her, then goes on, shaking off the pause: "Well, I'll see about that! I'll go up to the capital tomorrow and see my friends in the government. We'll see then what happens!" His fury passes suddenly, as if it had served its purpose. He spends the rest of the evening talking amiably and playing billiards with the camera man, who wins and therefore has his respect, because Don J—— is very good at billiards and it must be no ordinary man who can defeat him.

It is very late and I am in a large square bedroom with a balcony directly above the vat rooms where they ferment the pulque. I recognize the smell that has never left my nostrils since I came. It rises below through the thick drone of flies, sour, stale, like rotting milk, and this smell and this sound belong together. From the next window the Russian voices murmur along: the famous director loves to sit up all night talking over the work with his assistants. Below, next to the vat rooms, are the apartments of Don J—— and his lady, puffy with silk, glossy with polished wood, restless with trivial ornaments and tables and boxes of sweets and down pillows. There is a long, quiet wing above the terraces to the back, facing a garden with an old fountain, near the chapel, opening to the south on the old monastery garden and stone bath, where once surely it must have been pleasant to live, and could be so again. Yet all the life of the place clusters around this focus of decay and evil odors, as if to be reassured by touch, by smell, by the rumble of barrels and the shouts of the men, that pulque, the good river of life, is still unquenched. Pigs grunt and root in the soft wallow near the washing fountain, the women are still kneeling in the darkness, thumping wet cloth on the stones, talking, laughing. All the women seem to be laughing tonight; the high bright sound sparkles again and again from the long dark rows of huts down the corral. The burros sob and mourn to each other. I am attracted by a slight flurry at the arch of the inner patio. One of the polite expensive dogs has lost his dignity and is chasing a little fat-bottomed soldier back to his proper place, the barracks by the wall opposite the compound of the peons.

Can it be jealousy? For this soldier is part of the guard sent by the government to defend the hacienda against assault by the Agrarians, who have made Don J——'s life, and the life of all other hacendados in the district, a hell on earth of late years. During a ruinous season of war, Don J—— himself operated a machine gun from one of his towers, and the number of Agrarians he killed is matter for tall talk among his hangers-on. In a pinch these soldiers might fail him, but their presence is a visible sign of government approval, for which Don J—— must pay; he tolerates them and resents them, and so do the dogs.

He should be grateful to his ancestors for having gained the concession to make pulque instead of raising corn, or wheat, or sugar, or coffee, or tobacco, or cattle. Nowhere are the great haciendas so secure as in this maguey country. The Indians drink pulque. It is their traditional liquor, part of their ancient mode of living brought over the gulf of the Conquest. They account for its discovery in one of their most familiar legends. Even now, each vat room is decorated with a fresco, as unvarying as the Stations of the Cross in the chapels, relating how a young woman made this divine refreshment from the honey water of maguey, and was rewarded with semi-deification. Her apotheosis coincides with that of Maria Santísima, who stands always in a painted niche with a shrine lamp and paper flowers. Maria Santísima enjoys a formal preëminence, but the two live side by side in harmonious confusion. Both are anodynes: pulque and the merciful goodness of Maria Santísima. The Indians drink pulque and call upon the Mother of God. (These are of course peons, not the fighting Indians of the free villages.) I remember stories of how Zapata's tough warriors rose and pillaged, living on parched corn and brown sugar ground up together. On this food they broke up the corn and sugar haciendas of Morelos. No man wants to fight on pulque. He gets his bellyful and wants only to sleep. So the revolutionary government sends soldiers to help Don J—— when he is attacked by the Agrarians, and in turn Don J—— gives the government about a third of his income from the hacienda for the privilege of holding it, as do all the other hacendados of the district. The Indians drink the corpse-white liquor, swallow forgetfulness by the riverful. Pesos pour by the hundreds of thousands into the government treasury. When the Agrarians attack these haciendas, each peon is given a rifle and becomes a burning patriot, defending his little fatherland.

Julio Saldivar and an unidentified actress in the courtyard at Hacienda Tetlapayac. Saldivar, Don J—— of "Hacienda," and the actress "are dressed in the fashions of 1898" as in the stills from the film which, in the 1932 version of the story, A—— shows the narrator. For film publicity, this photograph was captioned, "The daughter of the Hacendado arrives at the plantation for the celebration of the Corpus Christi holiday. A scene from 'Thunder Over Mexico' directd by Sergei M. Eisenstein." Sergei Eisenstein Collection, Lilly Library, Indiana University.

What is the peon fighting for? Literally, for sixty centavos a day and a half pound of corn unless the corn is scarce. On this he lives with his family, all work and eat on this, with the help of pulque and Maria Santí-sima. He will not give this up lightly, to be thrown naked on the hard risks of the world, for he is an enslaved being, no longer by violence, for that is not necessary; he has consented at last. He is stabled worse than his own burro, but he eats his corn and cannot be persuaded away from it. For who would give him corn but the master?

This smell is abominable, stale sap-soaked mud, maguey juice and flies fermenting in the stinking, frothing bull-hide vats. But I have drunk pulque cold, freshened with strawberry juice, and remember yet the good taste in my mouth, the soft sleep that drew me away from all memories and dreams, the suave cure of my racked bones after days on horseback. Maria Santísima, why shouldn't they have their pulque? Or should such a man be ripped violently out of his sleep, all his poppy juice and maguey honey taken away, shaken until his teeth clatter, and told: "Look at this world by daylight. Is it not a beastly place? Come now, get ready to die changing it!" For he is the born victim, the first who will be killed. Shout slogans in his ear (slogans invented by bright young men in Universities to drape upon the figure-head of Zapata, who is safely dead and can no longer embarrass them by acting upon their theories): "Land and Liberty for all forever!" Quote an old epitaph at him: "It is more honorable to die standing than to live kneeling!" He can answer—does answer the Agrarians so, by means of bullets—that here are his mountains and the place where his mother bore him, here are the sorrows he is best acquainted with, here are his sixty centavos and his half pound of corn, here are pulque and Maria Santísima, here is Don J——, the master, who has friends in the government, who does everything properly: is even now in the village getting Justino out of jail. What would become of Justino if Don J—— did not take care of him?

While I am thinking about these things, I wrap myself in a blanket and sit on the balcony, huddled, knees under chin. It is growing cold, late, the tides have drawn away to the center of the earth. In the vat room the men are filling and counting the barrels, calling the numbers in a long chant, wailing and wailing again, like a litany: "twenty- . . . one!" A barrel is rolled down thundering and lifted on to the car under the window: "Ave Maria Santísima!" Before sunrise they are off to the station to send away the pulque. Other men and small boys are leaving for the maguey fields, driving their donkeys. They shout, and whack the donkeys with small sticks, but no one is really hurrying. The tired men are driving themselves, it is themselves they lash when they strike the donkeys.

Not long ago, an old schoolmate of the grandfather returned to this hacienda for a visit after sixty years of absence. He walked about looking at everything, and at last smiled and nodded his head. "How beautiful," he said, "Nothing has changed at all."

"My God!" says K——, over coffee in the morning. "Do you remember,"—he beats off a cloud of flies, and fills his cup with a wobbling hand—"I thought of it in the night and couldn't sleep—don't you remember," he says to the camera man, "those scenes we shot only two weeks ago, when Justino played the part of a boy who killed a girl by accident, tried to escape, and Vicente was one of the men who ran him down on horseback? Well, think of it—*think* of it! The very same thing has happened to the same people in reality! And"—he turns to me—"the strangest thing is, we have to make that scene again, it didn't turn out so good, and look, my God, we had it happening really, and nobody thought of doing it then! Then was the time. We could have got a close-up of the girl, really dead, and real blood running down Justino's face where Vicente hit him, and my God! we never even thought of it! Now what was the matter with us all, I wonder?" He looks accusingly at the camera man, who takes his elbows off the table and examines his coffee spoon attentively.

"Well," he says, "that would have been a little too much in cold blood, don't you think?" His eyes flicker open, click shut as if they had taken a snapshot of something.

"If you want to look at it that way," says K——, "but after all, there it was, it had happened, it wasn't our fault, and we might as well have had it."

"The light was poor, anyhow," says the camera man, "and we can always do it again when Justino comes back, and there is time for a rehearsal."

This is even better. "Imagine!" says K——, pouncing. "Just try to imagine that! When the poor boy comes back he'll have to go through the same scene he has gone through twice before, once in play and once in reality! *Reality!*" He licks his chops. "Think how he'll feel. Why, it ought to drive him crazy!"

Don J—— remembers something and thumps the table. "That imbecile judge," he says, "asked me why I worried so much about one peon. I told him it was my affair what I chose to worry about. He said he had heard we were making a picture over here with men shooting each other in it. He said he has a jailful of men waiting to be shot, and he'd be glad to send them over for us to shoot in the picture. He couldn't see why we were just pretending to kill people when we could have all we needed to kill really. He thinks Justino should be shot, too. Let him try it! But never in this world will I give him two thousand pesos!"

In the evening, Don J—— plays billiards with the camera man. A—— sits ats the piano and sings Russian songs. The wife of Don J—— is curled up on the sofa, with her Pekinese slung around her neck like a scarf. He snuffles and groans and rolls his eyes in a flabby swoon of enjoyment. The big dogs sniff around him with pained incredulity on their knotted foreheads. "They cannot believe he is a dog!" says the mistress in delight. I am learning a new card game with a thin dark youth who is some sort of assistant to the art adviser. "When Justino was here," says this boy, shuffling the cards, "the director was always having trouble in the serious scenes, because Justino thought everything was a joke. In the death scenes he smiled all over his face and ruined a great deal of film. Now they are saying that when Justino comes back we will never again have to say to him, Don't laugh, Justino, this is death, this is not funny."

Don J——'s wife turns her Pekinese over and rolls him back and forth on her lap. "He will forget everything, the minute it is over," she says gently, looking at me with soft empty eyes. "They are animals."

At midnight Don J—— is off somewhere. His powerful car roars past the vat rooms and flees down the wild dark road toward the capital. In the morning there begins a gradual drift back to town, by train, by car. "Stay here," each one says in turn to me, "we are coming back tomorrow, work will start again." By afternoon I too wish to go. I cannot wait for tomorrow, in this deathly air. "If you should be here again in about ten days," says the Indian driver, "you would see a different place. The green corn will be ready, and ah, there will be enough to eat again!"

Notes on Texts

Texts of all previously published pieces appear here as in their original appearance with the following exceptions. Single quotation marks have been changed to double quotation marks where required for American practice. Obvious misspellings have been silently corrected. Occasionally, missing pieces of punctuation have been supplied where necessary, but no attempt has been made to conform Porter's punctuation or that of the publishers' house styles to a standard editorial practice. Diacritical marks have been supplied or corrected where required for consistency within individual pieces. Most subheadings within the texts of articles, usually from newspapers, have been eliminated.

With Porter's previously unpublished pieces (and with "In a Mexican Patio," where a copy of the piece as it originally appeared has not been located and the manuscript version is the source of the text), the following practice has been followed. Obvious misspellings have been silently corrected. Porter's idiosyncratic punctuation, generally not considered standard practice, has been allowed to stand. Where there is omission of required punctuation (quotation marks, periods, commas), it has been silently added. Occasionally, capitalization for clarification or consistency has been made. In a few of the texts, new paragraphs have been created where none exist in the manuscripts, primarily to make clear which of several characters is speaking. Spacing errors have been corrected, and dropped letters inserted. Porter's extensive use of series of periods of varying numbers has been retained but standardized to three or four periods.

Angle brackets have been used to indicate insertions from separate drafts when more than one draft exists for a certain piece. Separate fragments are appended to the ends of texts following a line of three asterisks. Square brackets have been used to indicate editorial insertions for clarification or for conjectural readings where there are gaps in the copy text.

The unpublished manuscript materials are all housed in the Katherine Anne Porter Collection, Collection Management and Special Collections Division, University of Maryland at College Park Libraries.

The Shattered Star

This story was published in the children's magazine *Everyland* in January 1920. Porter's three stories published in *Everyland* were charmingly illustrated by the husband and wife team of Berta and Elmer Hader, personal friends of Porter. The illustrations are not reproduced here.

The Faithful Princess

Published in the children's magazine *Everyland* in February 1920, the story includes a note at the foot of the first page: "A Legend of India, Adapted from Donald A. MacKenzie's Translation." It is, indeed, Porter's interpretation of "Nala and Damayanti" from MacKenzie's *Indian Myth and Legend* (London: Gresham, 1913).

The Magic Ear Ring

Porter's adaptation of this "folk-story of Kashmir" was published in *Everyland* in March 1920.

The Adventures of Hadji: A Tale of a Turkish Coffee-House

Perhaps it was on the basis of this tale "retold" by Porter for *Asia*, where it was published in August 1920, that Porter received the commission to ghostwrite *My Chinese Marriage*. That work was serialized in *Asia* from June through September 1921.

Blasco Ibanez on "Mexico in Revolution"

This book review appeared in the English-language section of the Mexico City newspaper *El Heraldo de México* on November 22, 1920.

The Fiesta of Guadalupe

El Heraldo de México published this piece on December 13, 1920, in its "Foreign Section." This version served as the copy text for this volume. At the time, Porter was also writing the column "Talk of the Town" for the English-language pages of the newspaper.

No clear explanation exists for the introduction of the confusing error mentioned in the headnote to this piece. The manuscript copy of this essay among Porter's papers contains the same error; physically it resembles Porter manuscripts from the 1920s. However, it does not resemble those of her manuscripts and letters that can be dated to 1920, when the essay was originally published. A copy of this manuscript served as the copy text for Porter's *Collected Essays*. It is not clear from Porter's correspondence with Seymour Lawrence, her publisher for that collection, whether she actually read proof on it. She did make some autograph corrections to this piece in the manuscript for *Collected Essays*, but she did not correct this confusing passage.

Book Review: *Caliban* by W. L. George, *The Chinese Coat* by Jeanette Lee, and *The House of Lynch* by Leonard Merrick

Porter's second book review was published in *El Heraldo de México* on December 15, 1920.

The Funeral of General Benjamín Hill

This account appeared in Porter's "Talk of the Town" column in *El Heraldo de México* on December 17, 1920.

Striking the Lyric Note in Mexico

Co-authored with Robert Haberman, this political essay originally appeared in the Sunday magazine section of the Socialist newspaper *New York Call* on January 16, 1921.

The New Man and The New Order

An unabashedly positive picture of President Obregón, this piece was the featured article in the first issue of the *Magazine of Mexico*, published in March 1921.

In a Mexican Patio

There are two separate drafts among the Porter papers at the University of Maryland at College Park Libraries. One of seventeen pages, headed with her name and the address 12 St. Luke's Place, is a clean draft transcribed from an earlier marked sixteen-page one. The latter has been chosen as the copy text because it is an earlier version and probably closer to the version published in the *Magazine of Mexico* in April 1921. It includes several passages that Porter deleted from the seventeen-page draft.

Surviving military intelligence reports compiled in Mexico during this period document April 1921 as the date of publication. Unfortunately, a copy of this issue of the *Magazine of Mexico* has not been located at this time. The physical evidence in these two drafts and in Porter's letters written in 1924 suggests that both drafts date from the time Porter was submitting materials for the *Survey Graphic* Mexico issue (May 1924). The later draft may have been the one that Porter submitted in Spring 1924 to Paul U. Kellogg for possible publication in another issue of *Survey Graphic*. Porter biographer Joan Givner asserts that this piece was also published in Garfield Crawford's oil trade journal in the 1921–1922 period when Porter was living and working in Fort Worth.

Porter subtitled this sketch "Snatches from a Guadelahara [*sic*] Diary" on the draft used as copy text; on the later seventeen-page draft, she scored out "Guadelahara" and inserted "Mexico City" by hand. Space breaks appear where Porter placed a series of characters (# or %) in the draft used as copy text. The later draft contains breaks at the identical locations in the text, but the sections are separated by three asterisks.

Xochimilco

This literary sketch was published in the *Christian Science Monitor* on May 31, 1921.

Children of Xochitl

As the published version, "Xochimilco," appeared in May 1921, the internal evidence here indicates that the visit chronicled was taken in March 1921. As the eleven-page typewritten manuscript from which this text is taken has confusing strikeouts and insertions, the editors have retained some of Porter's strikeouts. Punctuation has been edited as necessary.

Trinidad

The typescript of this unfinished story is the messiest and most fragmentary of those published here. It is clearly a rough draft that Porter had worked over in her own hand. The manuscript contains many dropped letters, much missing punctuation, and many spacing errors. The editors have attempted to clean up the manuscript without making too many additions. The following types of corrections and emendations have been made silently in order to keep the manuscript relatively free of editorial intrusion: misspellings corrected; quotation marks, periods, commas, and capitalization added for clarification and consistency; spacing errors corrected; dropped letters inserted.

The manuscript consists of ten numbered pages of continuous text and six pages of fragments and notes. One of the fragmentary pages appears to be a clean transcription for part of a page of the continuous text. Part of that page is incorporated into the transcription of the ten-page text in angle brackets. In this portion of the piece, personal names in square brackets occasionally replace pronouns to make clear what the editors believe Porter intended (see pp. 87, 91). One confusing addition to the manuscript in Porter's hand has been slightly truncated by the editors. The manuscript reads: "His voice dipped again; he had come once more on the thing he wanted to tell, and this time." The edited version appears on p. 92: "[Felipe's] voice dipped again; he had come once more on the thing he wanted to tell."

The remaining five fragmentary pages have been transcribed as accurately as possible and appended to the more complete part. In four of these five pages of fragments, there is inconsistency in Porter's naming of the character who is called Felipe in the ten-page manuscript. Felipe placed in square brackets replaces the name Vicente in the transcriptions of the fragments; the editors believe Vicente is the character Felipe of the ten-page version.

Notes on Teotihuacan

We have used parts from what appears to be three separate drafts of these notes. There are six pages from a draft headed "Notes on Teotihuacan" numbered 1–5 and 7, a single unnumbered page, and two additional pages numbered 2 and 3. The insertion in angle brackets is made from another single fragment. Parts of the full manuscript from these notes may have been published as "Two Ancient Mexican Pyramids—the Core of a City Unknown until a Few Years Ago" in the *Christian Science Monitor* on September 19, 1922. Because of the condition of these notes, silent emendations and corrections have been made in capitalization, spelling, and punctuation.

The Dove of Chapacalco

The text here is taken from thirty-three pages of manuscript. The plot outline is taken from one page of text typed on stationery headed "Fort Worth Gas Company/192_," probably composed in late 1921 and early 1922 when Porter was living and working in Fort Worth after her first trip to Mexico. The completed section of the story is taken from twenty-nine consecutively numbered pages of manuscript. The three fragments are taken from three separate manuscript pages, one of which was also typed on the Fort Worth Gas Company letterhead.

The editors have made a conjectural reading for one of Porter's autograph insertions ("unendurable," see p. 115). The physical evidence in the manuscript indicates that it was Porter's clear intention to emend "inimical" to the extremely rare "inimicable" (see p. 115).

In this story Porter's inconsistent use of the British spellings for words such as *colour* has been standardized to American spellings (for example, *color* substituted for *colour*, *rigor* for *rigour*, *labor* for *labour*, etc.). In her collected works, which were published with Porter's active participation, American practice was adopted. Silent correction and emendation of capitalization, spelling, and punctuation have been made by the editors in several places.

A Letter from Mexico and the Gleam of Montezuma's Golden Roofs

Porter's letter, imbedded in George Sill Leonard's article, was published in the *Christian Science Monitor* on June 5, 1922. The editors have deleted anomalous opening quotation marks from the paragraph that begins "Strange how little the world has concerned itself with the art of the ancient Americas, of ancient Mexico and Peru" (see p. 134).

Outline of Mexican Popular Arts and Crafts

The *Outline* was published under the auspices of the Mexican Secretariat of Industry, Commerce, and Labor and printed by Young & McCallister in Los Angeles ("being completed November 10, 1922"). As explained in the headnote to this piece, a slightly freer hand has been exercised in editing it. The following is a complete list of the corrections and emendations the editors have made to the text.

Page	Reading in Copy Text	Corrected Reading
138	Bandolier	Bandelier
	Rivas Palacio	Riva Palacio
	Reville	Revilla
	archeological	archaeological
	Vincente	Vicente
140	Pre-Hipanic	Pre-Hispanic
141	archeology	archaeology
	Otomis	Otomís
142	motives	motifs
144	Yucatan	Yucatán
145	Huitzilopotchli	Huitzilopochtli
	theorised	theorized

Page	Reading in Copy Text	Corrected Reading
146	stylised	stylized
147	ancient Mexico	ancient Mexico.
	or	of
	Huitzolopotchli	Huitzilopochtli
	humming bird	hummingbird
148	Atzcapotzalco	Azcapotzalco
149	*ixchuintli*	*itzcuintli*
150	Page 73.)	Page 73).
	Rivas Palacio	Riva Palacio
152	Chichen Itzá	Chichén Itzá
	Labnáh	Labná
	Colonial Art/Part II.	*Part II: Colonial Art*
153	Tenochtitlan	Tenochtitlán
	Tenochtilán	Tenochtitlán
154	Quautitlán	Cuauhtitlán
155	stylised	stylized
158	ornaments	ornament
160	tile	tiles
	Tepozotlan	Tepozotlán
	Compaña	Compañia
	Barrocco	Barroco
168	irridescent	iridescent
	Michoacan	Michoacán
170	strait	straight
172	stylised	stylized
173	Rabelisian	Rabelaisian
175	Tonolá	Tonalá
	bouganvillea	bougainvillea
176	perrenial	perennial
	plate	plates
177	Michoacan	Michoacán
	nonchalent	nonchalant
178	puebla	pueblo
	Titzatlań	Titzatlán
179	Michoacań	Michoacán
181	Michoacań	Michoacán
182	Yucatan	Yucatán
183	San Luis Potosi	San Luis Potosí
	imporant	important
	bourgoisie	bourgeoisie
	pariotism	patriotism
185	fourth	forth
186	bull's heads	bulls' heads

Two Ancient Mexican Pyramids—the Core of a City Unknown until a Few Years Ago

The *Christian Science Monitor* published this essay on September 19, 1922. Among Porter's papers are the galley proofs for this article. The editors have chosen to use the text of the galley proofs as copy text because it includes three paragraphs that did not appear in the published version. The deletion of these three paragraphs, all from what would have been the last column of the essay as published in the newspaper, does not seem to have been a calculated editorial decision based on religion. Rather it seems to have had more to do with the physical space limitations in this particular issue. There is a large space-consuming illustration for the article. It simply appears that the three paragraphs of the last column were excised in order to fit advertising in the space they would have taken. The three deleted paragraphs include the one beginning "Another head is found here . . ." and the last two. In the published version of the essay, the word "flowing" is substituted for "glowing" in the last sentence of the paragraph beginning "The controversy makes" (p. 193).

Corridos

Porter's informative essay, with "Decorations by Adolfo Best-Maugard," was published in the *Survey Graphic* Mexico issue of May 1924.

To a Portrait of the Poet

The portrait published with Porter's translation of and notes on the Sor Juana poem (*Survey Graphic*, May 1924) was completed by Mexican painter Miguel Cabrera (1695–1768) in 1750 and hangs in the National Historical Museum, Chapultepec Castle, Mexico City. Printed beneath the portrait is Porter's translation of the text of the poem. The text of Porter's notes is printed to the left, below, and to the right of the poem, much as a Biblical commentary would be printed around a Biblical text. The following Spanish text of the sonnet appears in Alan S. Trueblood's *A Sor Juana Anthology* (Cambridge, Mass.: Harvard University Press, 1988), 94.

> Procura desmentir los elogios que a un retrato de la poetisa
>   inscribió la verdad, que llama pasión
>
> Este, que ves, engaño colorido,
> que del arte ostentando los primores,
> con falsos silogismos de colores
> es cauteloso engaño del sentido;
>   este, en quien la lisonja ha pretendido
> excusar de los años los horrores,
> y venciendo del tiempo los rigores
> triunfar de la vejez y del olvido,
>   es un vano artificio del cuidado,
> es una flor al viento delicada,
> es un resguardo inútil para el hado:
>   es una necia diligencia errada,

es un afán caduco y, bien mirado,
es cadáver, es polvo, es sombra, es nada.

The Lovely Legend

Porter worked sporadically on this story during the 1920s. Among her papers, there is a letter (apparently unsent) to Freda Kirchwey of about July 1923 outlining the story, then to be titled "The Enchanting Legend of Rosita." On one part of the existing manuscript, Porter noted in her own hand, "written 1925." However, two of her letters to Matthew Josephson of early 1929 (undated and March 19, 1929) mention working on the story for imminent publication. The editors have constructed the story from parts of four different drafts that are among Porter's papers; they contain very little overlap. The character we have chosen to designate Rubén is named Rafael in all but one draft. Consisting of one page, this draft is the only one that contains a title and a clearly designated opening to the story. It is free of the types of errors, omissions, and messiness characteristic of Porter's rough drafts. That evidence and the clear similarities between the artist character and the one named Rubén in Porter's "The Martyr" dictated the decision to adopt the name Rubén for the character named Rafael in the remainder of the manuscript.

Another draft has five pages numbered [1] to 5; it is dated 1925. A third draft seems to be closely related to the one dated 1925. It consists of one page numbered 3. The longest draft has fourteen pages numbered 3–16; this forms the major part of the text of the story published here.

To create that text, six sections, taken from the three less complete drafts, have been inserted into the fourteen-page draft in angle brackets. They are, in order of their appearance, (1) all but one line of the one-page opening, (2) about three pages from pages [1]–4 of the draft dated 1925, (3) one line from page 4 of the draft dated 1925, (4) approximately one page from pages 4–5 of the draft dated 1925, (5) three lines from the one-page draft numbered 3, and (6) four lines from page 5 of the draft dated 1925.

The following types of corrections and emendations have been made silently throughout the text in order to keep the manuscript relatively free of editorial intrusion: misspellings corrected; quotation marks, periods, commas, and capitalization added for clarification; spacing errors corrected; and dropped letters inserted. As in "The Dove of Chapacalco," Porter's inconsistent use of the British spellings for words such as *colour* has been standardized to American spellings (for example, *color* substituted for *colour*, *vapor* for *vapour*, *odor* for *odour*, etc.). This is the only text in this volume containing an ellipsis inserted by the editors (see p. 205).

The Evening

The copy text for this story consists of an eleven-page draft numbered consecutively. In three places in this draft, Porter inserted words above others but did not score out those below. The editors have incorporated the inserted words into the text printed here. Porter inserted "defects" above "faults" (p. 222), "that move" above "because it moves" (p. 223), and "caprices" above "laws" (p. 223). From the remaining fragments of this piece that are filed with this clean draft, one page of an earlier draft (numbered 4), from which the eleven-page draft was clearly transcribed, contains the following passage, which provides Porter's insight into her own character at a particular time in her life.

These men had caught her up, had carried her along on their wayward, sophisticated fancy. When she was with them, mere breathing became excitement, and for excitement she had an insatiable thirst. They talked to her, and for her among themselves with the indulgent tenderness one gives to a darling child, with always the subtle inference of her charm, her value as a beautiful woman. She was accustomed to love, but not to its intoxicating rituals and gestures. Her eagerness to be beautiful in their eyes, to draw them to her, made her ache. Her nerve-ends boiled and bubbled. But she kept her face calm as she watched them, serpent-feminine enough to know that her attitude of calm pleased them. Their poses of worldliness, their intelligent malice, their beautiful hands, all were thrilling to her senses. And she was compounded of sensualities, she wished only to be loved, to be loved in an atmosphere of jealousy, of intrigue, of art, of music and gay conversation. She wished to inspire love, not to love; she had in her that born talent for making intrigue; for to dance with one man while another stared in another direction with murder in his heart . . . that was the way she described it to herself—added another fillip of pleasure to the dance.

But she feared them a little: their solidarity of interest, of race, of sex. They were familiars to one another, but mysterious to her. She kept glancing from one to the other, each presented a separate problem. What would they be like, actually what would they be, apart from each other? Vicente had offered to paint her portrait, Ciro to teach her those mocking little Mexican songs. Roberto was beginning to expound to her as to a favoured disciple his brilliant, if unstable metaphysics. The little boy Lino made his caustic jokes which more than anything revealed the secrets of their philosophy to her. In these she discerned their inexplicable sense of ridicule, their natural hardness of heart, and it was a challenge to her vanity. She was unread, inexperienced in ideas. . . . Their derived theories came to her as from a clear fountain of original thought. But pure feminine mind is a caterpillar, and she absorbed voraciously all tints and dyes against the final spreading of her bright wings. Her education must come to her through the medium of sensation.

The Princess

The text has been assembled from one draft of ten pages misnumbered [1]–9 (there are two pages numbered 3), from a three-page section of an earlier draft that appears to have been the source for the ten-page draft, and from four separate fragments totaling six pages. The earlier draft is inserted into the text of the clean draft in angle brackets. The fragments are appended to the text composed of these two drafts. "Princess" placed in square brackets replaces "Queen" in the transcription of one of the fragments (p. 238); the editors believe that Porter intended to refer to the Princess and not to her mother.

Return

The manuscript for this piece is composed of five pages of relatively clean type-written copy numbered [1]–5.

Harcourt, Brace News

This snippet from a Porter letter was published in *South Dakota Club Woman* in September 1930.

Segment edited from "Leaving the Petate"

The manuscript for this excised part of Porter's essay consists of four pages numbered 3–6. The first and the last pages are not full pages of text. The remainder of the essay was published in the *New Republic* on February 4, 1931.

Parvenu . . . Review of *Mexico: A Study of Two Americas* by Stuart Chase

The manuscript of this review has four typescript pages. One line that was inadvertently repeated, probably when Porter retyped the review, has been excised by the editors.

Hacienda

This version was published in the *Virginia Quarterly Review* in October 1932.